Stories, Stats and Stuff About Colorado Football

By Dave Schaefer
Daily Camera
Foreword by Rick Neuheisel

Copyright © 1995 by The Wichita Eagle and Beacon Publishing Co., Wichita, Kansas 67201-0820. This publication may not be reproduced, stored in a retrieval system, or transmitted in whole or in part, in any form by any means, electronic, mechanical, photocopying, recording, or otherwise without prior permission of The Wichita Eagle and Beacon Publishing Co.

Printed in the United States of America by Mennonite Press, Inc.

ISBN 1-880652-45-5

PHOTO CREDITS Photograph on pages 7 and 14 were provided by the University Archive at the University of Colorado. Photographs on pages 12, 17, 36, 37, 39, 40, 41, 43, 45, 46, 48, 50, 51, 52, 55, 57, 59, 60, 61, 62, 64, 66, 70, 72, 74, 75, 77, 78, 82, 83, 87, 90, 91, 95, 97, 98, 100, 102, 104, 108, 110, 119, 125, 126, 130, 131, 136, 137, 142 were provided by CU's Sports Information office. All other photographs are from the files of the Daily Camera.

All names, logos and symbols attributable to the University of Colorado which appear in this book are trademarks of the University of Colorado and have been reproduced with the permission of the University of Colorado. This notice is for the purpose of protection of trademark rights only, and in no way represents the approval or disapproval of the text of this book by the University of Colorado.

ACKNOWLEDGMENTS

Several people lent their talents to this book and deserve to be recognized. First, thanks to Daily Camera sports editor Dan Creedon, who pitched this idea to me a few months ago at 1 o'clock in the morning when he must have known I would be foolish enough to accept.

Also, thanks to Daily Camera publisher Harold Higgins, executive editor Barrie Hartman, circulation director Jaime Naranjo, whose enthusiasm for this project was contagious, and his assistant Julie Reeser.

Providing experience and guidance from long distance was the Wichita Eagle crew. Thanks to Bill Handy, Kim Redeker, Lauretta McMillen and the book's design and layout tag-team of Jeff Pulaski and Jim Borger.

The University of Colorado's fine media relations department, headed by director Dave Plati and his staff, allowed me to "move in" and rummage through their files unchecked. The statistics in this book are reprinted directly from the CU media guide with Plati's permission.

Also, a special thanks to CU athletic director Bill Marolt and head football coach Rick Neuheisel, who authored the foreword.

This project simply would have been impossible without the work of the talented sportswriters and photographers who have chronicled the Buffs for over 100 years. A special thanks to Cliff Grassmick and the Daily Camera photo department.

Thanks to Mike Burrows, who swallowed his Big Red pride and served as author of the trivia questions and local copy editor, and to Fred Casotti, *the* authority on CU football history. Casotti's three entertaining books on the subject served as invaluable resources.

And finally, I'd like to thank my family and friends for their patience this summer. I look forward to reintroducing myself to them soon.

Dave Schaefer

For Mom and Dad
– D.S.

FOREWORD

When you talk about Colorado football, you're talking about a rich tradition. From Dal Ward to Eddie Crowder to Bill McCartney, there's been a real feeling of small-town environment coupled with big-time football. Put together, it creates an unbelievable atmosphere. You look at most of the great college football programs across the country - they start in small areas. That type of family environment and comraderie really brings a team and community closer together. That's what I'm most excited about – being a part of the Colorado family and tradition.

There have been hundreds of players that have made their mark on Colorado football. Even above what individuals have contributed, what's most important is the sense of community with the team. The Buffaloes belong to Colorado.

I have learned quickly that tradition is very important at Colorado. Byron "Whizzer" White, Bobby Anderson, the 1971 team and certainly Bill's teams in the late '80s and early '90s. There's a real sense of pride involved with Colorado football. Because of that, there's an obligation and responsibilty for all those who are charged with perpetuating it. You don't take it as a burden; it's an honor to carry on that tradition. That's why I'm very excited about the next era of Colorado football.

My goals are lofty. I would love to see Colorado win another national championship – if not more than one. I would love to keep us in the upper echelon of college football where we currently find ourselves. That isn't something you just talk about. You have to work at it. It's a day-to-day obligation. What I like most about my new situation is that I've been adopted. I feel very much a part of the Colorado football family. It isn't as though it's a closed unit and I'm on the outside trying to find my way in. The town and the state have embraced me and said, "Hey now, the Buffaloes are really important to us. Let's make sure we treat that spirit and entity with respect." I plan to.

Rick Neuheisel

TABLE OF CONTENTS

Chapter 1:
THE EARLY YEARS *(1890-1915)*...**6**

Chapter 2:
WARS AND WHIZZER *(1916-47)*..**17**

Chapter 3:
DALLAS WARD *(1948-58)*..**36**

Chapter 4:
SONNY AND BUD *(1959-62)*...**50**

Chapter 5:
EDDIE CROWDER *(1963-73)*...**60**

Chapter 6:
MALLORY AND FAIRBANKS *(1974-81)*......................................**78**

Chapter 7:
BILL McCARTNEY *(1982-94)*..**95**

Chapter 8:
RICK NEUHEISEL *(1995-   )*...**142**

Chapter 9:
BY THE NUMBERS *(Some CU Statistics)*....................................**152**

CU Quiz:
TRIVIA ANSWERS...**168**

The Early Years 1890-1915

Here's the first starting lineup CU put on the field on Nov. 15, 1890. CU lost 20-0 to the Denver Athletic Club in Denver and didn't advance the ball. The team didn't have a coach, and Edmundson served as captain.

End:
Ed Ingram
End:
John Nixon
Tackle:
George Darley
Tackle:
Delos Holden
Guard:
Harry Layton
Guard:
Howell Givens
Center:
Charles McConnell
Quarterback:
Tom Edmundson
Fullback:
Bert Kennedy
Halfback:
Homer James
Halfback:
Wesley Putman

Overall Record: 127-52-7 (.683 winning percentage)
Coaches: None (1890-93), Harry Heller (1894), Fred Folsom (1895-99, 1901-02 and 1908-1915), T.W. Mortimer (1900), Dave Cropp (1903-04), Willis Keinholtz (1905), and Frank Castleman (1906-07).
Conference Championships: 1894 (8-1), 1895 (5-1), 1896 (5-0), 1897 (7-1), 1901 (5-1-1), 1902 (5-1), 1903 (8-2), 1909 (6-0), 1910 (6-0), 1911 (6-0), 1913 (5-1-1)
Worst Seasons: 1890 (0-4), 1891 (1-4), 1915 (1-6)

  Football at the University of Colorado had such humble beginnings, it wasn't even football.
  In 1889, a CU medical student from England rallied some of his classmates from the dorm and tried to form the University's first "football" team. The game they played looked suspiciously like soccer. Unable to find any other teams to compete against in the state, the team quietly disbanded.
  The next fall, having run into similar scheduling problems, Colorado changed its game to Rugby and joined the State Association (and existing teams Denver Athletic Club, School of Mines and Colorado College). Practices on campus immediately commenced as the team hurriedly prepared for its first game.
  They needed more time.
  The 1900 Coloradoan, the student yearbook, noted, "There was no coaching, and as for teamwork all were most blissfully ignorant of the existence of such a thing." CU opened its first season and its history on Nov. 15, 1890 against the Denver Athletic Club in Denver.

The Denver Athletic Club Foot Ball Team Defeats the Boulder University Eleven

Headline in the Rocky Mountain News, Nov. 16, 1890

  "The day was an excellent one for the game and players, but a little chilly for the spectators, who numbered about 300.
  "The game was quite one sided as the Boulders

The 1891 CU team. Back row (from left to right): Howell Givens, captain Pat Carney, Bert Kennedy, Harry Gamble, Wesley Putnam, Ed Newcomb, Jim Garrett, Conrad Bluhm; sitting: Homer James, Bill McIntosh, V.R. Pennock, Clarence Perry, Charlie Easley, Harry Layton. CU president Horace Hale is seated in middle.

were too weak for their Athletic opponents.

"The university boys were not familiar with the game having practiced but two weeks, while most of the Denver team have played for several years... The university team was weakened somewhat by Edmundson spraining his knee, but they played a good game and deserve credit in keeping the score so low (20-0)."

Tom Edmundson, the quarterback and team captain, missed the rest of the season. He may have been fortunate.

BLOWOUT Mines, the state powerhouse of the day from Golden, visited Boulder the next week and handed CU its worst loss in school history, 103-0. Conrad Bluhm, a fullback, recalled CU's first home game, which was played on a dirt field on campus:

"With the greatest team Golden ever had, our showing of 103-0 in Golden's favor was not so bad," Bluhm wrote. "None of us knew the game except as we learned it in the progress of the game itself. Our line could not hold. It was full of big holes. Every play it looked as if the Kaiser's army rushed through the holes with nobody but myself as fullback to challenge their march to the goal. At the close of the game I was a rolled beefsteak, like the veteran of a thousand battles. But I became desperate and quickly got onto the low tackle, which put several of their players back to the sidelines."

Chapter 1: The Early Years 1890-1915

1. When the original Buffs lined up for their first varsity game, nine of their 11 starters were from Colorado towns. What were the hometowns of the other two starters?

Late in the game, Bluhm, once again buried beneath a pile of Miners, received an uncommon assist from the school's upper administration.

"In order to give me time to get my wind, President Hale threw off his coat, jumped the ropes and started to clear up the adversaries single-handed, and he weighed only 100 pounds."

PAYDIRT While another shutout defeat (44-0 to Colorado College), CU's third game marked the first time the University team actually advanced the ball, which was considered progress.

They closed the season on a high note, losing 50-4 in a rematch with Mines in a game that featured CU's first touchdown (worth four points in those days). Here's how John Nixon, an end on the team, remembered it in a Boulder Daily Camera article on Nov. 28, 1932:

> "The Mines halfback was tackled and as he was going down, George Darley, Colorado University end, grabbed the ball out of his arms, and with a clear field ran for a touchdown."

Officially, the play is in the CU record books as a 65-yard return of a fumble recovery for Darley, whose nephew, Dr. Ward Darley, became the school's seventh president from 1953-56.

The 1893 CU team (left) and the Colorado Aggies pose for a photograph before their Oct. 7, 1893, game in Boulder. CU won, 44-6.

COACHLESS, FIELDLESS AND NAMELESS CU didn't employ its first football coach, Harry Heller, until its fifth season in 1894, the same year games were moved off the rock and dirt campus site to the first "real" football field off-campus.

Although they were called many names, the football team (and all CU teams) didn't get the current nickname "Buffaloes" until 1934 when the student newspaper

sponsored a contest to name the team.

FIRST ONE'S THE TOUGHEST It wasn't until the fifth and final game of the University's second season that the team was able to enjoy its first win. In losing their first eight games, the team was outscored 319-10 and shut out six times.

But on Nov. 26, 1891, CU traveled to Colorado Springs and handled Colorado College, 24-4, to earn the first 'W.'

The Buffs have not had a winless season since their first, in 1890.

HELLER'S HEROICS Here's a switch: the player recruits the coach. In 1894, team captain Harry Gamble, using a persistent letter-writing campaign, lured Harry Heller to Boulder from Baker University in Kansas. The day Heller stepped off the train, he was recognized as the first coach in CU football history and summed up his coaching philosophy: "Our games are not to be full of tricks, but straight snappy football."

Heller instituted the earliest version of what players know today as "training table" where the team ate regularly together. The team was housed in the basement of Woodbury Hall (the second oldest building on campus), where they showered and were required to take naps in the afternoon before practice.

A new field in an area northeast of campus known as "Lover's Hill" was constructed, and CU would play its home games there for the next four seasons.

Heller led the 1894 squad to its first winning season and first conference championship with a 8-1 record. However, Heller declined a second tenure as coach to concentrate on his studies. He even suited up occasionally the next season as a player.

Fred Folsom, known as the "Father of CU Football," had a curious superstition on game days. At the start of the contest, Folsom would pick up five pebbles from the field and hold them in his hand the entire game.

1895: THE LEGEND ARRIVES

Heller helped establish Colorado football, in only its fifth year in existence, as the premier collegiate power in the state (DAC was a semi-professional team). But CU's stature was in jeopardy when Heller resigned before the 1895 season.

But out of the uncertainty, unknown and concern came Fred Gorham Folsom, who would not only immediately save the team but take the program to new heights which wouldn't be paralleled for nearly 100 years.

Born and raised in Maine, Folsom earned his bachelor's degree from Dartmouth while starring as an end on the football team when CU came calling.

Fred Folsom won nine conference championships in 15 seasons at CU.

The Silver and Gold newspaper, on Sept. 26, 1895, covered the hiring:

> "At the suggestion of Captain Caley, a letter was written to the Captain of the Dartmouth Varsity Eleven asking the names of available coaches and Monday the reply came that the only coach not yet engaged of whom he had heard was F. G. Folsom of the Dartmouth Eleven. Wednesday morning a telegram was sent calling him here at once so that he may be expected early next week."

Apparently, CU didn't have much choice, but the hire was still a good one.

Folsom revolutionized Colorado football. Until Bill McCartney passed him in 1993, Folsom was CU's winningest coach with a 77-23-2 (.765) record. Folsom coached at CU for 15 years, in three separate stints, and guided his teams to nine conference championships.

His legacy is everlasting: CU's football stadium, which opened in 1924, has carried his name since his death in 1944.

2. *The first six times Colorado played the Denver Athletic Club, the Buffs lost by 20-0, 42-0, 44-0, 42-6, 14-0 and 32-4 scores. When did CU finally beat the DAC?*

FAST START Folsom arrived too late to coach in the 1895 opener, which CU won 36-0 over Denver Manual High School. Despite inheriting a team that the Boulder Daily Camera said "had practically disbanded because of poor prospects," Folsom began his era the next week with a 32-0 victory over the Denver Wheel Club. Under Folsom, CU finished 5-1 that first year to defend its conference title.

FOLSOM, P.I. Besides coaching the football team, Folsom also worked toward a graduate degree in the CU law school, where he picked up the nickname "P.I." Here's how, according to the Colorado Alumnus:

> "His college nickname grew out of his original way of designating the place from which he came. When he entered the boys asked him where he came from. 'Way down East.' 'Well, where?' 'Way down East.' On looking on the map they found that the farthest 'down East' place was Prince Edward's Island. Accordingly, he was dubbed 'P.E.I.' and Pei he is. However, when asked to explain its meaning, he insisted that it meant 'Prince of Indians.'"

'P.E.I' evolved to 'P.I.,' which was later interpreted 'Penobscot Indian.'

Folsom was also called "Bill" – which he brought upon himself. The extremely intelligent, studious coach was also a bit flighty. He continually had trouble remem-

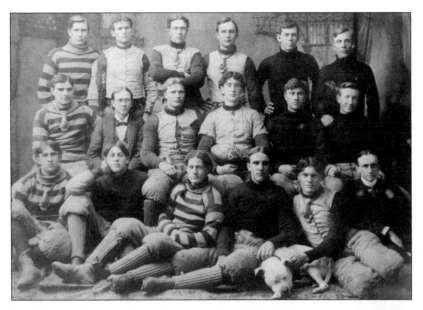

CU's first undefeated team, pictured above, outscored opponents 171-6 in 1896. Captain Harry Gamble holds the ball in the center.

bering players' names so he called them all "Bill," which, in turn, they often called him.

IT'S GOTTA BE THE HAIR Helmets weren't worn until 1896, and only sporadically then. They become mandatory issue in 1939.

In the early years, some players grew their hair long (relative to the custom of the day) in order to give the noggin some extra padding.

The Colorado Alumnus, in May 1929, reported "football hair" became a campus fad:

> "When football was introduced at the University in 1890, it brought an era of football hair, rotten egg fights, nose guards and enthusiasm ... The long, thick, matted hair protected the heads of those early football players in lieu of helmets. Football hair became popular among the students and even certain members of the faculty."

RULE CHANGES 1897 saw a major rule change that would put the University at odds with its conference brothers for the better part of the next 10 years. CU contested that the new four-year eligibility restriction should not apply to players already enrolled, which happened to include CU's best two players, QB and captain Harry Chase and center Robert Schaefer.

A day before the season finale against Mines, which would decide the conference championship, CU students, still upset about the new rule, voted to withdraw

3. It wasn't until 1898, their ninth season, that the Buffs played a non-Colorado opponent. Name that opponent.

Chapter 1: The Early Years 1890-1915

Folsom, in his familiar Dartmouth sweater in the right rear, led this 1897 team to a 7-1 championship season. They allowed just 10 points while scoring 188.

In 1898, CU's home games were played in this state-of-the-art facility for the first time, Gamble Field. Here, a sellout crowd watches a 1902 contest between CU and Nebraska.

from the conference at season's end. CU won 36-2 to clinch its fourth straight title, and withdrew. But by the beginning of the next season and with a compromise on the eligibility rule worked out, CU's "resignation" was ignored and the team was back in good standing.

Without Chase and Schaefer (a six-year starter), however, CU slumped to a 4-4 record, its worst since Folsom had arrived.

GAMBLE FIELD The team moved back to its campus home in 1898 when construction of a grass field (not as many rocks) was completed. It sat in the area which presently houses the University Memorial Center and extended into the quad west of Norlin Library.

It bore the name of Harry Gamble, CU's first star player as a fullback from 1892-96. The student newspaper campaigned successfully:

> "Those who are new in the University care little what kind of a name is given to the new park, but to those of us who are in the upper classes but one

CU's run of four-straight conference titles was stopped when the 1898 squad, short-handed because of new eligibility rules, managed just a 4-4 record.

name appeals. All unite in saying 'Name it Gamble Field.' To Harry Gamble alone belongs the honor. He who has ever striven to bring U. of C. athletics to a perfection standard."

Silver and Gold, 1898

BIG GAME CU fans and the citizens of Boulder have been seeing red for a nearly a century when it comes to neighboring powerhouse Nebraska. Leading up to the first meeting in the 53-game series between the two rivals, the Boulder Daily Camera on Nov. 16, 1898, reported how the city was ready to shut down for game day:

NEBRASKA IS COMING
Boulder People Will be Treated to the Game of the Season

"A petition was circulated among the business men today asking that all business houses be closed during the progress of the game. The petition was signed by practically every house in town so that all employees will be enabled to see the game."

In its first game against an out-of-state opponent, CU fell 23-10 to Nebraska before a record crowd at Gamble Field.

LONG ARM OF THE LAW After rebounding his team to a 7-2 record, Folsom, who had earned his law degree, abruptly quit as coach to enter private law practice in Denver. His absence was a short one, however, as he returned in 1901 after missing just one season.

CU carried on without Folsom in 1900 under the leadership of T.W. Mortimer, a high school coach from Chicago, who was selected by Gamble, the graduate manager of the team. Mortimer's team struggled to 6-4 and scored just 10 points in final five games of season. Mortimer, a record holder in the hammer throw in the Middle West Inter-Collegiate championship, went on to become the school's first track coach in 1902.

VISIONARIES Folsom's return as coach brought two-straight conference titles in 1901 and 1902. The only blemish on the 1902 schedule was a 10-0 home loss to Nebraska, a tightly-contested battle that inspired the 1902 Coloradoan to suggest that CU was ready for the big time:

> "The season of 1902 will have a far-reaching effect on football history. Our game with Nebraska and our magnificent showing in that game have done wonders in the advancement of our football reputation. That game showed conclusively that we should enter into an Intercollegiate League with Nebraska, Iowa, Kansas, Missouri, and, perhaps, Ohio. That we have a right to represent Colorado in this proposed League has been proven, beyond all doubt, by our past record."

CU entered the Big Six, making it the Big Seven, in 1948, joining Iowa State, Missouri, Kansas, Kansas State, Oklahoma and Nebraska. Oklahoma State joined in 1960 to form the Big Eight Conference, which expands to the Big 12 in 1996 with the addition of Texas A&M, Texas Tech, Texas and Baylor.

MAKING FRIENDS "We want Boulder to know that we can think of no language fit enough with which to characterize the muckerism, foulness and filth that her actions seem to evidence." – Colorado College Tiger, Saturday Evening, Oct. 25, 1902.

GOING HOME For the second time in his coaching career, Folsom skipped out of Boulder in 1903. This time an opportunity to coach his alma mater, Dartmouth, provided the lure.

At the same time, an athletic department, called the Department of Physical Training, was created, and Dave Cropp was hired as the first athletic director. His duties included instructing gym class for men and women, coaching the football, baseball and track teams and serving as treasurer of Gamble Field.

He turned out to be a good football coach, leading CU to a 14-4-1 record over his two seasons. His two major

Folsom (above) returned to Dartmouth to coach for four years. While he was gone, CU gained an historic win over Nebraska, 6-0, in 1904 when captain Everett Owens (below) plunged over the goal for the game's only score.

contributions: the institution of spring drills and the first win over Nebraska in 1904.

ROAD TRIP! A year before, Cropp boarded his boys on a train and headed to Lincoln for Colorado's first out-of-state road game. The actual contest, a 31-0 shellacking at the hands of the Huskers, was forgettable, but the road trip, recounted blow by blow through newspaper accounts in the 1905 Coloradoan, sounded memorable. Some excerpts:

> "Kingsbury, one of the halfbacks for the visitors, attracted much attention from the ladies on account of his beautiful hair." – Sterling Record.
>
> "The State University Football Team is a very democratic bunch of boys. They mingled freely and without the irksome medium of an introduction with the most unpretentious young ladies of our fair city" – Denver Times.
>
> "Strum, a big Colorado tackle, was arrested last night for disturbing the peace. Explanations proved that he was only dreaming a football dream and he was released from the city bastille this morning." – Lincoln Bugle.

MORE PROBLEMS For the only time in its history, CU did not participate in conference play in 1905, because of continuing disagreements with the State Intercollegiate Conference. Under new head coach Willis Keinholtz, the team romped through a make-shift schedule filled with small schools from the area to an 8-1 mark. The Buffs averaged a record 39.9 points per game, including a 109-0 win over Regis College, the most lopsided victory in school history.

When a new conference rule (behind which the University proudly considered itself the driving force) was adopted to mandate that a player must carry at least 10 hours of course work to be eligible, CU rejoined the conference the next year.

CU continued to search for a worthy replacement for Folsom as Frank Castleman was hired in 1906 as athletic director and head football coach (as well as track and basketball). Apparently overwhelmed by the rule change that made it necessary to cover 10 yards instead of five to keep the ball, Castleman's first team struggled through four scoreless ties in 1906 and finished 2-3-4, CU's first losing season in 13 years.

HE'S BACK After coaching Dartmouth to a 29-5-4 record over four years, Folsom (for a $1,000 coaching salary) returned to Boulder for the third and final time in 1908.

Frank Castleman's CU teams of 1906-07 struggled to a 7-6-4 record including four scoreless ties. When Folsom indicated a desire to return as head coach in 1908, Castleman stayed on as athletic director.

Chapter 1: The Early Years 1890-1915

Castleman remained as athletic director, but made way for Folsom to coach.

Good move.

Folsom immediately produced some of the best CU teams in history. The 1909 team is the only undefeated, untied and unscored-upon CU squad ever. They gave up one field goal (called a "Princeton" then) to Wyoming the next season while going 6-0 again and followed up that in 1911 with another 6-0 run, which was tarnished by a Wyoming Princeton and a safety against in an 8-2 win over Colorado College.

Add on a victory in the final game of the 1908 season and two wins to open the 1912 campaign, and it totals an all-time best 21-game winning streak. For three-straight seasons, the team didn't allow a touchdown.

BAD BLOOD Following a particularly bitter 14-10 defeat at Gamble Field to Denver University, a brawl broke out between the two student bodies. Combined with the fact that CU believed DU was circumventing the 10-hour player eligibility restrictions of the conference, the incident severed the athletic relationship between the two schools for six seasons.

END OF AN ERA Folsom never matched the magic of the 1909-11 run again, but his 1913 team, with a climactic 20-0 win over Mines, secured Folsom's ninth (and final) conference championship.

Folsom, increasingly more involved and interested in his job as a member of the law faculty, nearly quit after that season. But Castleman convinced him to stay, which he did until failing health forced him off the sidelines in 1915, his worst season ever at 1-6. Amazingly, five of Folsom's 15 career conference losses came that season.

Folsom hardly rode off into the sunset. He remained intensely involved with the University, both as a law instructor and chairman of the athletic board. It was in that role that, in 1923, he managed the financial planning for the building of CU's new football stadium.

Two years after Folsom retired and less than two weeks following his death, the CU Regents officially renamed Colorado Stadium "Folsom Stadium," on Nov. 24, 1944.

> "It was a most fitting tribute to this man," law professor and former CU football star Walter B. Franklin said. "Alumni of this University will join with me in satisfaction that the name Fred G. Folsom and the things he stood for will be perpetuated as a tradition in the University of Colorado."
>
> Boulder Daily Camera, Nov. 26, 1944

Dr. George Norlin, CU president and driving force behind the construction of Colorado Stadium and the formation, in 1910, of the Rocky Mountain Faculty Conference, on football's place within a university:

"There is no truth in the idea that winning football teams tend to attract more students than does a University which does not turn out winning teams. Students choose their college for its standing and not for its athletic prowess."

Wars and Whizzer 1916-1947

Overall Record: 154-86-15 (.604 winning percentage)
Coaches: Bob Evans (1916-17), Joe Mills (1918-19), Myron Witham (1920-1931), William Saunders (1932-1934), Bunnie Oakes (1935-1939), Frank Potts (1940, 1944-45), and Jim Yeager (1941-1943, 1946-47).
Conference Championships: 1923 (9-0), 1924 (8-1-1), 1934 (6-1-2), 1935 (5-4), 1937 (8-1), 1939 (5-3), 1942 (7-2).
Worst Seasons: 1916 (1-5-1), 1918 (2-3), 1927 (3-5-1), 1932 (2-4).

Two of CU's greatest athletes crossed campus after World War I, Lee Willard (left) and Walt Franklin (right).

4. Other than a part of their name, what do CU's Folsom Field and Oklahoma's Owen Field have in common?

5. Eddie Evans was CU's standout quarterback in 1915 and 1916. What happened to Evans in 1918?

With legendary coach Fred Folsom moving into the background after his resignation in 1915, the next era of Colorado football would be dominated by the boys who played it rather than the men who coached it.

Sandwiched in time between two world wars, several players grabbed the spotlight during each of their tenures on the CU campus: Lee Willard, Walt Franklin, Art Quinlan, Bill McGlone, Hatfield Chilson, William "Kayo" Lam, and Orvill Nuttall.

And, of course, Byron "Whizzer" White.

The game of football was changing around the time of World War I as it developed the style which modern day fans would recognize. The forward pass had been legalized, offenses needed 10 yards, not five, to make a first down, and the four-year eligibility rule was strictly enforced.

The days of the flying wedge and plowing, prodding offenses were numbered. In a freer, more wide-open style of game, attentions turned toward the athletic ability of the players.

CU had some good ones.

THE GREATEST?... LEE WILLARD

Headline in The Denver Post, 1961

Lee Willard was the first and only CU athlete to earn 16 varsity letters.

Lee Willard arrived on campus in 1918. He left four years later as the most decorated athlete in CU history. Willard, a quick 155-pounder who was rejected for war service in the Navy because of an unconfirmed illness, is the only CU athlete ever to earn 16 letters.

He was captain in four sports (football, basketball, baseball and track) and all-conference in three. Willard was also president of his senior and sophomore classes and a member of Beta Theta Pi. Some days he had to pull double duty:

> "At the time (Willard) competed, the CU athletic plant was located on Gamble Field, site of the new memorial building. It is said that on days when both the baseball and track teams were at home, (Willard) would compete in his track specialty between innings of the baseball game."
>
> *Boulder Daily Camera, Dec. 13, 1951*

Willard, a 9.8 sprinter in the 100 as well as an all-conference broad jumper and javelin thrower, began his football career as an end, moved to the backfield and finished as a quarterback his senior year. He was the basketball team's leading scorer for three years from his forward position and an accomplished center fielder. Upon graduation, Willard earned $600 for a 30-day tryout with a professional baseball team, but he decided instead to pursue his interest in the oil business.

While many consider Byron "Whizzer" White (CU's first All-American in 1937) the most gifted athlete in school history, Willard has his supporters.

Wrote high school friend Alan Loucks in 1961 during another of his failed attempts to see Willard enshrined into the Football Hall of Fame, "The greatest all-around athlete in CU history was Lee Willard."

It was a title and debate from which Willard always shied.

Willard, then the Vice President of the Cities Service Gas Co. in Oklahoma City, did his best to quell the debate in a letter to the Boulder Daily Camera on Dec. 27, 1951:

> "An attempt to compare athletes of the past with those of the present is entirely impossible. Unquestionably, there are many more (great athletes) at the school who are equally deserving. The songs of the old timers were sung loud and strong during their time. Anyway, thanks for the memory."

Preparations for the 1918 season were interrupted for several days because the players needed to recover from receiving government-mandated inoculation shots.

FIREBALL The task of trying to fill the sizeable coaching cleats of Folsom in 1916 fell on M.C. "Bob" Evans, a high school coach from Kentucky. Evans arrived in August, just over a month before his first game, apparently with a good deal of excitement for his new job:

> "Personally the mentor is a fellow of medium size with a pair of broad shoulders and a general appearance of fine physical condition. He is a good deal of a cyclone in his actions, getting around quickly and expressing himself in the same way with plenty of decision and force.
>
> "And generally speaking, he acts like a fellow who is either going to put a punch into the University of Colorado eleven or know the reason why."
>
> *Boulder Daily Camera, Aug. 22, 1916*

Evans' first CU team proved to be punchless, going 1-5-1 in 1916, but they rebounded in 1917 with a 6-2 record which Evans parlayed into a head coaching job at Stanford.

Joe Mills, the basketball coach at the time, took over as interim football coach and athletic director, but with World War I in full swing, few hardly noticed or cared that Mills' teams went 4-6-1 over two years, and he resigned quietly to enter private business.

His given first name was Melbourne, but CU's 7th coach went by Bob Evans.

MR. FRANKLIN While the war considerably thinned the ranks of players, Willard wasn't the only talented football star on campus during that time. He was joined by Walt

Walt Franklin was a behind-the-scenes workhorse in the construction of Folsom Field, the Men's Gymnasium and the CU Fieldhouse.

Franklin, a hard-nosed lineman from Durango, who earned all-conference accolades at two positions, center and end.

Both student body president and a conference heavyweight boxing champion, Franklin was a rare mix of brains and brawn. His biggest contributions came after his graduation in 1922 when he served as graduate manager of athletics until 1940, as assistant line coach from 1922-30, as well as stints as boxing and golf coach.

He was a driving force behind the construction of Folsom Field, and spoke at the stadium's dedication Homecoming Day 1924. The field directly east of the stadium, which served as the football practice field for so many years, was named "Franklin Field" in his honor.

Both Willard and Franklin are members of CU's All-Century Team, selected in 1989.

1920-31: THE WITHAM ERA

It worked once with a Dartmouth man, so why not try again? In 1920, CU's search for a coach who could rekindle Folsom's glory days centered on a fellow Dartmouth grad and former All-American quarterback who played for the CU legend. Myron Witham, a pint-sized, scholarly man who had been out of football working as a civil engineer for 14 years, was Folsom's choice to head the program.

Good choice.

In what would be a 12-year stint at Colorado, Witham nearly equaled Folsom's coaching record. His 63-26-7 record stands fourth all-time in terms of victories and included two conference championship teams (1923 and '24). His 1923 9-0 team remains CU's only undefeated team in the last 71 years. CU also played its first post-season game, in 1924 at Hawaii, during Witham's tenure.

Myron Witham is tied for fourth with Dal Ward on CU's all-time winningest coach list with 63 victories.

"The University is particularly fortunate in securing a man of Mr. Witham's calibre," Folsom said of the hiring. "I have known him for years. He was a wonderful athlete, made good as a coach, and has been exceptionally successful in his engineering capacity. He is one of the finest men of my acquaintance."

Boulder Daily Camera, March 9, 1920

Witham, ever the scholar, authored the 1921 season recap for the 1922 Coloradoan, and he took the opportunity to scold those boosters who held expectations that were too high:

"An overzealous enthusiasm on the part of the team's most ardent supporters, leading to the coining of the phrase of 'the wonder team' showed its effect in the first games and acted as a severe handicap during the remainder of the season."

Witham's squad finished 4-1-1, but a 0-0 tie against rival Utah midway through the season denied CU the conference championship. Witham had this to say in the yearbook:

> "As has been the case in previous games in Utah, poor officiating marred the contest, apparently decreasing the effectiveness of each team."

PERFECTION Led by a dynamic pair of quarterbacks, Art Quinlan and Hatfield Chilson, CU carved out its first conference championship in 10 years in 1923, posting a perfect 9-0 record along the way.

6. What was Colorado Stadium's seating capacity when it opened in 1924?

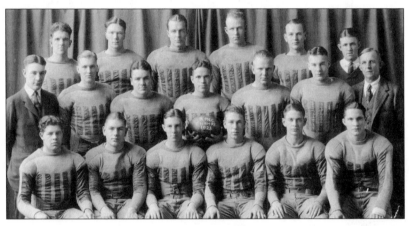

The Buffs, masters of the forward pass in Witham's aggressive offensive system, averaged 31 points per game; they allowed 27 all season.

Quinlan, the senior captain, broke his hand in a 47-0 rout of Mines, a week before a showdown with conference power Utah. With Quinlan available only for place-kicking duties, Chilson, a sophomore, stepped in and led a comeback victory sparked by this tricky play:

> Trailing 7-0, "Quinlan trotted out on the field with his arm in a sling, and prepared to place-kick. The ball came back to Chilson, who bent to touch it to the ground, then straightened up and tossed it over the line to (Bill) Bohn for a touchdown, and the score was tied."

G.E. Helmer, sports editor of the Silver and Gold, in the 1924 Coloradoan

CU went on to win 17-7, including a field goal from the slinged-up Quinlan.

CU's 1923 undefeated championship team boasted three "All-Century" players: manager Walt Franklin (middle row, far left), guard Bill McGlone (middle row, third from left) and quarterback Hatfield Chilson (bottom row, third from right).

Chapter 2: Wars and Whizzer 1916-1947

Two weeks later in the season finale in Fort Collins against the Colorado Aggies (CSU), Quinlan, without the sling, broke off a 67-yard punt return in the fourth quarter. He then kicked the winning field goal with 45 seconds left (after his first try was blocked but he recovered) to secure the championship with a 6-3 win and cap the undefeated season.

AGGIE RIVALRY As is true today, the CU-CSU rivalry was a hotly contested one in the 1920s. After whipping the Aggies 36-0 in 1924, CU held a fairly dominant 21-4-2 edge in the series. But the Fort Collins Express-Courier, in an article published on Nov. 13, 1925, wasn't all that impressed:

From the 1923 CU yearbook, "The Pass That Made Chilson Famous."

"During the past few years the Colorado University team has been very fortunate in its games with the Aggies and have tied or won the games by various tricks and breaks when they found themselves outplayed. They have outsmarted the Farmers until now. They hold the Aggies in some contempt and consider themselves able to win by their brains when main strength will not get the game.

"This year, however, with the experienced Hyde, Brown and Montgomery in the backfield, Boulder will have to win the game to get it. In the (Colorado College) Tiger games there has been a jinx at work, and no doubt about it, but with the Boulder bunch it has been no jinx, just simply more experience, tricks and quick thinking, when the game could not be otherwise garnered in."

The Express-Courier was onto something. With Chilson out with an injured arm, CSU beat CU 12-0 in 1925.

Explaining away a 7-0 CU win in 1922, the paper had this to say about CU's opening touchdown on a kickoff return, which featured a cross-field lateral:

7. Colorado has played Front Range rivals Wyoming and Colorado State a combined 91 times. What is CU's record in those games?

"Witham had devised the trick the night before when he saw it was to be a muddy field and had rehearsed and practiced it behind closed gates."

CU was a fired-up bunch in 1924 when the team capped an undefeated, untied regular season with a convincing 36-0 win at Fort Collins, according to the 1925 Coloradoan:

"The slogan of the campus of the entire 'Hill' became 'Beat Aggies.' The expression was used as words of greeting on walks, in class rooms, and over telephones. It was emblazoned in immense letters on the pavements and sidewalks. Ten thousand hand bills were printed with the two words, and were put on every tree, post, and window in Boulder, Ft. Collins, and other northern state towns. The Aggie campus was invaded and placarded with the bills, and the pavements decorated in white-wash. Colorado University had gone wild."

THE TEAM HOUSE One of Witham's contributions was the construction of a team house, an athletic dorm off-campus which was called the "C" House. Purchased in part by the booster club (another Witham innovation), Boulder businessmen, and from student funds, the house on 14th street boarded 30 players.

Its advantages were numerous: the house was open before the dorms in the fall so the football players could return to campus earlier for drills. In the winter, the basketball team moved in and the track and baseball teams had the run of the place in the spring. Meals and tutoring sessions were centered in the house.

Wrote the Coloradoan, "It is a forward move in the attempt to place Colorado athletes supreme in the Rocky Mountain Conference."

EVEN BETTER CU followed its undefeated conference championship of 1923 with an even more impressive year in 1924. CU marched through the regular season and conference campaign undefeated and unscored upon. But a 0-0 tie at Denver blemished a perfect record.

CU was the only team in the nation to not allow a point all year.

The team opened with a 31-0 win over Western State in the last game played at Gamble Field, CU's home since 1898, and then christened the new stadium the following week with a 39-0 rout of Regis.

In its early years, CU's football stadium was known as Colorado Stadium and, during a stretch in the late 1930s, Norlin Stadium in honor of Dr. George Norlin, the school president, who was so instrumental in forming the Rocky Mountain Faculty Athletic Conference in 1910. In 1944, it was officially named Folsom Field.

CU's amazing 1924 season was rewarded by a post-season trip to Hawaii in December. Witham, assistant coach Walt Franklin, 18 players and the team doctor were treated to a week in paradise, where "The Withamites" (as they became known) whipped a group of military all-stars before the fun and sun got the best of them and they lost to the University of Hawaii, 13-0, on New Year's Day 1925.

"It is reported that one of the men, a fast, pass-

CU's 7-0 loss at Utah on Nov. 8, 1919, was "viewed" by 1,200 Colorado fans in Macky Auditorium. Students from the Silver and Gold newspaper received the play-by-play of the game by wire from Salt Lake City and recreated the action using a mimic field.

Myron Witham was forced out after 12 seasons, largely because of his inability to beat rival Utah.

THE NICKNAME

In 1934, it was worth five bucks. Today, most CU fans consider the nickname "Buffaloes" priceless.

The student newspaper, the Silver and Gold, sponsored a name-the-team contest in 1934 and offered a $5 prize for the winner. Of more than 1,000 entrants (which included "Puddle Jumpers," "Tanks," "Boulders," "Zephrs," and "Flatirons"), "Buffaloes" was selected by a four-man committee headed by athletic director Harry Carlson.

Boulder resident Andrew Dickson, a printer at the Boulder Daily Camera newspaper, pocketed the $5.

For the final game of the 1934 season, some students rented a buffalo calf (and its owner) and paraded "Mr. Chips" along the sidelines of CU's 7-0 Thanksgiving Day win over Denver. The first "Ralphie" wouldn't debut until 1966, and "Mr. Chips" continued to make an occasional appearance.

Before 1934, CU athletic teams didn't have an official nickname, although they were known most often as the Silver and Gold and, at times, by some other creative monikers: Moose, Yellow Jackets, Greyhounds, Silvertips, Arapahoes, Sour-Doughs, Big Horns, Grizzlies, and, in the early days, Tea Sippers.

Buffaloes stuck in 1934, but several variations have cropped up over the years, starting obviously with "Buffs" and including "Bison," "Thundering Herd," and "Golden Buffaloes."

grabbing end, and a campus women's favorite, lost his heart to a fair damsel on the island, and that he plans to return during the summer months."

1925 Coloradoan

So it wasn't a total loss.

8. Name the last season Folsom Field had a natural-grass playing surface.

ACHILLES HEAL Witham had several good seasons left in him, but no more great ones like he enjoyed in 1923 and '24. During his last seven seasons in Boulder, Witham compiled a very respectable 34-19-3 record, but seven of those losses came at the hands of conference bully and hated rival Utah.

It was Witham's 2-9-1 career record against the Utes that finished him after the 1931 season, when the Regents chose not to renew his contract, or in other words, fired him.

Witham headed home to Vermont, where he lived until he died at age 92. He left Boulder disappointed and angry, leaving only this terse reply: "My friends don't need a statement, and the others don't deserve one."

REBUILDING Athletic Director Harry Carlson plainly stated what he felt the prerequisites were for Colorado's next coach: "We want a man who is young, who has a good character, who has experience, who can do personnel work with the men under him, who will work hard and who will accept the job at a maximum salary of $4,800."

From a list of over 70 applicants, William Saunders was found to be that man. The former coach of Colorado Teachers College in Greeley (UNC), Saunders was a fun-loving Southern gentleman who played his college football at Navy.

Saunders first team floundered to a 2-4 record, losing their final four games and not scoring in their last three. But thanks largely to the talents of scat-back William "Kayo" Lam, CU re-emerged as a conference contender with a 7-2 mark in 1933 and went 6-1-2 in 1934, which was good enough to earn a tie for the conference title. CU also beat Utah for the first time in 10 years, 7-6.

TRIBUTE The Aggies down in Stillwater were extremely impressed with the work of Frank McGlone, a powerful blocking back on CU's 7-2 team in 1933. After McGlone leveled several Aggies to lead a 6-0 victory, the Oklahoma A&M student newspaper ran this poem in honor of McGlone the following week:

> "Grosvenor, a troubador,
> Makes touchdowns in the battle,
> But for a fight just any night,
> From Boulder to Seattle
> We'd pick the lone and lean McGlone
> To make the rafters rattle.
> There is a name that sounds the same
> As a left hook to the chin,
> An Irish-Scot, who, like as not
> Goes in a fight to win.
> For Frank McGlone just has a tone
> Of fists thrown out and in.
> For he's a bold bad man, a des-pee-ray-do
> From Bloody Gulch in Col-e-ray-do."
>
> *Colorado Alumnus, December 1933*

STEPPING DOWN Saunders coached his teams to a 15-7-2 record over three years. At the height of his success, Saunders unexpectedly resigned after his third season in 1935, saying he wanted to tend to his ranch in New

Myron Witham was 2-9-1 against Utah, a record which led to his dismissal as coach in 1931:
1920 L, 0-7
1921 T, 0-0
1922 L, 0-3
1923 W, 17-7
1924 W, 3-0
1925 L, 7-12
1926 L, 3-37
1927 L, 13-20
1928 L, 6-25
1929 L, 0-40
1930 L, 0-34
1931 L, 0-32

Good-guy William Saunders coached Colorado to a 15-7-2 record between 1932-34 before stepping down to tend to his ranch in New Mexico.

Mexico although he returned to coaching in Denver two years later.

He apparently didn't notice a big, strong kid by the name of White on the freshman squad that year who would be moving up to the varsity next season.

KAYO LAM

Before Whizzer there was Kayo.

William "Kayo" Lam, all 115 pounds of him, emerged from tiny Glenrock, Wyo., and helped lead CU football into the big time in the early 1930s. By his senior year in 1935, Lam (up to 160 pounds) was such a star that he relegated backfield mate Byron "Whizzer" White, then a sophomore, to backup duty.

Lam led the nation in rushing as a junior with 906 yards. In a 58-0 win over Mines that season, Lam ran for four touchdowns and threw for another in just 12 minutes of action.

One of CU's more interesting personalities off the field, Lam came to CU as a band drummer and continued to play Boulder hotspots with his band. When he added vocals to his act, he became known as "The Crooning Quarterback."

While his team struggled to a 5-4 record in 1935, Lam blossomed as the featured player. He was CU's first 1,000-yard rusher as he led the nation again in rushing (1,043) and in all-purpose yardage (2,225) and became the first CU player invited to the East-West Shrine Game in San Francisco.

Said his coach Bunnie Oakes, who played with the great "Red" Grange at Illinois and later coached White, "He's the best runner I ever saw." After graduation, Lam worked in the CU athletic department, serving as assistant dean of men and business manager for 30 years up to his retirement in 1970.

William "Kayo" Lam, depicted in this Jan. 16, 1966, Boulder Daily Camera cartoon, was CU's first 1,000-yard rusher in 1935 before becoming a fixture in the CU athletic department for 30 years.

THE WHIZZER OF AH'S

No other athlete, possibly no other Colorado alum, reached the heights that Byron White achieved on the CU campus and beyond.

Born in Ft. Collins, White was raised in a tiny, neighboring farming community of Wellington (sportswriters often referred to him as the "Duke of Wellington"). His father managed a lumber yard, and White grew up stacking two-by-fours and developing the body White's freshman coach, Frank Potts, later described as "hard as iron all over."

His resume is overwhelming.

White became CU's first All-American in 1937, leading the nation in rushing (1,121 yards) and scoring (122 points) while captaining an undefeated Buffs team to its first bowl appearance. He graduated as the school's second all-time leading rusher, leading scorer, leading punter, and leader in total offense, all-purpose yardage, interceptions and punt returns.

White was also all-conference in basketball and baseball and earned nine varsity letters. His No. 24 is one of three numbers retired, and when the university selected its "All-Century Team" on its 100-year football anniversary in 1989, White was the leading vote-getter, receiving 5,812 out of a possible 6,265 votes.

He studied, too. White, the student body president and valedictorian, graduated with a 3.968 grade-point

Probably CU's most famous athlete ever, Byron "Whizzer" White, came from Wellington, Colo., population 300.

Chapter 2: Wars and Whizzer 1916-1947 27

Whizzer White breaks through an opening on a snowy track at Colorado Stadium in 1937.

White served on the U.S. Supreme Court from 1962-1993.

average (180 hours of A, six of B) and became a Rhodes Scholar in 1938, all the while working in a fraternity cafeteria.

White postponed his Rhodes Scholarship work at Oxford and played one season of professional football for the Pittsburgh Pirates in 1938. As a rookie, he led the NFL in rushing and was named to the all-NFL first team. He then went to England, but his education was interrupted by World War II, so he returned to the NFL for two more seasons with the Detroit Lions and led the league in rushing again in 1940 while attending law school at Yale during the off-season.

White was inducted into the National Football Hall of Fame in 1952.

White enlisted as a naval intelligence officer during World War II and served in the South Pacific. He was instructed to write a report on the sinking of a P.T. boat captained by John Fitzgerald Kennedy. Thus began a relationship that climaxed in 1962 when White was nominated by President Kennedy (and approved by Congress) for the United States Supreme Court.

After 31 years on the bench, Justice White retired in 1993.

MY LITTLE BROTHER, THE JUSTICE Byron's older brother, Clayton (who was also called Sam), starred at CU between 1931-34 and distinguished himself as a Rhodes Scholar in 1933. It says a lot about Byron's legacy that a gifted student and athlete such as Clayton White is remembered mostly as Byron White's older brother. But Clayton saw it coming: "If you think I'm good, wait until you see my kid brother," he said in 1933.

ANOTHER ERA For the second time in four years, athletic director Carlson was searching for a football coach before the 1935 season. His choice was Bernard "Bunnie" Oakes, an ex-Marine who ran his practices like one.

Oakes played collegiately at Illinois in the days of the great Red Grange, and his five-year coaching stint at CU was blessed with two pretty good runners in their own right, Lam in 1935 and White from 1935-37.

The Buffs were 25-15-1 and captured three conference titles under Oakes, but he was arguably the least popular coach in the first 50 years of the program. After the White-led, magical season of 1937, which ended in a Cotton Bowl loss to Rice, Oakes signed a new five-year contract. But his 1938 team slumped to 3-4-1, and dissension among the players ran rampant.

Several players quit, and a petition circulated among the team called for Oakes' ousting (one of the reasons they gave was the coach held longer practices than conference rules allowed).

The athletic board wanted to fire him immediately, but the Regents held off until after the 1939 season. The team, minus contributing players Marty Brill and Orvill Nuttall, rallied from an 0-3 start to win its last five games and the conference championship.

Oakes, however, couldn't rally. The last three years of

A 1935 season ticket, for five home games at Colorado Stadium, cost $5.50. Including tax.

"Whizzer" White's 102-yard kickoff return for a touchdown in a 7-6 loss to Denver in 1936 remains the longest in CU history.

White was also an all-conference basketball and baseball player in addition to his football exploits. He earned nine varsity letters.

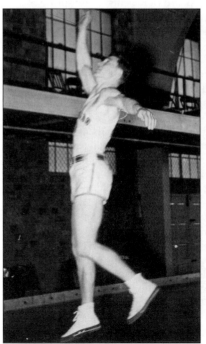

Chapter 2: Wars and Whizzer 1916-1947

CU coach Bunnie Oakes and his star, Whizzer White, in 1937. Oakes rewrote his entire playbook in 1937 to feature the multi-talented White.

9. One of the earliest NCAA records was 246.3 all-purpose yards per game, established in 1937 by CU senior Whizzer White. That record wasn't broken until 1988. Name the player who erased White's record, 51 years later.

his contract, worth $5,000 a year, were bought out in an agreement with the Board of Regents in the spring of 1940. Oakes returned to coach in the Rocky Mountain Athletic Conference (formed in 1936) with Wyoming from 1941-46.

BREAKING OUT White's sophomore season, his first with the varsity, was cut short by a knee injury, although he recovered sufficiently to participate in basketball and baseball.

White burst on the national scene the following fall on a snowy November Saturday in a game against Utah. He accounted for all his team's points in the 31-7 victory on two punt returns for touchdowns, a 90-yard kickoff return for another score, a 38-yard TD run and a 35-yard TD pass to Art Unger. He also kicked one extra point.

Wrote The Denver Post: "A gold streak, 'whizzing over the field of falling snow,' this boy White ... "

But that's not where White got the name Whizzer.

Two years earlier, Leonard Cahn, a Denver sportswriter, commented to his editor after seeing White in a freshmen game, "That guy's a real whizzer!" The name stuck, but Byron's close friends know never to call him Whizzer in person. White detests the nickname.

HIGH PRAISE Frank Potts, White's freshman coach who would head the program in 1940, watched White develop from the fields of Wellington to national stardom. His assessment:

> "To my mind, (White) was the perfect combination of brains, strength and coordination," Potts wrote. "He had the strongest forearms and chest development I ever saw. He was hard as iron all over. His straight-arm was like a mule's kick.
>
> "He was just plain mean and ornery and tenacious. He knew everybody's assignment and he'd knock the block off any guy who didn't do his job. He wasn't dirty, just mean. Ask anybody who ever tried to tackle him. He made every play sting."

Coach Frank Potts, a legendary CU track figure, predicted great things for Byron White when he was just a freshman in 1934.

YOU COACH, I'LL PLAY White and Oakes enjoyed a fine player-coach relationship. Not surprisingly, Oakes designed his offense around the vast talents of his quarterback, and White took charge on the field, often demanding his teammates to play harder, just as Oakes commanded in practice.

Oakes taught White to field punts on the run, whenever possible. It was an innovation that made White the most dangerous punt returner of the day.

But when it came to his studies, Whizzer was his own coach, as this story related by Carlson in a Denver Post column by Harry Farrar illustrates:

> "I remember one time," CU Athletic Director Harry Carlson said, "when Byron had hurt a knee and was sitting in the whirlpool for treatment. He was studying a textbook. Coach Bunnie Oakes came in and snorted that Byron should be doing something worthwhile, such as boning up on football plays.
>
> "Byron very quietly told Oakes, 'You take care of the football. I'll take care of the books.'"

GOING BOWLING CU's 1937 season had a magical feel from the very beginning. An opening 14-6 win at Colorado Stadium over highly ranked Missouri, featuring a school record 84-yard punt by White, set the tone. White was already a national figure; his team was about to join him.

Oakes surrounded White with a capable supporting cast. Fullback Ervin Cheney opened plenty of holes and had a knack for getting into the end zone in tight situations. Nuttall assisted White in the backfield.

CU's surprising 8-0 romp through the regular season ended with a 34-7 rout of Denver, and White capped his

10. *In what season did CU lead the NCAA in total offense, rushing and scoring?*

Chapter 2: Wars and Whizzer 1916-1947 31

The 1937 Buffaloes, CU's first Orange Bowl squad.

magnificent career with three touchdowns to bring his record totals to 16 TDs and 122 points.

For their efforts, the Buffs were invited to the Cotton Bowl in Dallas for a New Year's Day matchup against Rice. The team voted to accept, and later voted as to when they would leave for the game and where they would practice. Democracy ruled in those days.

SAYS IT ALL On Nov. 3, 1937, national columnist Henry M'Lemore for United Press was dispatched to get the scoop on Colorado's legendary runner near the end of White's senior season. Here is M'Lemore's article in its entirety:

"Here in the land of the eternal snows, they are making an eternal fuss about a young man with the rather unusual name of Whizzer White.

Whizzer, who was christened Byron, quarterbacks the undefeated, untied and almost unscored upon University of Colorado football team and has displaced Pikes Peak, Estes Park and Buffalo Bill's final resting place as the state's outstanding attraction.

He's in the headlines more than Mr. Roosevelt and declarations that he is the greatest football player in the country are more common than silver dollars. There are many critics who rate him as better than Earl "Dutch" Clark, the fellow who went from Colorado College to become the standout performer in the professional ranks.

I came here to take a look at him and was besieged with stories of his prowess. How he played but 13 minutes last Saturday but found that sufficient time to score 21 points and take third place among the nation's leading scorers with 62 points. How he would have already scored well above 100 points this year were he not an unselfish fellow who refuses to call his own signal when the ball is in scoring position. Time and again he has carried the number of fullback Ervin Cheney for the scoring plunge. Cheney has 42 points to his

This recognizable cheer, created by student Joe Bounds, was first heard in the 1931 Homecoming Parade:
FIGHT! FIGHT! FIGHT!
Fight! C.U. down the field
C.U. must win!
Fight! Fight for victory,
C.U. knows no defeat,
We'll roll up a mighty score,
Never give in!
Shoulder to shoulder we will
FIGHT! FIGHT! FIGHT!

credit.

And he is not only a football player. He is an all-conference third baseman in baseball and all-conference basketball guard.

Moreover he is the best student on the campus. This I learned from none other than president George Norlin.

'Whizzer is an A student. He is certain to make Phi Beta Kappa next month and he will try for a Rhodes Scholarship,' president Norlin said. 'He is the busiest man on the campus, what with working his way through school by waiting tables at a fraternity and serving as president of the student body.'

Between halves of the Utah game last year, president Norlin said he visited the team's dressing room and found Whizzer stretched out on a rubbing table studying his calculus."

WHIZZER ARRIVES White didn't make the trip to Dallas with his teammates. He was in San Francisco taking his Rhodes Scholarship tests and arrived a few days later.

"FORTH WORTH, Texas, Dec. 22-About the biggest news to break in this country since Sam Houston copped a close decision from the Mexicans in 1836 to get out of the chile and tamale league, popped here today when a retiring blond youngster rushed off a plane at the Fort Worth airport."

"Byron (Whizzer) White was the distinguished young aerial passenger and the reception he received eclipsed the greeting accorded another famous air traveler, Charles Augustus Lindbergh, in 1927, at Fort Worth's Meacham Field. Photogs and sports writers were as thick as the muggy mist which shrouded Northern Texas last night and this morning, and White was put thru his paces like a trained seal."

Rocky Mountain News, Dec. 23, 1937

BIG GAME PERFORMER Despite the constant attention and pressure, White closed out his brilliant college career in fine fashion, albeit in a losing effort, against Rice. White tossed an 8-yard TD pass and returned an interception 47 yards for another score in the first quarter as CU built a 14-0 lead that eventually disappeared in the 28-14 loss to spoil an undefeated season.

"Surrounded by autograph hunters, the blond star remained popular even in defeat with countless Dallas football fans who pushed and fought to

During World War II, CU had to be creative in finding enough opponents to play to fill out its football schedule. Between 1943-45 against military teams, CU was 1-2 vs. Ft. Francis Warren, 1-0 vs. Lowry Air Force Base, 0-1 vs. Second Air Force Base, and 1-0 vs. Peru State.

11. Name the five Buffs who became Rhodes Scholars.

Chapter 2: Wars and Whizzer 1916-1947

Byron "Whizzer" White was a triple-threat offensive player. He was equally effective passing, punting and kicking. He also played safety on defense.

12. In his magical senior season of 1937, CU's Whizzer White led the nation in rushing (1,121 yards), in total offense (1,596 yards) and in what other category?

get his signature on scraps of paper and programs.

He was delayed getting to the dressing room because of the scores who crowded around him.

He accepted congratulations quietly from admirers and said little until after his shower.

'It was a good game and I enjoyed it, but I wish we could play them again tomorrow,' the Whizzer told this writer.

'I am sorry this is my last game but it's over and there's no hard feeling about it.' "

Denver Post, Jan. 2, 1938

1940-47: TRANSITION TIME

CU trudged through the 1940s in almost a post-Whizzer hangover, and its next savior, Dal Ward, wasn't to arrive until 1948. Oakes' messy dismissal had tarnished the program and set it back a stride or two. And with an obviously more serious issue such as World War II, clouding the spirits of everyone, CU football lost some of its luster.

CU lost some players and its coach, Jim Yeager, to war-time service. The Buffs began the decade by promoting track coach and faithful athletic department employee Frank Potts to the head football coaching post for the 1940 season. CU had a good team back, bolstered by the return of anti-Oakes players Brill and Nuttall, but all they could muster was a 5-3-1 record, which the Regents called a "splendid" job.

Potts declined an offer to stay on as coach, choosing instead his first love, track, and CU turned its eyes to "Gentleman Jim" Yeager, the head man at Iowa State.

Yeager's tenure ran from 1941-43, was interrupted in 1944-45 when he went off to the war (Potts filled in), and picked up again in 1946-47. An immensely popular coach, Yeager's best season was his second, in 1942, when the 7-2 Buffs shared the conference crown with Utah.

But Yeager lost the recruiting war to Uncle Sam and watched many of best players, including powerful backs John Zeigler, Walt Clay and Carl "Steamroller" Stearns, leave the program. The ranks were so depleted across the league that conference play was suspended for three years.

Jim Yeager left his CU coaching duties to serve in World War II from 1944-45.

39 SAILORS, 36 MARINES AND 18 CIVILIANS SEEKING BERTHS ON U. OF COLORADO GRID TEAM

Headline in The Denver Post, Sept. 11, 1943

College teams, including Colorado, stocked their teams with mostly inexperienced military students training on campus who had the time to play on the team.

"To begin with, our football will be pretty fundamental," Yeager said. "We'll probably work into a system as the season progresses. ... I never saw a group in higher spirits."

Yeager returned from a two-year stint in the Navy in 1946, but he was never able to recapture the success he and his teams enjoyed before the war. After a 4-5 season in 1947, Yeager resigned to enter a profitable clothing business in town, and the search to find the man who could dress up the Buffs as winners again began.

13. The Buffs began recording attendance figures at Folsom Field in 1946. In what season did the first recorded sellout take place?

Dallas Ward
1948-1958

Overall Record: 63-41-6 (.600 winning percentage)
Conference Championships: None.
Best Seasons: 1951 (7-3), 1956 (8-2-1).
Worst Seasons: 1948 (3-6), 1949 (3-7), 1950 (5-4-1).

Welcome to the big time.

Dallas Ward, CU's 14th head football coach, brought his Midwestern conservatism and football philosophy to Colorado in 1948 from the state of Minnesota, where he had been a highly successful high school coach and college assistant during the Golden Gophers' best years in the Big Ten, the toughest conference in the nation at the time.

In Boulder, it certainly was a time of transition. Ward's first season also marked CU's debut in the old Missouri Valley Conference, or the new Big Seven, joining Iowa State, Kansas, Kansas State, Missouri, Nebraska and Oklahoma.

In order to compete with the "big boys," Ward, 42, instituted the offense he had coached under Minnesota head coach Bernie Bierman, the single wing. Critics, and Ward had plenty over his 11 years in Boulder, referred to the single wing as a "horse-and-buggy" offense.

Dal Ward's first team in 1948 emerged from the post-war era by posting a 3-6 record. The squad was CU's first to compete in the Big Seven and finished fourth with a 2-3 record. Ward stands in the middle of the back row.

With it, the Buffs rode into the big time.

Oklahoma, coached by Bud Wilkinson, absolutely dominated the conference (and the nation) during the late 1940s and 1950s, a run highlighted by OU's 12 straight conference championships and a 47-game undefeated streak. But no Big Seven team put more fear in the heart of Wilkinson and his talented Sooners than did Ward's Buffaloes.

Dal Ward was born in Lexington, Ore., and starred on and coached his high school football team. Having began his high school playing career in the seventh grade, Dal was deemed experienced enough for the coaching job by the time he actually attended high school.

Ward overcame his modest physical abilities to become a three-sport athlete at Oregon State, starting for three years as a 170-pound end. He turned down contracts to play minor-league baseball and professional football to become a football coach at Marshall High School in Minneapolis. After winning back-to-back city league championships and years of supplying the University with numerous quality players from his program, Ward was hired as freshmen coach at Minnesota in 1936.

When Colorado called, Ward saw it as another challenge to take on. The program was down, having lost nine games over the two previous years under Yeager, yet was about to jump into Big Seven competition. More than one fan, newspaper writer and alum thought the Buffaloes were diving in over their heads trying to compete with the Oklahomas and Nebraskas.

But Ward, a quiet yet stern leader, ignored the rumblings and prepared to do what he did best – coach.

Dal Ward, who coached from 1948-1958, brought a simple but effective offense from Minnesota and became one of the most successful coaches in CU history.

DALLAS WARD, WHO CLIMBED FOOTBALL'S HEIGHTS THE HARD WAY, WILL LEAD C.U.'S BUFFALOES INTO THE TOUGH BIG SEVEN

Rocky Mountain Empire Magazine, Sept. 19, 1948

"The fact that Colorado will undertake the most difficult football schedule in her history as the Buffs make their debut in the Big Seven conference does not dampen the optimistic spirit of the new coach.

"... Ward describes himself as 'one of the luckiest guys alive' and supplements his good fortune with abundant hard work, strict attention to detail and the use of thorough coaching methods that mark him as a perfectionist."

Dal Ward was a wanted man at Colorado. Ward reportedly turned down six head coaching offers while he was at CU. They were from Southern California, Oregon State, Indiana, Southern Methodist, Wyoming and Washington.

Dal Ward's All-Star team of players that he coached, from a Feb. 3, 1975, Denver Post article:
Ends: Don Branby, Alabama Glass, Jerry Leahy, Frank Merz, Gary Knafelc and Frank Clarke;
Tackles: John Wooten, Jack Jorgenson and Bob Salerno;
Guards: Dick Stapp, Roger Hunt and Dick Knowlton;
Centers: Roy Shepherd, Jim Uhlir and Dick Punches;
Linebackers: Sherm Pruitt and Bill Mondt;
Quarterback: Boyd Dowler; Tailbacks: Carroll Hardy, Zack Jordan and Bob Stransky;
Wingbacks: Woody Shelton, Eddie Dove and Frank Bernardi;
Fullbacks: Merwin Hodel, John Bayuk, Emerson Wilson and Chuck Weiss.

ROUGH START Ward's horse-and-buggy single wing broke down as the 1948 Buffs opened with a home 9-6 loss to lowly New Mexico, followed by a 40-7 whipping at the hands of Kansas in their Big Seven debut. But the next week, led by tiny back Harry Narcisian, the Buffs flashed signs of the improvement to come with a 20-6 win over heavily-favored Nebraska at Folsom Field. CU defeated just one more conference foe, Kansas State, the rest of the season and finished 3-6 and 2-3 in its new conference, good for fourth place.

Year Two in Ward's rebuilding effort was even more disappointing. CU opened promisingly enough by nipping Kansas 14-13 in Boulder thanks to two blocked extra-point attempts, but there were few more bright spots. Sophomore Merwin Hodel, a bruising fullback, emerged on the scene, but his and the Buffs' best years remained ahead. CU finished 3-7 and in sixth place at 1-4 in the conference to mark Ward's second-straight losing season. It would be his last.

BENCH WARMER He didn't see one minute of action all season, but there was a sophomore scout-team quarterback on that 1948 squad who would make an indelible mark on the CU program. Bud Davis, who would eventually be known as Dr. William Davis, president of Idaho State and New Mexico Universities, finally earned a varsity letter in 1950, thanks to just enough service on the Buffs' PAT defensive team.

In an Oct. 6, 1968, first-person article in The Denver Post, Davis, who authored the definitive history of the University called "Glory Colorado," recounted his "playing" days:

"The fact is that among the fans watching Colorado football from 1948 to 1950, those who even knew I was in the game included only my wife, my parents, and fraternity brothers.

"After three years of varsity service, my jersey, No. 25, was untouched, unsoiled and unknown, probably the only jersey in almost 80 years of football at my alma mater that never had to be cleaned.

"...I well remember my first interview with Coach Ward. Frustrated that the full potential of my 145 pounds of dynamite and enthusiasm was going unnoticed, I cornered him one day after practice. 'Coach,' I said with dignity, 'I'm not sure whether I should be playing fullback or quarterback.'

"He looked me up and down critically before replying, 'Frankly, I don't think it makes a hellova

Ward works the sidelines as assistant Frank Prentup listens in.

During Dal Ward's era, CU produced four All-Americans (Don Branby, John Bayuk, Bob Stransky and John Wooten) and 24 All-Big Seven selections.

lot of difference.'"

Following the firing of coach Sonny Grandelius amidst a recruiting scandal after the 1961 season, Davis, then serving as alumni director, was hired as interim head coach. One of his assistants was Dal Ward.

SINGLE WING AND A PRAYER By 1950, Ward's offense was catching on and the Buffs were catching up. A modest 5-

The first coaching staff under Dal Ward (from left to right): Bus Gentry, Ray Jenkins, Ward, Marshall Wells and Frank Prentup.

Chapter 3: Dallas Ward 1948-1958 39

Ward horses around with Ward Waldrof.

4-1 record belied the large steps the Buffs took to gain respectability. Once again, CU upset a favored Nebraska team, 28-19, to rekindle interest on campus and in Boulder. The Buffs then took a 3-2-1 record into their first conference meeting against mighty and third-ranked Oklahoma (scheduling conflicts kept CU and OU from playing the first two years of the Big Seven).

FOOTBALL HISTORY TO BE WRITTEN AS COLORADO MEETS NATION'S NO. 3 TEAM;
SOONERS CAN SET MODERN RECORD WITH WINS; BUFF VICTORY WILL BE MAJOR UPSET

Boulder Daily Camera, Nov. 3, 1950

"Grid history will be made Saturday in Folsom Stadium when the football teams from two great state universities clash. Oklahoma, seeking an all-time modern football record 27 straight, and Colorado, seeking to stage the biggest football upset of the season.

"...Tomorrow's classic, played before the greatest crowd in Boulder history, 29,000, finds Oklahoma, the nation's number three grid power, giving regional fans the best exhibition of football ever presented before in the Rockies. Oklahoma is to football what Hogan and Snead are to golf, the Yankees are to baseball or Phillips' to basketball. They are champions all the way."

A Hodel touchdown gave CU an early 6-0 lead and sophomore Zack Jordan passed for 139 yards and averaged 42 yards a punt, but the Sooners escaped with a 27-

14. Name the lineman who played for the Buffs from 1950-52 and later became an astronaut featured in the 1995 movie, Apollo 13.

18 win before a record crowd of 29,500 at Folsom Stadium. A disappointing, but promising, result.

BRIGHT LIGHTS CU made its first-ever national television appearance in 1951 at Nebraska. The Buffs overcame bitter cold temperatures and an early deficit to drill the Cornhuskers 36-14 at Memorial Stadium to take the season-finale and finish 7-3 and in second place in the conference.

BIG FOOT Colorado's fine tradition of producing punters didn't start with Zack Jordan in the early 1950s, but it may have peaked then. When his family moved to Boulder, Jordan transferred from California to CU in the spring of 1950. He quietly walked on the football team but left heralded as one of the best offensive backs, and especially punters, in CU history.

As a sophomore, Jordan led the nation in punting with a 48.3 yard average, a national record at the time. His 57.2 yard average in a 28-25 win over Arizona was also a single-game NCAA record.

Several long boots came on third-down quick kicks, a

Zack Jordan, the first of a long line of nationally heralded CU punters, led the nation in punting in 1950 and narrowly missed out on repeating the feat in 1952. Jordan earned a spot on CU's All-Century team as a punter, but he was a fine halfback who could pass, too. Jordan also signed a professional baseball contract after he graduated.

trademark Ward strategy. A blocked punt against Nebraska (the lone block in his career) two years later kept Jordan from winning national honors again as he fell one-tenth of a yard short of USC's Des Koch at 43.4 yards.

Jordan's 3,035 yards of total offense stood as a CU record until Gale Weidner broke it in 1961.

Jordan was an All-Big Seven pick as a senior in 1952 after accounting for all three touchdowns (two rushing, one passing) in CU's historic 21-21 tie with Oklahoma. He punted seven times for a 56-yard average in that game, including a 77-yard quick kick from his own 1-yard line, which set up his tying score.

In the final 1:51, Jordan drove the Buffs 62 yards to the Sooner 21 when time ran out and CU had to settle for the tie.

CLOSE BUT NO... The Buffs under Ward never did beat Oklahoma, posting an 0-8-1 record, which is greatly misleading. The series featured just three routs: 55-14, 56-21 and 23-7. In addition to the 21-21 tie in 1952, CU lost 27-18, 27-20, 13-6, 27-19, and 14-13. In six of nine

DON BRANBY

Whizzer White stood alone as CU's only All-American for 15 years until 1952 when a quiet, versatile athlete from Glenwood, Minn., named Don Branby joined the legend.

Branby, a stout defensive end who made running around his side of the Buffs' defensive line a futile effort for three years, earned a spot on the Associated Press All-American first team in 1952.

"I never thought it was possible," Branby said from the Daily Camera lobby, where he heard of his honor. "It is the greatest thrill in my lifetime."

While White was the star of stars, Branby toiled in as much obscurity as a player of his talents possibly could. That didn't stop him from collecting nine varsity letters (matching White), as he played on CU's basketball and baseball teams as well.

As a senior, Branby was named to virtually every all-opponent team on CU's schedule. In his final game, he intercepted two passes and recovered two fumbles in CU's 61-0 rout of Colorado A&M.

Branby's relentless hawking of Oklahoma quarterback Eddie Crowder, the future CU coach, highlighted the Buffs' 21-21 tie with the mighty Sooners.

"He was the fiercest competitor I have coached in 25 years," Dal Ward said.

games with Oklahoma, CU scored the first touchdown and led in eight of the nine games, including once by 19-6 at halftime. Four times, CU led in the fourth period.

RELOADING Following in Jordan's footsteps were Carroll Hardy and Frank Bernardi, a dynamic pair of runners known as CU's "Twin Torpedoes." Both were All-Big Seven in 1954.

Hardy, who was the first CU freshman to play under the new Big Seven eligibilty rules in 1951, scored a touchdown the first time he touched the football, scampering 12 yards to ice away Colorado A&M. Later, he scored CU's only touchdown, a 55-yard run, in a 45-7 loss to national champion Michigan State.

"I wouldn't trade him for any other back in the country," Ward said during Hardy's junior campaign. Bud Wilkinson called Hardy, "One of the most dangerous, if not the most dangerous, back we have played against or I have seen."

Hardy averaged 9.2 yards a carry as a senior (including a national-record 10 carries for 238 yards in the season finale), complemented nicely by Bernardi's 8.9

Alabama Glass, an end from 1951-53, said Ward, known as a tough disciplinarian, had two nicknames for him: That-A-Boy Bama and Goddammit Glass.

Carroll Hardy (left) and Frank Bernardi (right) were known as CU's "Twin Torpedoes" in 1954, and the backs led the Buffs to a 7-2-1 record.

Chapter 3: Dallas Ward 1948-1958

Carroll Hardy will forever be known as the only man to pinch hit for Ted Williams.

Between 1946 and 1959, Oklahoma wasn't beaten in 75 consecutive conference games, but they were tied twice. By Kansas (13-13) in 1947 and CU (21-21) in 1952.

average. They scored 16 touchdowns between them.

Bernardi, a 5-9 halfback/defensive back, typically played nearly all 60 minutes of a game and was known for his toughness as well as his 669 yards of total offense, which led CU in 1953.

In 1954, Bernardi denied Missouri a trip to the Orange Bowl and preserved a 19-19 tie by blocking a late extra point attempt. Bernardi broke his nose on the play, and lore has it that he blocked the ball with his face, but he actually swatted the ball away with his hand and smashed his face on teammate Wally Merz's knee.

In any event, Bernardi didn't miss a start and went on to an improbable professional football career with the Cardinals and Denver Broncos. Hardy played one season in the NFL before taking his skills to the major leagues as a right-handed hitting outfielder for the Cleveland Indians, Boston Red Sox and Minnesota Twins.

He's also the answer to one of the best trivia questions of all-time: "Who was the only man to pinch hit for Ted Williams?" In the first inning after Williams removed himself from a 1960 game after fouling a ball off his foot, Hardy grounded into a double play.

"Ten years from now," Hardy said in a 1980 newspaper story, "that won't be a double play I hit into. It'll be a home run."

Hardy, incidentally, also pinch hit twice for a young Carl Yastrzemski in 1961, doubling both times. "Yaz" wouldn't be pinch hit for again until 1978.

GRACIOUS Bernardi earned second-team AP All-American honors in 1954 but it was hard to distinguish his performance from that of Hardy, who was named honorable mention. Both played in the East-West Shrine Game.

> "Bernardi said 'Gosh, that's a great honor, but I don't deserve it,' when he learned of his AP selection. Then, in the next breath he asked about Hardy.
>
> " 'Carroll's as good as any football player in the country, in my opinion,' Bernardi said."
>
> *Boulder Daily Camera, Dec. 9, 1954*

HANDS ON Frank Prentup, an assistant for Ward all 11 years and long-time baseball coach, recalled Ward's teaching methods in a Boulder Daily Camera article in 1983:

> "We were working late one day after practice with the punters," Prentup said. "They were having a bad night. (Ward) came over and was kind of grumbling and grouching. Well, somebody kicked a ball and it bounced into his hands. He picked it

up, booted a perfect spiral about 50 yards, said 'That's the way you're supposed to do it,' and walked off the field."

IN SEARCH OF ORANGES CU returned just three regulars in 1956 – Wally Merz, Dick Stapp and hard-charging fullback John Bayuk – so expectations weren't real high. They certainly didn't get any higher when Oregon raided a newly expanded Folsom Field (capacity 45,000, although crowds of 45,500 and 47,000 watched the Buffs play that year) and hung a 35-0 pasting on the young Buffs.

CU rebounded, led by its talented backfield of Bayuk, Eddie Dove, Bob Stransky and quarterback Boyd Dowler, who actually lined up under center on occasion as Ward mixed in some "T" formations with his single wing. The Buffs marched to five straight wins, setting up the yearly showdown with No. 1 Oklahoma, which would be played in Boulder before 47,000 fans.

End Jerry Leahy blocked a quick kick, and Bayuk pounced on it to give CU its customary early lead, which was stretched to 19-6 by halftime. But a gutsy call by Wilkinson to go for a fourth down deep in OU territory at the beginning of the third quarter fueled the Sooners to a 27-19 victory and their 58th consecutive game without a loss.

Still, a CU win or tie at Missouri the following week would give the Buffs a trip to the Orange Bowl as Oklahoma was again ineligible after playing in Miami the previous year.

Fullback John Bayuk was nicknamed "The Beast" when, as a sophomore, he ran for 71 fourth-quarter yards and scored the final touchdown at Kansas. After the game, an elderly female KU fan visited the Buffs' team hotel and asked to speak with the "beast who wears number 30."

BUFFS AIMING FOR ORANGE BOWL AFTER SCARING MIGHTY OKLAHOMA

Boulder Daily Camera, Nov. 5, 1956

The starting CU backfield for the 1957 Orange Bowl: Eddie Dove (11), John Bayuk (30), Bob Stransky (20), Boyd Dowler (44) and center Jim Uhlir.

Chapter 3: Dallas Ward 1948-1958   45

Twice in the decade after his coaching days at CU were over, Dal Ward was prematurely pronounced dead. In 1965, a massive heart attack struck Ward. Bud Wilkinson, the former Oklahoma coach, heard a report that he was deceased and sent flowers to Ward's wife Jane. Four years later, a blood clot in Ward's brain landed him back in the hospital. One doctor told Jane her husband was dead, only to have another doctor predict recovery. Ward lived 14 more years until his death in 1983.

"So many adjectives have been used to describe the play of the Buffs that there are only a few left. In the minds of many, it was the greatest performance ever given by a Colorado football team...

"Tex Maule, of the national Sports Illustrated, said, 'Dal, I came out here from New York looking for a possible upset. Well, we didn't quite make it but I have an idea this was the best football game played this year.' "

CU got its tie with Missouri, coming back to make it 14-14, then won its final two non-conference games to earn the Orange Bowl berth, only the Buffs' second bowl trip ever. In what Ward called the highlight of his career, CU opened a 20-0 lead on Clemson, fell behind 21-20, and then rallied when John Wooten covered an on-side kick to set up Bayuk's scoring plunge to win 27-21. Stransky's interception capped CU's 8-2-1 season.

"T"-EED OFF Speaking to 800 coaches at the National Football Clinic, Ward contested that he was fired after the 1958 season in part because of his single wing formations, which fans and alumni considered outdated compared to the modern "T" formation.

"Our dear alumni," Ward said. "... want us to go out there and throw the ball around, dream up all kinds of fancy formations and take all kinds of chances to make the game interesting for the spectators."

With the versatile Dowler at quarterback, Ward's 1957 team led the nation in rushing and was second in total offense. Stransky, nicknamed "Stop and Go," went for 1,097 rushing yards, joining Kayo Lam and Whizzer White as CU 1,000-yard rushers. Despite all the offensive firepower, the Buffs managed only a 6-3-1 record, losing

Coach Dal Ward was carried off the field after the Buffs beat Clemson, 27-21, in the 1957 Orange Bowl. It was CU's first bowl victory.

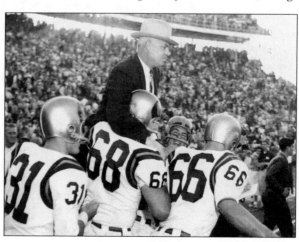

Bob Stransky earned first-team conference honors in 1957 as a running back. When CU's offense featured the pass in 1958, quarterback Boyd Dowler followed in his footsteps.

twice by one point and once by three.

Over their last 28 games, Ward's teams averaged 28 points per game and nearly 400 yards while using a multiple offense.

"If that is supposed to be conservative football, then this is a mighty peculiar game we're playing these days," Ward said.

A SUDDEN END Ward's final two seasons – 6-3-1 in 1957 and 6-4 in 1958, including home losses to Colorado State and Air Force to end the year – disappointed all who were still on an Orange Bowl high and expected more from the experienced teams. Still, very few followers close to the program expected what happened on Jan. 23, 1959, when the Board of Regents voted 5-1 to dismiss Ward for "the best interest of the university."

Here is the entire statement Dal Ward issued in response:

> "The request to step down as football coach came as a complete surprise to me.
>
> "I'm stunned.
>
> "I have not talked to any member of the Board of Regents since the Orange Bowl game in Miami two years ago. At that time they expressed complete satisfaction with the manner in which the football program was being conducted at the University of Colorado.
>
> "I think it is unfortunate that the Board did not follow the normal procedure in making a decision of this type immediately after the close of the sea-

Howard Cook, All-American Bob Stransky's successor in 1958, exploded for 25 points in CU's 65-12 mauling of Arizona. Cook's 25 points (4 TDs, 1 PAT) tied Whizzer White's school record, and the 65 points CU scored as a team marked a modern-era record.

The Buffs went a record 84 games without being shut out between 1947 and 1955, when Colorado A&M blanked CU 10-0 on Nov. 26. Dal Ward–coached teams were shut out only twice; the second time came in their next game, a 35-0 loss to Oregon to open the 1956 season.

son. This would have allowed the members of my staff to locate another position at a time when more positions were open. Nearly all college coaching changes are made before this date and this action is going to create a real hardship for some very capable football coaches and their families.

"I would like to take this opportunity to thank the many loyal alumni and friends of the University for the very solid support they have given me during my tenure at the University of Colorado.

"I would also like to express my appreciation to the grand group of young men who have competed in football here under me. It is largely through their efforts that the University of Colorado occupies the favorable position in football that it enjoys today.

"They represent the very highest type of young American manhood and I am happy to have been associated with them. It has been a very gratifying period my life."

A huge public outcry and immediate support for Ward on the part of the newspapers demanded the Regents rescind their decision. They refused.

Ward, who compiled a 63-41-6 record over 11 sea-

FRANK CLARKE

A list of Colorado football pioneers would be incomplete without the name of Frank Clarke, the first black football player at the University.

Clarke transferred from Trinidad (Colo.) Junior College in 1955. He not only broke through the color barrier, he was instrumental in carrying the Buffs to the 1956 Orange Bowl.

At six-foot, 206 pounds, Clarke was the fastest player on the roster and made a career of turning short passes into long gains from his end position. Clarke led the Buffs in receiving with 13 catches for 407 yards and five touchdowns as a junior. His two TD catches against Missouri the following year gave CU a 14-14 tie with the Tigers and an Orange Bowl berth.

He also handled the kickoff chores and developed into one of the Buffs' best pass rushers on defense.

Clarke, of Beloit, Wis., began his college career at Wisconsin University before transferring to CU via Trinidad JC. He went on to an 11-year career in the NFL with the Cleveland Browns and the Dallas Cowboys.

All-Century teamer Boyd Dowler quarterbacked CU between 1956-58. In the NFL, Dowler was a star receiver. At left, Dowler scores a touchdown in Green Bay's 1967 NFL Championship win over Mike Gaechter and the Dallas Cowboys.

sons, remained as a tenured physical education teacher and later helped future head coaches Bud Davis, Eddie Crowder and Bill Mallory. He was an assistant athletic director until his retirement in 1975, the year he was inducted into the Colorado Sports Hall of Fame. After battling several illnesses, Ward died in 1983 at the age of 76.

Upon his firing, Ward left his best-ever recruiting class, a group which would produce eight starters and 18 players overall for the 1961 undefeated Orange Bowl team. Ward had taken the Buffs to the big time.

JOHN WOOTEN

Affectionately known as the "Hatchet Man," John Wooten carved up opposing defenses for three seasons, paving the way for Buff runners.

Wooten, who became an All-Pro guard with the Cleveland Browns, gained All-American status as a senior in 1958. Wooten's crunching blocks helped CU back Bob Stransky, a close friend, gain over 1,000 yards in his All-American 1957 season.

Along with Franke Clarke, Wooten was among the first black players to play in the Orange Bowl when CU beat Clemson on New Year's Day 1957. It was a bittersweet experience. Wooten and Clarke didn't attend a couple of pre-game team functions at Miami country clubs because blacks weren't permitted.

Wooten's recovery of a Clemson on-side kick in the fourth quarter stuffed the Tigers' momentum and set up CU's winning score in the 27-21 victory, CU's first bowl triumph ever.

Sonny and Bud
1959-1962

When he took over at CU in 1959, 29-year-old Sonny Grandelius was the youngest coach in the nation.

Overall Record: 22-19 (.537 winning percentage)
Coaches: Sonny Grandelius (1959-1961) and Bud Davis (1962)
Conference Championships: 1961 (9-2).
Worst Seasons: 1959 (5-5), 1962 (2-8).

Everett "Sonny" Grandelius brightened Colorado's football picture in 1959, but he would soon be gone amidst ominous storm clouds.

Plucked off the coaching staff at Michigan State, the 29-year-old Grandelius, the youngest coach in the nation, seemed to be everything his predecessor, Dal Ward, was not: young, innovative, charming, ambitious, and, best of all, an aggressive recruiter.

In Grandelius, an All-American halfback for the Spartans in 1950, CU believed it had found the All-American boy. He was hired less than 24 hours after he had been interviewed.

"Oklahoma can be had," Grandelius said when he was hired on Feb. 9, 1959, "and I believe they can be had by CU; If I don't believe it, who will?"

Grandelius, preaching the virtues of the mighty Michigan State machine, talked dollars out of the pockets of boosters and alumni immediately. Grandelius promised to bring glory to Colorado, but there would be a price.

The 1959 Buffaloes, Sonny Grandelius' first team, were the first to wear black as part of their uniform colors. Grandelius junked the old silver and gold uniforms, the grayish plain uniforms that were an eyesore to many fans, and replaced them with black and silver.

Two mediocre seasons of rebuilding and recruiting laid the foundation for CU's 1961 undefeated run through the conference to the Orange Bowl. But as the Buffs were closing in on their first Big Eight (Oklahoma State had joined the Big Seven) championship, the NCAA was closing in on Grandelius' program.

SONNY'S DEBUT Grandelius knew he needed all the charm and fast-talking he could muster to keep CU fans happy through that first season. The schedule was brutal. The Buffs, led by Ward's leftover talented sophomore class, opened against Rose Bowl-bound Washington, a good Baylor team and Oklahoma. The baptism by fire left the Buffs a toasty 0-3, including this 21-12 home loss to Washington:

> "Grandelius' debut was not an artistic success but the 27,000 fans in Folsom Field saw plenty to buoy their hopes for Big Eight activity. Three of the 17 sophomores who played–(Gale) Weidner, end Chuck McBride and tackle John Denvir–were gilt edged standouts and many of the others acquitted themselves well.
>
> "The Buffs showed a passing attack that will keep Big Eight foes jumpy at all times."
>
> *The Denver Post, Sept. 20, 1959*

YOU'VE GOT HOW MANY? Grandelius' recruiting efforts caught his new school by surprise. When the coach's first recruiting class totaled 60 freshmen, he was informed by school officials there were only 17 scholarships to offer.

"With Sonny and his new staff coming in," athletic director Harry Carlson said, "it was a big year for them to

Above, Grandelius (seated in center) addresses the media for the first time. Below, Grandelius conducts his first practice in the spring of 1959.

Chapter 4: Sonny and Bud 1959-1962

get as many freshmen players as they could. We went ahead with the idea that any recruiting over the 17 scholarships would be taken care of by alumni and friends."

"THE WHIP" Grandelius brought a modern, pass-oriented offense to Boulder, and his teams were always stocked with several talented quarterbacks. It didn't take long to recognize that Gale Weidner, a 6-1, 195-pounder, was the best of the bunch.

Buffs Win 1st, 20-17;
Weidner's Passes Fatal to K-State

Headline in The Denver Post, Oct. 11, 1959

"MANHATTAN, KAN.– Gale Weidner, Colorado University's brilliant sophomore quarterback, was a one-man show Saturday as he led the young Buffaloes to a 20-17 football triumph over Kansas State for their first triumph under Coach Sonny Grandelius.

"The 19-year-old Troy, Mont., sensation had a hand in all the scoring, climaxing his amazing performance with a 20-yard touchdown pass in the final period for the winning points in the come-from-behind victory. Weidner ran for the first two Colorado touchdowns and passed for a two-point conversion after the second."

The game revealed two Weidner trademarks, which

Gale Weidner, nicknamed "The Whip," was CU's first pure passing quarterback. Known for leading miraculous comebacks, Weidner left CU as the Buffs' leader in all-purpose yardage.

CU fans would be treated to for the next three seasons: Weidner's strong throwing arm, which earned him the nickname "The Whip," and the quarterback's ability to produce victories late, often using a favorite Grandelius device, the shotgun formation.

Weidner and sophomore guard Joe Romig were both named to the All-Big Eight first team, the conference all-academic team and shared most valuable player honors in 1959. Romig went on to a become a three-time All-Big Eight performer and saw his jersey, No. 67, retired. Weidner was a two-time All-Big Eight pick and left as CU's leading passer and total-offense leader.

Weidner's favorite targets included Ken Blair, McBride and All-American end Jerry Hillebrand. It was Hillebrand that Weidner found for a 17-yard touchdown to cap a 20-point fourth-quarter comeback win over Kansas to preserve the undefeated 1961 conference season. The 20-19 victory is still considered by some the most exciting game in Folsom Field history.

Weidner was named the national back-of-the-week and Grandelius called it "the finest one-game performance I've ever seen by a quarterback."

IMPROVEMENT The Buffs finished the 1959 campaign by going 4-1 and narrowly missed out on an Orange Bowl bid when they fell behind early and lost 14-12 to Nebraska on a cold day in Lincoln. Behind Romig's blocking, Weidner's passing and Teddy Woods' running, the following season started well as the Buffs jumped out to a 5-1 record, highlighted by CU's first win over Oklahoma (7-0) since the schools' first meeting in 1912.

Fullback Chuck Weiss scored the game's only touchdown and made a TD-saving tackle in the fourth quarter on Bennett Watts' 69-yard run.

BUFFS GET THE JOB DONE, 7 TO 0!

Headline in Rocky Mountain News, Oct. 30, 1960

"It finally happened here this moist, overcast afternoon. Colorado University scored its long-sought football victory over Oklahoma's proud Sooners.

"Colorado 7, Oklahoma 0!

"Those much cherished numerals flared brightly on the Folsom Field scoreboard as thousands

Chet Nelson, a Rocky Mountain News columnist in an article titled "Tiddly Winks or Football?," pointed out that Sonny Grandelius was hired to win football games, not popularity contests: "Grandelius was an ambitious young man in a big hurry from the moment he took over at CU, and there is no doubt but that he always looked out for No. 1 first.

"One of his friends remarked midway of last season: 'Sonny aims to make a million before he's 50 and don't bet he won't do it. He can be selfish and ruthless.'"

15. Name the only CU team to appear in the final Associated Press poll from 1938-60.

JOE ROMIG

Little can separate Colorado's two most successful football alums, Byron White and Joe Romig. Both were All-Americans, both won Rhodes Scholarships, both had their jersey numbers retired, both are members of the Football Hall of Fame, and both went on to wildly successful careers after their playing days were over.

But White was nicknamed "Whizzer" while Romig, a 5-9, 196-pound fireplug, carried the moniker "Toad."

Romig, a two-way star playing offensive guard and linebacker, is CU's first three-time All-Big Eight player and two-time All-American (1960 and '61). Romig was sixth in the 1961 Heisman Trophy balloting, an unusually high finish for a line player.

Romig, a Lakewood, Colo., product who carried a 3.8 grade-point average at CU, shunned a professional football career and earned his masters degree from Oxford in plasma physics before he returned to CU to pursue a Ph. D. in astrogeophysics. The man who built his own telescope while at CU still lives in Boulder, where he works as a physicist.

Joe Romig, the only player in CU history to captain two teams and earn All-American honors both seasons, is one of only three Buffs to have his jersey retired (top photo with AD Harry Carlson). In bottom photo, Romig accepts the CU team MVP trophy in 1961 with Grandelius, banquet speaker Ray Eliot and 1962 captain Ken Blair.

TED WOODS

Ted Woods, CU's leading rusher during the Orange Bowl season of 1961, had to talk his way onto the Buffs' track squad as a sophomore in 1960.

A few months later, CU track coach Frank Potts watched Woods run an NCAA meet-record 45.7 seconds in the 400 meters. Woods, who would later hold a world record in the same event, qualified for the 1960 Olympics in Rome as a member of the United States' 1,600-meter relay team. But at the last moment, he was replaced on the team and watched from the infield as the U.S. raced to a gold medal.

Woods, who actually played guard in high school until his senior year, was recruited to CU from the projects of Pittsburgh by Dal Ward. But when Ward was fired, Woods exploded on the scene in Sonny Grandelius' offense. It was Woods' 96-yard kickoff return against Nebraska that gave CU a 7-0 victory and helped preserve an undefeated conference run.

Woods left CU a semester before graduating for a successful CFL career, but returned to Boulder after his playing days to earn his diploma and a law graduate degree. He died in 1988 at age 47 of a heart attack.

Ted Woods averaged 4.5 yards per carry over his two-year CU career in 1960-61. An explosive runner, Woods set an NCAA record in the 400-meters in 1960 only months after first lacing up track spikes.

One of CU's most embarrassing losses came in Grandelius' first year when Iowa State ran all over the Buffs, 27-0, using Dal Ward's old offense, the single wing. It was the Cyclones' first conference victory in two seasons, first over CU since 1950 and marked the first time CU had been shut out since the 1956 opener.

In what might be the most lopsided 7-0 victory ever, the Buffs outgained Nebraska 343-31 and didn't allow the Huskers a first down in a 1961 win in Lincoln.

poured from the stands and the tenacious Buffs hoisted their young coach, Sonny Grandelius, on their shoulders.

"It was a fanatical climax to a golden hour in Colorado's collegiate football history."

Several key injuries, however, derailed CU's momentum in 1960 as the Buffs stumbled to a 6-4 record and left their fans wanting more.

ORANGES AND OUSTING With usual powerhouses Oklahoma and Nebraska experiencing a down year in 1961, CU's stiffest competition in the conference was provided by Missouri and Kansas. No matter, the Buffs stampeded through them all.

Weidner's and Hillebrand's heroics over Kansas set the tone for the magical season. Bill Harris, who didn't even make the traveling squad for CU's 9-7 win at Miami, returned and rushed for 74 yards and two touchdowns to beat Kansas State 13-0. Harris said he was inspired by watching high school buddy Herman Johnson of Michigan State run wild over Michigan on television when he sat idle in his dorm room the previous Saturday.

A 5-0 CU team prepared for a showdown against Dan Devine's 10th-ranked Missouri Tigers, who featured a senior center named Bill McCartney. Harris struck again, hauling in a 21-yard touchdown pass from Weidner to give CU a 7-6 win on way to its first Big Eight championship and a trip to Miami.

The Orange Bowl was anti-climatic. The Buffs had ruined a perfect season by inexplicably losing to Utah, 21-12, at home following the Missouri triumph. With the NCAA setting up offices and asking a lot of questions back in Boulder, LSU, a 13-point favorite, jumped all over CU, 25-7, and buried the Buffs, who finished 9-2. The Sonny watch officially began.

NO BACKING DOWN With the hammer from the NCAA about to come down, and rumors that the CU Regents were prepared to fire Grandelius, the newspapers scrambled to get reaction from Grandelius. At the time, he was escaping the storm on the Colorado Western Slope, where he was on a recruiting tour:

"As I said when I arrived in Boulder to become head coach, the easiest thing in the world is to walk away from a problem and quit. It takes some intestinal fortitude to stay and see things through. That is exactly what I intend to do.

End Jerry Hillebrand earned All-America honors in 1961. He was also a two-time All-Big Eight selection and one of the best pass rushers in CU history.

"There's nothing that I've done to cause me to resign. I have a contract through 1966, and I intend to fulfill it."

Rocky Mountain News, March 16, 1962

Grandelius never got the chance. Even before the NCAA levied any sanctions, the CU Board of Regents, which had conducted an independent investigation, called an emergency meeting on March 17, 1962, and by a 5-to-1 vote (ironically the same as in Ward's ousting), fired Grandelius.

When the NCAA sanctions hit, they agreed with the university's findings, the biggest of which was that several CU football players had been receiving illegal payments from a "slush fund" administered by an assistant coach at a local drugstore, all with Grandelius' knowledge.

All but six of the returning 35 lettermen were ruled ineligible for the 1962 season.

16. *Despite never playing for the Buffs, Fred Casotti was awarded a game ball after CU beat Missouri, 7-6, at Folsom Field in November 1961. It was CU's first ABC-televised game. What was Casotti's job at the time?*

Chapter 4: Sonny and Bud 1959-1962 57

1962: PICKING UP THE PIECES

A rushed, unorganized coaching search finally settled on William "Bud" Davis, the university's alumni director. In a span of a month, the university had fired its championship football coach and replaced him with the alumni director.

Captain Ken Blair stormed out of the Regents' meeting, where it was announced Davis would be the interim coach, screaming, "You have yourself a football coach. Now get yourself a team!"

CU was the target of more than a few jokes.

It wasn't Davis' fault. An extremely intelligent man who would serve as president of two universities, the good-natured and likable Davis accepted his impossible task and took his lumps. There were plenty. With most of the team ruled ineligible, many observers predicted a winless 1962 season. CU scratched out a 2-8 record that included back-to-back 62-0 and 57-0 losses to Oklahoma and Missouri, and an uplifting 34-10 season-finale win over Air Force.

Fred Casotti, CU's football historian, rated Davis' farewell game as CU's "Sweetest Saturday" in "Football, CU Style," the first of three books Casotti authored on the history of CU football.

Bud Davis is CU's all-time losingest coach after leading the Buffs to a 2-8 record in 1962.

COLORADO FOOTBALL'S GALLOPING DISASTER
Memoirs of a Big-Time Coach

Harper's Magazine, October, 1965

By Bud Davis

From April 1, 1962, to April 1, 1963, Bud Davis at Colorado served as Alumni Director, Head Football Coach and Dean of Men. He received paychecks from three different departments in a year, but no two at the same time.

"I believe I might be the first coach in the history of intercollegiate football to be hung in effigy *before* he got the job. Bonfires, student rallies, and protest meetings of the football squad accompanied the news of my appointment. ...

"We limped into the final week of a disastrous season, a season which the sports writers daily reminded the public was the worst in the history of Colorado football. The ball players eagerly rushed home from practice to read the evening papers and find out whether I had been fired, or whether the authorities would wait until after the final game to announce the decision.

"... I was all choked up as I launched into my final speech to that squad. 'Lads,' I said, 'if you beat the Air Force today, I'll resign after the game.'

"They went out and fought like hell. The final score was Colorado 34, Air Force Academy 10."

Davis was carried off the field on the shoulders of his players. Blair, who threatened a mutiny when Davis was hired, presented his coach with the game ball saying, "You got a raw deal, Coach."

FRED CASOTTI

It's possible that somebody has witnessed more Colorado football games than Fred Casotti. But it's not very likely.

First as CU's longtime and popular sports information director (1953-68), then as an associate athletic director and as CU's official historian after his retirement in 1987, Casotti has seen 469 CU football games (including just a handful on television) between 1953 and 1994.

He brings an in-person streak of 239-straight home games into the 1995 season if you count a 1960 game against Air Force when he checked into a hospital at halftime suffering from kidney stones.

Casotti served as CU publicist under coaches Dal Ward, Sonny Grandelius, Bud Davis and Eddie Crowder while helping several players achieve conference and national honors. It was with a young Crowder that Casotti worked closest, and when Crowder was promoted to athletic director, Casotti later served as his confidant and "right-hand man" in the athletic department.

Known throughout the country as "The Count," Casotti spiced up his weekly press releases with a poem or two. Here's an example from the 1972 season after a particularly tense game, from the "Bard of the Buffaloes:"

"Even Ralphie showed some pre-game jitters,
Had the crowd in nervous titters,
Referee remarked while smiling
He should get 15 yards for piling."

Casotti has authored three books on CU football. "Football, CU* Style" was published after the 1971 season and offered a fun, personal perspective (The CU* stands for Casotti Uncensored, appropriately so). In 1980, "The Golden Buffaloes" provided more of a straight, historical look at the program, and his third book, "CU Century," celebrated the first 100 years of CU football and came out on the heels of the Buffs' 11-1 season in 1989.

Eddie Crowder
1963-1973

Eddie Crowder began a 21-year relationship with CU when he was named head coach in 1963. He retired as athletic director in 1984.

Overall Record: 67-49-2 (.571 winning percentage).
Conference Championships: None.
Best Seasons: 1967 (9-2), 1969 (8-3), 1971 (10-2).
Worst Seasons: 1963 (2-8), 1964 (2-8), 1973 (5-6).

Oklahoma assistant Eddie Crowder, 27, withdrew his name from the list of Colorado coaching candidates in 1959 because he didn't feel he was ready for the job. That opened the door for 29-year-old Sonny Grandelius.

Four years later, CU again turned to Crowder and asked him to rescue a program put in disarray by Grandelius. With little hesitation this time, Crowder, 31, accepted on Jan. 2, 1963, the day after the Sooners lost in the Orange Bowl to Alabama.

A search never materialized. CU finally had its man.

Crowder, who grew up in Muskogee, Okla., and was affectionately known as the "Okie from Muskogee," turned a sparkling prep football career into a chance to drive Bud Wilkinson's football machine at the University of Oklahoma for two years. Crowder led the Sooners to 8-2 and 8-1-1 records in 1951 and '52 and earned 1952 All-American honors. Not known for his passing, Crowder tossed four first-half touchdown passes against CU in a 55-14 rout in 1951.

17. Ralphie's first appearance at Folsom Field came in what season?

He was on Wilkinson's coaching staff when CU came calling the second time.

After two rebuilding years, Crowder's 1965 CU squad went 6-2-2, and he was named the Big Eight Coach of the Year. The Buffs were never able to unseat Oklahoma or Nebraska atop the conference standings but Crowder delivered the Buffs to national prominence with a 10-2 record in 1971, good enough for a No. 3 ranking behind No. 1 Nebraska and No. 2 Oklahoma in a rare conference sweep.

Crowder was an All-American quarterback in 1952 for Oklahoma. He threw four touchdown passes against CU in a 55-14 1951 win.

Crowder produced five bowl teams and a steady stream of players who made the school one of the top three producers of NFL talent in the 1970s.

Crowder succeeded long-time Athletic Director Harry Carlson in 1965 and held the AD's job until 1984, long after he stepped aside as coach in 1974.

Crowder poses before his first practice in the spring of 1963.

OVERLOAD Crowder's hiring in January of 1963 gave CU the somewhat dubious distinction of having four head football coaches on the payroll at the same time: Dal Ward, dismissed in 1959, was an Assistant Athletic Director; Grandelius remained on leave of absence until March 1; Bud Davis' resignation wouldn't become effective until March 31; and the newly appointed Crowder.

A QUIET MAN Crowder, with his prematurely balding dome, wasn't much of a public figure in Boulder in his early coaching years. Grandelius could be found at every university function or hawking merchandise on television, and Davis was already well-known when he took the job.

But Crowder preferred the isolation and serenity of coaching and studying game films over the public aspects of the job, as Harry Farrar's Denver Post column on April 10, 1963, pointed out:

> "Eddie Crowder was hired last January as head football coach at Colorado University. Yet, somehow, he is still virtually anonymous. Some coaches rival Elizabeth Taylor in the race for newspaper space and their profiles are almost as well known as Richard Burton's.

CU's 1963 finale at Air Force was postponed a week due to President John Kennedy's assassination. Air Force took a 17-14 decision on Dec. 7.

18 Jersey numbers CU has retired are 24, 67 and 11. To whom do they belong?

"But Crowder and assistants can be forgiven for violating the coach's code in failing to practice personal press agentry. They have been going about their business so quietly and diligently they haven't had time to undergo psychoanalysis by the press."

When he was mistaken for a biology professor at a social function, Crowder explained, "I think it's wrong to impose yourself upon the press. I don't think a coach should deliberately drum up personal publicity."

Crowder, immersed in recruiting, ended the spring press conference by saying, "I'd like to talk to you fellows from the press some more but I have a date right now with a prospective All-America end."

THE LAWN DOCTOR Crowder couldn't have asked for a tougher opponent to make his coaching debut against than John McKay's Southern Cal Trojans, the defending national champs who were ranked No. 1 again in 1963.

However, the playing field was leveled, so to speak. A week's worth of rain leading up to the September opener drenched Folsom Field. By game time the field was soggy and the grass unusually long, not exactly a fast track for McKay's speedy backfield, which included eventual Heisman Trophy winner Mike Garrett.

Whether it was CU's good fortune or good planning depended on whom you asked. A livid McKay, despite his 14-0 victory, couldn't decide what was worse: the field or the officiating (USC was charged with 12 penalties for 107 yards and had two touchdowns called back).

"You can bet your life it won't happen again," McKay said, referring to the all-Big Eight officiating crew. "We play them out there (in Los Angeles) next year and we will reciprocate. ... I've never seen a field in worse condition. The sooner we get out of here the better."

The Trojans' departure from Boulder, however, was delayed nearly 45 minutes when one of their two team buses wouldn't start. Several players had to push the bus out of Balch Fieldhouse to get it going.

ODE TO JOHNNY Fred Casotti, CU's clever sports information director between 1953-68, couldn't resist taking one more jab at McKay. As was his tradition in his weekly press releases to the media, Casotti penned a poem prior to the 1964 rematch with the Trojans in Los Angeles in McKay's honor:

"Don't blacktop the Coliseum, Johnny
Even though you like it fast,
We know our field was muddy,

Fred Casotti

But John, what's past is past.
Remember, John, you won it,
And you were wet from rain not sweat,
And, John, My God, you wrecked our sod.
What more was there to get?
So have a heart, please, Johnny,
Don't go and be a hog,
Just beat us nice is my advice,
No blacktop, heat, or smog."

McKay took Casotti's advice: No. 13 USC won nicely, 21-0.

HONEYMOON They say every new coach enjoys a honeymoon with the fans before the real pressure mounts. Crowder pushed his to the limit. USC wasn't the only team beating up on Crowder's first two squads as Crowder got out of the gate with back-to-back 2-8 seasons. Added to Davis' 2-8 season in 1962, the Buffs struggled through their worst (to that point) three-year stretch at 6-24. Chuck Fairbanks and Bill McCartney would combine to start the 1980s off 6-26-1.

"First," Crowder explained, "you have to stop getting beat before you can start winning."

In a 27-14 win over CU in 1968, Missouri set a NCAA record by running the ball 99 times (for 421 yards). The Buffs possessed the ball for only 14:15 of the entire game, their lowest total ever.

BREAKTHROUGH "We're looking forward to winning. Everybody here is sick and tired of losing. This whole squad loves to play football." – Three-time U.S. Open champion Hale Irwin, before the 1965 CU football season.

The Buffs, with a future PGA Tour star playing safety, scratched out their first winning season since 1961 with a 6-2-2 record in 1965. Irwin was named Big Eight Back of the Week for making two interceptions in a 13-0 road win over Oklahoma, Crowder's first against his alma mater.

The Buffs were back with a third-place league finish and Crowder was honored as the conference's Coach of the Year. Columnist Bob Hurt on Nov. 5, 1965:

"In the early fifties, Eddie Crowder befuddled Oklahoma football foes with his quarterback sorcery. Opponents needed a search warrant to find the football. It was like tackling a mirage.

"Now, at 34, Eddie's only disappearing act concerns his receding hair line. But he's up to his old Houdini-like trickery. He's making Colorado reappear as a football power.

"What's Crowder's secret?

" 'There are no secrets in rebuilding a program,' he said. 'You've got to get the right kind of people

19. What is Joe Romig doing now?

and you've got to get them to believe in your program.'"

ALL HAIL HALE Boulder's Hale Irwin, a tough little safety with a great short game, was an example of "the right kind of people" Crowder lured to CU.

Irwin was named twice to both the All-Big Eight and All-Academic teams.

During the summers he kept himself busy by winning just about every imaginable amateur golf tournament in Colorado. Irwin captured the 1967 NCAA individual golf crown.

But the 6-foot, 180-pounder took football very seriously. He would cut short his golfing summers when fall football practice arrived. He took CU's 1966 season-

Hale Irwin (10) gained his fame as a professional golfer. But he was also a good safety at CU. Irwin, along with guard John Beard (60), captained the 1966 Buffs.

opening loss to Miami (24-3) particularly hard when a newspaper reporter pressed him for a golf analogy for CU's woes.

"Forget that golf stuff," he said. "The golf season ended in August, remember?

"Look at these hands. They're more like a baseball catcher's than a golfer's. I don't even think about golf after the middle of August. We play football now. And we didn't play it very good Saturday."

Irwin, who began his career as a quarterback out of Boulder High School, is a member of CU's All-Century Team, selected in 1989.

Hale's younger brother, Phil, followed in his footsteps and was a standout linebacker between 1968-70. Phil Irwin is the first CU athlete ever to get his picture on the cover of Sports Illustrated after CU upset Penn State in 1970. Phil's son, Heath, is a senior offensive guard on the 1995 Buffaloes.

BUFFALO BROTHERS: DICK AND BOBBY ANDERSON

As Eddie Crowder was suffering through his first season in the fall of 1963, the Andersons of Boulder High were grabbing all the local headlines while leading their school to a state football championship. Dick, a senior fullback, and Bobby, a sophomore quarterback, were on their way to help Crowder revive the CU program.

Dick arrived as part of one of Crowder's (and CU's) finest recruiting classes as a sophomore in 1965. With Wilmer Cooks handling the fullback duties, Anderson moved to safety and collected 14 career interceptions, including a Big Eight-leading seven in his All-America senior season of 1967.

That was the year younger brother Bobby joined him on campus. The duo promptly carried CU to a 9-2 record and its first bowl appearance in five seasons. It's not as if they weren't expecting great things, as Dick pointed out prior to the season opener: "All I know is the last time we were teammates, we won the state title."

Anderson played in three post-season all-star games in 1967 and was the MVP of two of them, the Senior Bowl and the Blue-Gray, in which he returned two punts for touchdowns.

Drafted in the third round by the Miami Dolphins, he made eight interceptions and was named 1968 co-AFL Rookie of the Year. Anderson played on the Dolphins' 1972 undefeated team and was named the NFL's

Hale Irwin, U.S. Open champion, and Dick Anderson, NFL All-Pro with the Miami Dolphins, were teammates on Boulder High School's 1962 state championship golf team.

20. Who was the first No. 1 draft pick of the Denver Broncos in their first draft as an NFL team?

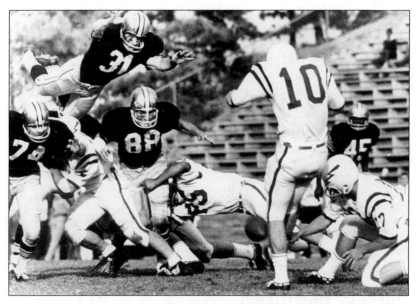

Dick Anderson blocked this Air Force field goal to preserve a 10-9 win in 1966.

Dick Anderson.

Defensive Player of the Year in 1973. He intercepted four passes (tying an NFL record) against Pittsburgh in the first half of a Monday night game.

An influential member of the NFL Players Association, Anderson served in the Florida state senate after his playing days.

All this, and the guy is widely known in CU annals as Bobby's older brother.

THE SUPER SOPH In the 1967 season-opening 27-7 win over Baylor, Bobby Anderson rushed for 83 yards, passed for 129 more and scored three touchdowns to earn Big Eight Back of the Week honors. Anderson and the Buffs were on their way to a 5-0 start and a No. 3 national ranking.

But lowly Oklahoma State shocked CU, 10-7, followed by a 23-0 whipping from Oklahoma. The senior-dominated Buffs regrouped to finish the regular season 8-2 and earn a Bluebonnet Bowl meeting with Miami. Anderson, who missed the team bus to the stadium after oversleeping and was slowed by an ankle injury, came off the bench in the second half and immediately led CU on an 80-yard scoring drive to regain the lead, 17-14. Anderson's 38-yard TD run in the fourth quarter put CU ahead for good for its second bowl win in 10 years, 31-21.

The loss of 24 seniors took its toll in 1968 as CU slumped to a 4-6 record and fourth-place finish in the

Big Eight. With Anderson running the offense, scoring was rarely a problem. But, unfortunately, the same was true for CU's opponents. The Buffs gave up 244 points including 141 over the last four games (all losses) of the season. The Buffs allowed 388.1 yards per game, the most until the 1980 squad surrendered an unbelievable 464.4.

Bobby Anderson began his CU career as a quarterback and graduated to the NFL with the Denver Broncos as a running back.

MAKING THE SWITCH A 1-1 start, including a 27-3 beating courtesy of Franco Harris and No. 2 Penn State, left Crowder searching for answers. His solution was a risky, yet brilliant, one: Anderson moved to tailback and Paul Arendt, a much better passer than Anderson, was inserted at quarterback before Wednesday's practice prior to a Week 3 showdown with Indiana.

Playing his first game (high school or college) at tailback, Anderson trudged through a huge Boulder snowstorm and the Hoosiers defense for 161 yards and three TDs in the 30-7 whitewashing. Crowder's gamble paid off. Three more Anderson TDs and 132 yards helped the Buffs upset No. 5 Missouri on way to a 7-3 finish, including losses to Oklahoma (42-30) and Nebraska (20-7). The Buffs made their second bowl appearance in three years, facing Bear Bryant's Alabama Crimson Tide in the Liberty Bowl.

Defensive end Bill Brundige and guard Dick Melvin joined Anderson on the All-Big Eight team. Anderson, who rushed for 854 yards and scored a school record 19

Bobby Anderson

touchdowns, was a consensus All-American choice. Not bad for a rookie running back.

"I'm more of a meat ax now. I still use my head, but in a little different way. I don't have to worry about all the memorization work ahead of each game. It's no longer my job to recognize defenses and check plays at the line of scrimmage. I'm required to use my head on opponents."

Boulder Daily Camera, Dec. 7, 1969

BUFFS PROVE 'UNBEARABLE' TO TIDE, 47-33

Headline in the Boulder Daily Camera, Dec. 14, 1969

"Colorado, smashing more than a dozen Liberty Bowl offense records along the way, drove the Bear – Alabama Coach Paul (Bear) Bryant – into hiding early Saturday afternoon by burying the Crimson Tide 47-33 for one of its most prestigious football victories of all time.

"With tailback Bob Anderson bruising the 'Bama defenders for a school record 254 yards on the ground and scoring three touchdowns in perhaps his greatest performance ever, the Buffs stemmed the Tide in the fourth quarter to pull out the come-from-behind win after squandering an earlier 17-point lead."

The win vaulted Colorado back into national prominance, eight years after scandal had threatened to bury the Buffs. Anderson capped his magical career with his best performance ever. With players such as Cliff Branch, Herb Orvis, Charlie Davis, and John Stearns entering the program, the Buffs were headed into what Crowder later called their "Glory years."

RETIRED Anderson left CU the owner of 18 school records, including career rushing, total offense and touchdowns. "Oh, they'll be nice to look back on, but most of them will be broken soon by better athletes anyway," Anderson told the Boulder Daily Camera. He was right. Only his four touchdowns scored in a game against Tulsa in 1969 still stands, and 11 others have matched it.

Bobby Anderson scored 10 touchdowns in the three season openers he played.

CU quarterback Jimmy Bratten on beating Alabama in the 1969 Liberty Bowl: "We think Crowder is a great coach and we had heard so much about Bear Bryant being a god. We wanted to show him for Crowder."

But Anderson will always be a CU immortal. Including bowl game statistics, he accounted for over 5,000 yards of total offense, the first Big Eight player to do so.

And he joined Byron "Whizzer" White and Joe Romig as the only CU players to have their jersey retired on May 9, 1970, during halftime festivities of the spring game.

After watching his No. 11 retired, Anderson paid tribute to his older brother, "I've always felt if Dick had been given a chance on offense, they might also have already retired his No. 31, too."

NOT IN AWE Before Crowder took over, CU had beaten Oklahoma only three times in 17 meetings. But the former OU All-American quarterback proved the Sooners were human by beating them four times in the next 11 years.

After Crowder resigned, the Sooner dominance picked up again as OU won 14 of the next 15 in the series until Bill McCartney coached the Buffs to a string of five wins and a tie.

"I knew they weren't invincible," Crowder told The Denver Post in an Oct. 27, 1989, article. "I knew they were just normal human beings. I didn't have any sense of being uptight about playing against Oklahoma, and I think I could pass that along to the players."

However, there was another Big Red monster. In 11 games against Nebraska, Crowder's teams won only once.

Dick Anderson (right), winner of the Alumni "C" Club Award as CU's outstanding senior in 1968, presents the same award for 1970 to younger brother Bobby at the 1970 Varsity-Alumni spring game.

Bobby Anderson ranks fifth among CU's all-time rushers with 2,367 yards (in three years). He scored 34 touchdowns and was a unanimous All-American selection in 1969.

STREAK BUSTERS A generally disappointing 1970 season was interrupted by one terrific Saturday as the Buffs, who returned 40 lettermen off the Liberty Bowl team, plodded to a 6-5 record.

Fourth-ranked Penn State, owner of the nation's longest undefeated streak at 34 games, visited Folsom Field the second week of the season. Before a national television audience, the Buffs destroyed Joe Paterno's troops 41-13 to snap the streak. Speedy wideout Cliff Branch, a junior-college transfer, delivered the backbreaker by returning the second-half kickoff 97 yards for a touchdown.

Branch, considered the best game-breaker in CU his-

RALPHIE

Possibly the most famous Buffalo of them all is a buffalo.

"Ralphie," CU's stampeding mascot, has been a fixture at Folsom Field (and occasional bowl venues) since Oct. 1, 1966, when the six-month-old buffalo  calf first appeared on the sidelines during CU's 10-0 win over Kansas State. The buffalo, named Ralph by the students, didn't begin leading the team out on the field (and through opposing teams' huddles) at the start of both halves until the next season.

The student body, somewhat surprised to find out the buffalo was actually female, quickly adapted by changing her name from Ralph to Ralphie. It was a popular discovery. Ralphie was voted Homecoming Queen in 1971.

In Fred Casotti's book, "The Golden Buffaloes," Boulder rancher Bud Hays, Ralphie's owner and trainer, claimed Ralphie knew when game day arrived.

"She would come to the fence and make some funny noises just like she knew the handlers would be coming soon with the trailer," Hays said. "I'll swear there was some way she could tell."

Considered one of the greatest spectacles in college football, the "Ralphie" tradition has continued through three buffaloes. Ralphie, a 13-year veteran, retired after the 1978 season. Ralphie II, which debuted with a 20-16 loss to Iowa State in the '78 season finale, died following CU's 31-17 win over Stanford on Sept. 19, 1987.

Ralphie III, which was being trained to take over in 1988, was rushed into duty in time for CU's 27-10 victory over Missouri on Nov. 7, 1987, and is entering her eighth full season. Ralphie III, who weighs about 1,300 pounds and owns an impressive 36-5-3 home record, has made road trips to the Orange and Fiesta Bowls.

tory, returned one more kickoff (a 100-yarder against Kansas) and two punts for TDs in 1970. He added four more punt-return TDs in 1971 (a national record) to give him eight touchdowns on kick returns, which still stands as an NCAA career record. And Branch did it in two years.

Including plays from scrimmage, Branch, who once held the 100-yard world indoor record at 9.3 seconds, averaged 17.9 yards everytime he touched the ball.

CU's return trip to Memphis and the 1970 Liberty Bowl didn't rekindle any of the old magic, but instead appropriately capped a frustrating season. Tulane beat CU, 17-3.

In the 105-year history of CU football, 58 and 98 are the only two jersey numbers from 1 to 99 that have never been worn.

BE ALL THAT YOU CAN BE During a summer tour of Europe along with some other college coaches, Crowder discovered defensive end Herb Orvis in Berlin, where the high school dropout was playing with an Army service team.

Orvis had written to several American colleges about gaining a scholarship but got no response. Crowder, however, didn't waste any time in signing the 6-5, 240-pounder. Orvis received his discharge from the Army and became an anchor on CU's defensive line from 1969-71 and made over 200 tackles. At age 25, Orvis, a CU senior, earned All-American honors in 1971.

WELL-GROOMED For most of Crowder's tenure, a strict edict disallowing facial hair and restricting hair length was in effect. But during spring practice in 1971, a player uprising forced Crowder to change the policy. The football players finally were able to join their "free-living" classmates and grow their hair long (just above the shoulder). Moustaches, providing they were trimmed, and sideburns even with the earlobe were also permitted.

1971: THE PINNACLE

A murderous schedule of road games at No. 9 Louisiana State and No. 6 Ohio State, as well as conference road tests at No. 2 Oklahoma and No. 1 Nebraska, greeted Crowder and nearly 50 CU sophomores in 1971.

From that recipe for disaster, CU cooked up an amazing 10-2 season and No. 3 national ranking, the Buffs' highest final ranking to that point.

Sophomore quarterback Ken Johnson and classmate Charlie Davis ran CU's option attack all over LSU for a stunning 31-21 opening win.

Davis' 174 rushing yards were the most by a Big Eight back in his debut in 21 years, John "Bad Dude" Stearns

Following CU's 10-2 1971 season, which it finished ranked third in the nation, bumper stickers started popping up in Boulder proclaiming "The Buffalo Is Coming" and "CU No. 1 in '72." CU slipped to a disappointing 8-4 record.

grabbed two interceptions, and Branch chipped in a 75-yard punt return for a touchdown. But the game ball went to junior tailback Jon Keyworth, who broke his leg and missed the entire season.

The young Buffs also clipped Ohio State in Columbus, 20-14, behind Johnson's 39-yard touchdown sprint to get off to a 5-0 start. But once again, Oklahoma and Nebraska jumped up to put the Buffs in their place (third place) with convincing 45-17 and 31-7 victories.

Davis exploded for 342 yards in a 40-6 rout of Oklahoma State to set the school's single-game record (which still stands) and the Big Eight record. He finished with 1,386 yards on the season, also team and conference records. Columnist Jim Graham of the Denver Post was impressed:

Cliff Branch, possibly the most spectacular player to ever wear a CU uniform, returned an NCAA-record eight kicks for touchdowns in just two years (1970-71).

"Charlie Davis doesn't rhyme with Heisman, but he's sheer poetry in motion when it comes to carrying the football.

"...Your observer has been watching college football for 40 years and has never seen a sophomore running back with better moves than Charlie Davis."

The 9-2 Buffs could now look forward to a New Year's Eve date in the Astro-Bluebonnet Bowl against hometown Houston, ranked 15th in the nation.

Option quarterback Ken Johnson (1971-73) owns the Big Eight record for most yards gained per attempt in a career. Johnson averaged 9.1 yards per rushing attempt.

BAD DUDE Before he became known as one of the toughest catchers in the National League with the New York Mets in the 1970s, John Stearns was CU's "Bad Dude."

Even before he played his first college game, Stearns achieved a measure of national fame when he was quoted in Sports Illustrated's 1970 college football preview as saying he wanted to be known as "one bad dude."

Stearns went on to say his goal was to be remembered as "the most insane hitter in the history of college football."

In a 1972 Boulder Daily Camera article, Stearns, then a senior, called the comment "the biggest mistake I ever made."

"I had heard 'bad dude' a few times, but I really didn't

After their CU careers, safety John Stearns (left) went on to be a "Bad Dude" for the New York Mets and running back Jon Keyworth (right) starred with the Denver Broncos from 1974-80.

Chapter 5: Eddie Crowder 1963-73

Tennis hustler Bobby Riggs beat Bobby Anderson 6-2 in a charity tennis match in 1975 wearing Anderson's Denver Broncos uniform (helmet and shoulder pads included) and an ankle weight for good measure.

Tailback Charlie Davis was named the 1971 Bluebonnet Bowl MVP after running for 202 yards in a 29-17 win over Houston to cap a 10-2 season for the Buffs.

know what it meant," he said. "I wish it never happened. It doesn't bother me now, but it's real bush league to come out the way it has. Good players don't have to talk like that."

But Stearns did his most "insane" hitting as a catcher on the Buffs baseball squad, which helped make him the No. 2 overall pick in the baseball draft. "Bad Dude" once broke big Dave Parker's jaw in a football-like collision at home plate.

Playing safety, Stearns was a fierce hitter in the Buffaloes' secondary and was an All-Big Eight first teamer in 1972. He remains CU's all-time leader in career interceptions with 16.

But the biggest play in his career may have come in punt formation in the fourth quarter of the 1971 Bluebonnet Bowl, with his team clinging to a 23-17 lead. On fourth-and-9 and punting from his own end zone, Stearns gambled and ran for a first down. The Buffs then drove for an insurance TD.

Led by another brilliant effort by Davis, who ran for 202 yards, CU won 29-17. The final polls showed a Big Eight sweep of the nation: No. 1 Nebraska, No. 2 Oklahoma and No. 3 Colorado.

PACKING THEM IN The Buffs averaged 26,000 fans during Crowder's first year in 1963. By 1966, attendance was up

to 39,000. And by 1972, an average sellout crowd of 51,000 watched the Buffs.

ALL-DECADE TEAM A panel of sportswriters and broadcasters compiled a Big Eight All-Decade football team for the 1970s, and CU placed two players on the first team.

Defensive end Herb Orvis, an All-American in 1971 and two-time All-Conference selection, anchored the defensive line. J.V. Cain, who died just months before the team was selected, earned a spot at tight end. He was also an All-American (1973) and two-time All-Big Eight pick.

Earning second-team honors were running back Tony Reed (1975-76) and defensive backs Cullen Bryant (1970-72) and Mark Haynes (1976-79).

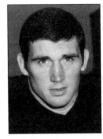

Herb Orvis

MELLOWING Prior to the 1972 season, The Denver Post ran a two-part series titled "The Mellowing of Coach Eddie Crowder" in its Sunday "Empire Magazine."

Frank Haraway, longtime CU beat writer, offered this perspective on the changing Crowder:

> "There's no doubt about it. Eddie Crowder just isn't the same breed of cat he was a couple of years ago. We strolled into Eddie's inner sanctum (his office) ... and there he was, feet propped on his desk, sweet-smelling smoke curling from his pipe, soothing music emanating from a newly installed stereo system, not a soul in the room and the

Herb Orvis, pictured below clobbering an Oklahoma State quarterback in 1971, is a member of CU's All-Century Team.

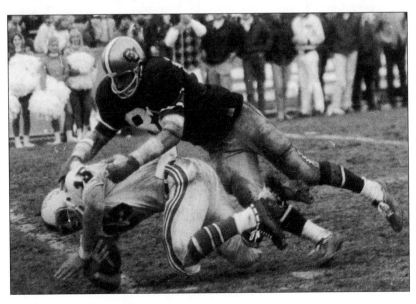

Chapter 5: Eddie Crowder 1963-73

During most of his time in Boulder, coach and athletic director Eddie Crowder was a part-owner of a restaurant called "Eddie's Mexican Cafe."

season's opener with Indiana roughly 100 hours away.

"It was incredible. This just couldn't be the uptight guy who guided CU football for the first half dozen years of his regime with an approach that seemed to border on grimness. Has he gone soft? Don't think that for a second. It's just that he has a new approach to football."

QUOTABLE In the same article, on Aug. 27, 1972, Crowder gave his perspective on how some of his players were anticipating not one, but two, possible national championship runs after finishing third in 1971:

"They've been caught up in the excitement of the national championship race because we played Nebraska and Oklahoma, and there was always talk about it at that time. I look at it this way: I've always wanted a date with Raquel Welch and never done much about it. Neither has she."

The pass combination of Ken Johnson (right) to tight end J.V. Cain (left) connected 61 times for 873 yards and three touchdowns between 1971-73.

The Buffs weren't able to regain their lofty height of 1971. Crowder's final two teams dropped to 8-4 and 5-6. CU lost its last four games of 1973, including a 17-14 season-ender at home to Kansas State.

Crowder woke up one morning with a "For Sale" in the front lawn of his house. He didn't give up his house,

only his job as football coach in mid-December. One writer described Crowder's press conference as being like a funeral "but the corpse was being interviewed."

GOING AWAY PARTY Crowder, thinking he was attending a formal welcoming party for new head coach Bill Mallory, was treated to a surprise Eddie Crowder Night at the Denver Hilton in August of 1974.

Among the 1,100 in attendance were former OU coach Bud Wilkinson, several of his OU teammates, Arkansas coach and good friend Frank Broyles and a host of former CU players, including Bobby Anderson and Hale Irwin. Even President Gerald Ford sent a congratulatory telegram.

"You know, we came so very close," a surprised and overwhelmed Crowder told the crowd. "We reached for the stars, but didn't quite touch them. And that you people here think enough of our efforts to do something like this is something I can't express my gratitude for."

BO MATTHEWS

On the same December Saturday that Colorado trounced Alabama 47-33 in the 1969 Liberty Bowl, the Crimson Tide and legendary coach Paul "Bear" Bryant made history by signing their first black recruit.

His name was Bo Matthews, a fullback from Butler High School in Huntsville, Ala., but he never played a down for Bryant. Instead, he starred for three seasons in the Colorado backfield.

"The pressure was on everybody around me," Matthews said in a 1972 Boulder Daily Camera article. "The school had convinced my parents that Alabama was the place to go. ... I'm glad I didn't go there. I didn't necessarily want to go in the first place."

Matthews backed out of his commitment to Alabama and attended Colorado without the benefit of a scholarship his first year. In three years, Matthews rushed for 1,339 yards and nine touchdowns while blocking for dazzling halfback Charlie Davis.

He didn't put his name in the history books as he would have as a trailblazer in Alabama, but Matthews carved out a nice career at CU. In 1974, the San Diego Chargers grabbed Matthews with the second overall NFL Draft pick, the highest ever selection for a CU player.

Mallory and Fairbanks 1974-1981

Young Bill Mallory led the University of Miami (Ohio) to a 12-0 record in 1973. In 1974, he was hired by CU. His intense demeanor was exactly what CU fans were looking for when he was hired. Five years later, the same personality had put off most of Mallory's supporters.

Overall Record: 42-47-1 (.467 winning percentage)
Coaches: Bill Mallory (1974-1978) and
Chuck Fairbanks (1979-1981)
Conference Championships: 1976 (tie, 8-4).
Worst Seasons: 1974 (5-6), 1979 (3-8), 1980 (1-10), 1981 (3-8).

To many people, the 1970s was a forgettable decade: bell bottoms, disco music and Watergate. Fans of Colorado football during that time have even more reason to wish for selective amnesia.

After the miserable end to the 1973 season, Crowder escaped to a mountain retreat for almost two weeks to contemplate his and the program's future. He decided he was no longer the best coach to get the job done. He also began thinking about Bill Mallory, who was wrapping up a perfect 12-0 season in his fifth year as the head man at Miami (Ohio).

Under Mallory, Miami had been the stingiest defensive team in the nation in 1973, and Mallory was generally regarded as one of the best defensive coaches in the country.

Other favorites for the job included Frank Kush of Arizona State, and Washington State's Jim Sweeney was led to believe he would get the job. In fact, an erroneous wire service report claimed that he would in half the newspapers in the country one day during the wild coaching search.

But Mallory was Crowder's choice all the way – even after he turned down the job once. Mallory explained the strange circumstances a couple of years later:

"I came to Boulder and was interviewed by both Eddie Crowder and President (Roland) Rautenstraus.

"Eddie offered me the job but he wanted a decision right away. I've never been one to make a snap decision and so I said I would have to turn

it down.

"I went back to Ohio, but I had Colorado on my mind. ... I knew I had made a mistake and I wasn't worth a damn for two weeks.

"Then I went to the NCAA Convention in San Francisco and I knew CU still hadn't named a coach. I was just hoping for an opportunity to talk to Crowder again.

"When I checked into the hotel, there was a note in my box which said Crowder wanted to see me. I couldn't get there fast enough and I told him if Colorado still wanted me, I was ready to come."

Rocky Mountain News, Dec. 19, 1975

On Jan. 12, 1974, Mallory became the 18th head coach in Colorado history. He packed a lot into a relatively short five-year tenure. He won a good percentage of his games (35-21-1, .623) but not enough "big" ones. He coached CU to its first Big Eight title in 15 years, capturing a share of the crown in 1976. But only a year later he had effectively alienated fans, media, boosters and university officials alike, and he would be gone well before the turn of the decade.

Mallory's CU teams were 0-5 against Nebraska and head coach Tom Osborne. The Huskers outscored CU 173-77 between 1974-78.

WHAT COULD HAVE BEEN From the You Never Know Department: If Crowder had hired Sweeney, he probably

Bill Mallory, left, was regarded as a defensive mastermind when he came to CU in 1974. Sophomore tailback Billy Waddy told the Daily Camera that the new coach didn't stop there: "Don't get the idea that Bill Mallory doesn't pay any attention to offense. He does. If you mess up on offense, Bill Mallory tells you about it. Man, does he tell you about it."

would have brought Washington State assistant Jack Elway to Boulder with him to coach his passing offense. Which meant Elway's son John, a pretty fair quarterback for Stanford and the Denver Broncos, would have enrolled at Boulder High School and may have been tempted to attend Dear Ol' CU.

WHAT COULD HAVE BEEN, PART II There was another coach in the Mid-America Conference who didn't get much consideration despite his CU ties. Don James, an assistant for three seasons under Crowder who had moved on to Kent State in 1971, wanted to return to Boulder desperately. But Crowder really had eyes only for Mallory. James, of course, went on to a great coaching career at the University of Washington.

Crowder wanted Mallory to keep two of his assistants, Jim Mora and Steve Ortmayer, in hopes of providing some continuity in the program during the transition. But Crowder insisted on bringing his entire Miami staff with him, and CU was out two of its better assistants and recruiters. Mora and Ortmayer moved on to the NFL.

21. Fred Lima, arguably CU's greatest placekicker (1972-73), led the nation in 1972 in field goals (15) and kick scoring (80 points). What was Lima's jersey number?

COACHING CRADLE Miami of Ohio boasts a prestigious list of big-time coaches among its head-coaching alumni: Weeb Ewbank, Woody Hayes, Sid Gilman, Bo Schembechler and Ara Parseghian among others.

In 1974, Mallory was the 11th former Miami of Ohio coach to move on to coach at a larger school.

"NOT A BULLY" Mallory, who played under Paraseghian and coached on Hayes' staff, insisted he was "not a bully" but instead just a tough, intense coach. Columinist Bill Connors of the Tulsa Daily World on July 29, 1976, relayed these observations:

> "Bill Mallory zipped through his football lectures at the Oklahoma Coaches Association clinic at a fierce, no-nonsense pace. No jokes or amusing stories; just technical information on drills and techniques.
>
> "Colorado's 40-year-old coach spoke in a manner that left no doubt about the devotion he brings to his job or the extraordinary fitness of his vocal cords. He was all business, and urgent; befitting the taskmaster that he is.
>
> "Mallory took his 'iron-fisted discipline' to the Big Eight Conference's most liberal campus. Lifestyles in Boulder were a decade ahead of the rest of the Big Eight. The thought of Mallory trying to be a disciplinarian in Boulder was fascinating. Something had to give. It was Colorado."

John Elway nearly called Colorado home in 1974.

Mallory moved the football players into a dormitory and imposed a curfew. He instituted regimented schedules for his players, including nightly bed checks (married players excluded). "I don't want to be responsible for any divorces. I think I caused a couple of players to get married a year early."

Said tailback Billy Waddy, a sophomore during Mallory's first year: "I haven't had bedchecks since ... well, since I was just a little kid."

When Penn State coach Joe Paterno publically denounced athletic dorms, saying they isolate the players and deny them a well-rounded college experience, Mallory shot back.

"I am sick and tired of hearing Paterno say what everyone should and should not do. Everybody seems to think Paterno has all the answers. He doesn't."

THE TASK AHEAD Mallory entered a Big Eight which looked more like the Big Two (Oklahoma and Nebraska) and the Other Six. Mallory accepted his challenge of trying to take Colorado to that next level. "I realize the challenge ahead in competing in the Big Eight," he said. "I consider it the best conference in the nation, since it's better balanced than the Big Ten or Southeastern, which have only a couple of standout teams."

However, only one of Mallory's 18 Big Eight wins came against the Big Two.

TRAGEDY CU's first practice of the fall was marred by

In an effort to pep up Bill Mallory's weekly television show called "CU 76," the show's producers hired veteran Los Angeles television personality Stu Nahan to host the show in 1976. Nahan would fly to Denver each week to tape the episodes.

Chapter 6: Mallory and Fairbanks 1974-1981

A decade of tragedy began when sophomore Polie Poitier collapsed and died during a 1974 practice.

tragedy when sophomore defensive back Polie Poitier collapsed on the track while running an 880 during conditioning.

Poitier never regained conciousness and died in less than 24 hours after suffering cardiac arrest related to sickle cell trait. Doctors said it was an extremely rare complication that occurs in less than one percent of cases.

Poitier, a fine option quarterback for Coral Gables (Fla.) High School, told reporters after leading his team to a big victory as a senior, "I had a dream this morning that something serious was going to happen to me. It's not a case of fear. You just never know what might happen."

GETTING STARTED It was under this dark cloud that CU opened the 1974 campaign, which was imposing enough with road games at No. 9 Louisiana State and No. 6 Michigan. The 42-14 and 31-0 blowout losses were expected and accepted.

Billy Waddy ran for 1,537 yards between 1973-76, good for 21st on the all-time rushing charts. Waddy, whose talents were often overlooked during his playing days, was rewarded with a spot on CU's All-Century Team in 1989.

82 Buffaloes Handbook

Waddy, honored by Sports Illustrated as the nation's Back of the Week a year earlier after running for 202 yards in a win over Wisconsin, helped beat the Badgers again as CU came from 11 points down to upend 11th-ranked Wisconsin 24-21 in Boulder for Mallory's first victory.

Waddy struck again the next week, bolting for a 67-yard touchdown, and quarterback David Williams added scores of 44 and 23 yards as CU nipped Air Force, 28-27, in the finale of spirited series between the two schools. Air Force officials begged out of the series (which was usually played the final week of the season) after CU won 12 of the 16 meetings.

Billy Waddy

"AIR FORCE ACADEMY – For the first time in 10 years Saturday, the Colorado-Air Force Academy football series had a new ingredient, competition.

"But, at the finish, five seconds after AFA place-kicker Dave Lawson missed what would have been a game-winning field goal from 50 yards out, Colorado was on top, just as it has been through most of the 16-year rivalry which officially died at 4:27 p.m., Saturday afternoon at Falcon Stadium."

Boulder Daily Camera, Oct. 6, 1974

Mallory's first team finished a respectable 5-6 after taking its requisite beatings from Oklahoma (49-14) and Nebraska (31-15).

RAISING EXPECTATIONS With LSU, Michigan and Wisconsin replaced on the 1975 schedule with the likes of California, Wyoming and Wichita State, the Buffs jumped out to a 3-0 start before running into No. 1 Oklahoma in the Big Eight opener in Norman.

The slimmest of margins, a missed extra point by CU's Tom MacKenzie with 1:19 left, separated OU from taking a 21-20 win for its 33rd-straight victory and CU stunning the top-ranked Sooners.

Some consider the 1975 Buffs the most talented CU squad ever assembled. Eleven seniors were drafted into the NFL in the spring, including first-rounders defensive tackle Troy Archer, center Pete Brock and offensive tackle Mark Koncar. Wide receiver Dave Logan went on to an All-Pro career while linebacker Gary Campbell, tight end Don Hasselbeck and fullback Terry Kunz were All-Big Eight picks.

And they got beat 63-21 by Nebraska. David Williams gave the Buffs a 7-0 lead with a 74-yard touchdown on the fourth play of the game in Lincoln before the Cornhuskers scored the next 63 points.

In the 1977 season-finale 23-0 win over Kansas State, workhorse running back James Mayberry set a CU record by carrying the ball 40 times. He rushed for 1,299 on the season, joining Byron White, Kayo Lam, Bob Stransky, Charlie Davis and Tony Reed as 1,000-yard rushers in CU history.

An original wild-man, defensive lineman Troy Archer wreaked havoc in Big Eight offensive backfields in 1974-75. Archer's NFL career with the New York Giants was cut short by a fatal car crash in 1979.

It was hard to take and harder to figure, although the suspensions of Archer and Campbell, stemming from a bar fight that week on the hill, and star running back Tony Reed, who was charged with shoplifting, didn't help.

CU recovered, whipped its next four Big Eight foes, and earned another trip to Houston for the Astro-Bluebonnet Bowl, where another inexplicable beating at the hands of Earl Campbell and Texas awaited. The Buffs dominated the first half as Williams hit Logan and Hasselbeck with TD passes to take a 21-7 lead, but then tripped all over themselves in the 38-21 loss. Campbell ran for 95 yards.

FAMILY AFFAIR Mallory's wife, Ellie, and their four children were fixtures at CU games both home and away. The Mallory family would often travel to road games on the team's charter. Ellie Mallory told the Boulder Daily Camera on Sept. 15, 1974, she'd have it no other way:

"I yell a lot at games and it's better if I'm right there.

Ellie Mallory, wife of head coach Bill Mallory, was one of CU's biggest fans.

The first of three Brock brothers to play at CU, Pete Brock was an All-American center in 1975 before playing 12 NFL seasons with New England. Younger brothers Willie and Stan followed.

Screaming in your living room startles the neighbors."

A Mallory family tradition included hosting a Christmas dinner for all the seniors. "You cook for two days and it's gone in 45 minutes," she said.

MORE TRAGEDY A horrible string of tragedy, beginning with Poitier's sudden death in 1974, hit too many CU athletes over the next 10 years.

Archer's promising NFL career with the New York Giants was cut short when he died in a car crash in 1979. A month later, J.V. Cain, an All-American in 1973, collapsed during practice with the St. Louis Cardinals and died two hours later of an apparent heart condition on his 28th birthday. Melvin Johnson, a wideout at CU from 1974-77 who had moved on to the Kansas City Chiefs, died during routine hand surgery in 1978. Meningitis killed CU running back Derek Singleton on New Year's Day in 1982.

WILD FINISH CU didn't have any plans on winning a

22. When the Denver Broncos made their first Super Bowl appearance, XII, their starting center was an all-Big Eight Conference offensive tackle from Colorado. Who was he?

share of the Big Eight title in 1976. It just sort of happened. The season turned on Oct. 16 in Stillwater. The 3-2 Buffs trailed 10-6 in the final minutes and appeared dead when quarterback Jeff Knapple had a fourth-down pass intercepted in the OSU end zone. But the Cowboys' defensive back, instead of kneeling down, tried to return

DAVE LOGAN

Dave Logan can do it all. He knows this, having tried it all.

A two-sport star at Colorado between 1972-75, Logan enjoyed a nine-year All-Pro NFL career with the Cleveland Browns and Denver Broncos. After one year with the Broncos, Logan retired in 1985 and made the transition to talk radio, where he's become one of Denver's most popular radio personalities over the last 10 years.

Logan, the CU football television analyst in addition to his dual role as Broncos color analyst and midafternoon talk-show co-host with Scott Hastings for KOA Radio, is the head football coach at Arvada West High School in his "spare time." In the winter, he works regional Big Eight basketball broadcasts.

A hectic schedule isn't anything new for Logan. The 1975 All-American wideout lettered four times and left CU as the school's second-leading receiver with 71 catches for 1,098 yards. A three-year letterman for Sox Walseth's CU basketball team, Logan was drafted out of Wheat Ridge High by the Cincinnati Reds.

He was the first freshman at CU to letter under the new eligibility rules in 1972 and started two games as freshman.

"There isn't anything Dave Logan can't do," Eddie Crowder, his coach in 1972 and '73, said.

Dave Logan was able to stretch his on-field talents to a successful career after his playing days.

Running back James Mayberry was CU's MVP in 1978, Mallory's final season. Mayberry ran for 1,299 yards as a junior and finished his career as CU's second-leading rusher behind Charlie Davis. His 2,548 career yards now rank him fourth.

it and CU's Steve Gauntry forced a fumble which Waddy recovered on the OSU one-yard line.

Two plays later, fullback Jim Kelleher scored. CU added a 25-yard touchdown return of an interception by linebacker Frank Patrick for an improbable 20-10 win. Riding the momentum, CU defeated 16th-ranked Iowa State 33-14 and No. 13 Oklahoma 42-31, Mallory's only win over the Sooners. After stumbling against Missouri, CU needed and got an OU win over Nebraska on Thanksgiving Day to finish in a three-way tie with OU and OSU for the title. Having swept both teams, CU headed for Miami to face Woody Hayes and Ohio State in the Orange Bowl.

Once again, CU took an early lead (10-0) and crumbled 27-10 in Mallory's second bowl trip in two years. As it turned out, it was the beginning of the end.

LOSING FRIENDS On the surface, CU's 7-3-1 record in 1977 looked pretty good. But looks can be deceiving. For example, after Oklahoma destroyed CU 52-14 the second-to-last game of the season, Sooner assistant coach Larry Lacewell was quoted as saying, "It was a lot easier than it looked."

And Mallory was in a lot more trouble than it seemed.

The Buffs started 5-0 but a 17-17 tie at Kansas followed by two straight losses to Nebraska and Missouri began the downward spiral. Following the OU loss, Mallory's routine meeting with the Boulder Buff Club raged out of control, with boosters verbally attacking Mallory and Mallory shouting down the non-believers.

"You know I'm here to run the show," Mallory report-

With Bill Mallory's job on the line, CU rallied from a 27-7 deficit to beat 13th-ranked Missouri 28-27 in Columbia on Oct. 28, 1978. Mallory was named UPI coach of the week for what turned out to be his last win at CU.

The largest home crowd in Colorado history, 53,553, watched the Buffs lose to Oklahoma, 28-7, on Nov. 4, 1978.

edly told the crowd of 120. "It's going to come right here. And when you people aren't pleased with me, then buy up my contract and I'll leave and go somewhere else."

One fan, standing face-to-face to Mallory, said, "I'm going to tell you something. We've got the best group of kids on that football team that anybody in the country has got. And if any blame goes anywhere, it's not going to go to the kids. It's the coaching."

Mallory agreed.

"Hey, what'd I tell you?" he said. "I told you that before. I'll take the blame. We're not perfect."

Mallory could have survived, however, if he would have kept just one very important booster happy. Continental Airlines Board Chairman Robert Six was called "the greatest college football booster of all-time" and he, along with Denver businessman Jack Vickers, were major players in the inner workings of the football program.

Crowder, who worked closely with Six when he was coach, catered to Six, who lived in California. When Six couldn't attend CU games in his private box, Crowder would call him after each quarter with updates.

Mallory spent one year living on his farm after he was fired in 1978 before resuming his coaching career at Northern Illinois in 1980.

> "The Colorado football program has no more avid supporter than Six. In addition to helping foot the bill for the Mallory TV show through Continental Airlines, he also provides summer jobs for nearly three dozen CU players. It's no accident practically every out-of-state player on the CU roster comes from an area where Continental has an airline stop. And, when asked, Six can also be a most persuasive recruiter for the CU football program."
>
> Boulder Daily Camera, Sept. 8, 1976

Crowder realized what Six's support for the program meant. Mallory didn't want to be bothered. When Six asked for daily phone updates and suggested Mallory and his coaching staff could benefit from a course at Continental's public relations department, Mallory scoffed at both. Six pulled his sponsorship of Mallory's TV show and cut off the program.

PRESSED BY THE PRESS Mallory's troubles didn't end there. Having instituted a closed locker room policy for reporters following losses, Mallory alienated the media, as well, and was routinely lambasted after losses not only for losing the game but for sheltering his players.

The locker room reopened in 1978, but the losses came even more frequently as the Buffs once again started fast against a light non-conference schedule at 5-0, gained a No. 12 national ranking and proceeded to lose five of their last six to finish 6-5.

"The natives are getting restless, and darkness is closing in on him.

"The University of Colorado's 52-14 defeat Saturday by Nebraska, the previous upset at Oklahoma State and the prospect of bad times against Missouri and, ye gads, Oklahoma, have all but decided the coach's fate.

"Like the wind, he's gone."

Denver Post, Oct. 25, 1978

Three days after losing 20-16 at home to Earle Bruce's Iowa State Cyclones, Mallory met with Crowder for 12 minutes on a cold Tuesday morning and was blown out of Boulder. Crowder, in an official statement, said, "After a review of our football situation, it has been decided that a change is necessary. Coach Mallory, his staff and players have made an outstanding effort, and yet our program is not progressing as it must."

Mallory said, "I want to make it clear that I was released. I didn't resign. There is no way in the world I'd ever quit."

1979-1981: CHUCK FAIRBANKS

"If the University of Colorado has the best football team that money can buy, the dollar is in more trouble than anyone thought."

N.Y. Times, October, 1979

With the program in steady decline since the Orange Bowl appearance in 1976, Crowder wanted to make a big, national splash with the hiring of Chuck Fairbanks, the former OU boss who was coaching the New England Patriots.

Crowder succeeded, for all the wrong reasons. Fairbanks still had four years left on his contract, and the Patriots were willing to fight, in court, to keep him. A long, drawn-out battle resulted in the Patriots receiving $200,000 from CU (paid by boosters), and Fairbanks gave up $100,000 remaining on his contract (which CU compensated). So $300,000 lighter in the pocket, CU put Fairbanks officially to work on April 2, less than a week before the start of spring drills and nearly four months after he had been hired.

BIG, BIG PROBLEMS Fairbanks produced 3-8, 1-10, and 3-8 seasons, but CU's miserable failures on game day were

23. *In Super Bowl XII, a starter for the Broncos at running back was a former Buff who never made All-Big Eight. Who was he?*

Chuck Fairbanks failed in his effort to make the transition from big-time pro football coach with the New England Patriots to big-time college coach with Colorado in 1979-81.

24. *Chuck Fairbanks was 7-26 (.212) in three years (1979-81) as the CU head coach. What was his record in Big Eight games?*

little more than comic relief for their serious problems off the field.

Arnold Weber, who became CU's president in 1980, Fairbanks' second season, put things in perspective for a story by the Boston Globe's Ron Borges, reprinted in the Daily Camera, Dec. 27, 1989:

"I got a crash course in big-time football," Weber, then the president at Northwestern, said. "My first day, literally, I was told of an (NCAA) investigation into 132 alleged infractions.

"My second day, I was told the athletic department budget was $5.5 million with a $1 million deficit. That was immediately followed by a lurid article in Sports Illustrated that dealt with alleged expenses. Some were mistaken or exaggerated, like Chuck wearing new shirts and shoes every day, but one truth was the $50,000 office which I never had the stomach to visit.

90 *Buffaloes Handbook*

"Another was something called the team (locker and weight) room. It was budgeted at $125,000 and came in at $624,000. The program was clearly in extremis."

Colorado was hit with NCAA probation for the second time in 20 years. Only this time, nobody really noticed the Buffs were banned from national television and bowl appearances. They weren't getting any anyway.

CHUCK'S STORY In the same article, Fairbanks explained his point of view:

"The biggest mistake I ever made in my coaching career was going to Colorado, because I didn't go there for the right reasons.

"I'd already made up my mind I wasn't going to stay with the Patriots with the way we were having to do our business. I guess Colorado was just convenient. So I did it without investigating as thoroughly as I should have. That's what caused the problems.

"Turns out they weren't really committed to win! I should have known better because Bill Mallory was a damn good football coach. If he couldn't be successful there, why the hell did I think I could be?"

"I knew I was leaving, but I didn't know what I'd do. Then Colorado called. It sounded good, so I took it."

Fairbanks: "Arnold Webber came there from Carnegie-Mellon. If they had football there, I don't know who in the hell they ever beat."

Weber: "We beat Notre Dame. In 1928. We're still talking about it."

DEFIANT Big Eight Skywriters predicted CU would finish last in the Big Eight in 1980, and a few went so far to say that Fairbanks' second team could go winless.

Running back Lance Olander found it hard to stomach.

"There's just no way we can lose every game," he said in a St. Louis Globe-Democrat story. "I don't accept it at all. I don't want to go down the list of people I think we can beat, but there is no way we'll be last. I think we'll be no lower than fifth. And that's the bottom."

The Buffs beat Iowa State 17-9 to finish 1-10 overall, 1-6 in the Big Eight, which gave them a tie for seventh in the conference.

25. *Until the Buffs won the 1990 national title, what was their highest finish in the national polls?*

Fairbanks led CU to a three-year record of 7-26.

Chapter 6: Mallory and Fairbanks 1974-1981

Quarterback Charles Davis, not to be confused with star tailback Charlie Davis, averaged 3.1 yards per rush and completed 44 percent of his passes, including four TDs and 13 interceptions between 1978-81.

THE ARTICLE In what might be the most forgettable week in the history of CU football, the Buffs lost home games to Indiana (49-7) and Oklahoma (82-42) back-to-back in 1980. In between, a Sports Illustrated article, authored by 1963 CU journalism grad and current Boulder resident Doug Looney titled "There Ain't No More Gold in Them Thar Hills," portrayed Fairbanks as a "non-stop, out-of-control spender" and Crowder as an administrative incompetent.

Fairbanks called it "pure, unadulterated filth" and told reporters, "This should make you ashamed of your profession." Weber described Looney's work as "scurrilous" and "a garbage can of innuendos" and went so far as to ban Looney from stepping foot on campus. Looney, in fact, has returned many times and even teaches a sports writing class in the journalism school.

The magazine hit the newstands Thursday. The Sooners hit the Buffs Saturday. OU established NCAA records for total offense (876 yards) and rushing offense (758 on 73 carries). The teams combined to score 124 points and 18 touchdowns, both NCAA marks which still stand.

Headline in the Daily Camera, June 2, 1982: CUers Can't Hide Glee at Coaching Change

Fairbanks, after watching his team practice all week, said he saw it coming. "Quite frankly, I'm not surprised at our inability to defend against Oklahoma's team."

PICK YOUR ROCK BOTTOM While it wasn't devoid of solid,

and some great, players, the state of the program bottomed out in the late '70s and early '80s. Cornerback Mark Haynes earned All-American honors in 1979 to cap a spectacular four-year career at CU before heading to the pros. Stan Brock, Pete's little brother, joined Haynes on the 1979 All-American team.

But as Fred Casotti wrote in his 1989 book "CU Century," "The less said about Fairbanks' three seasons the better.

"The Buffs were 7-26-0 during that time. Horror followed horror. Did the Buffs bottom out when they lost two straight games to lowly Drake in 1979 and 1980? Or was it in the 1980 opener at UCLA when they trailed at the half, 56-0? Or was it that same season when they swept Davis' 1962 team out of the record books by four points in permitting 282? ... Or was it an 0-59 Nebraska,

A familiar cheer from the CU student section during the Buffs' miserable 1-10 season in 1980: "Two, four, six, eight, score before we graduate."

LEON WHITE

An All-American center at CU in 1977, Leon White appeared NFL-bound and on his way to joining the rich and famous.

White never gained his fortune. But "Vader" did.

White, believed to be the only player in Big Eight history to letter at three different positions since the player platoon system started, missed his entire junior season with knee surgery and then injured his other knee a month before the NFL Draft. Eight months and 14 knee operations later, White's career was doomed.

And another one was born.

In a Daily Camera article on July 13, 1985, the 350-pound former Buff explained why he was entering the world of professional wrestling:

"I'm a ham. Since I was eight years old, I've been in front of a crowd playing something and I miss it," said White, who lettered as a guard, tackle, and center. "It's not a whim. There are people in the game today who couldn't carry my proverbial jock.

"Besides, I've got to get into wrestling just to feed me. It's 50 or 60 bucks a day."

Known as "Bull Power" (a derivation of his college nickname "Baby Bull") and most recently as "Vader," White commands a seven-figure salary to play the bad guy opposite Hulk Hogan most Saturdays on TBS.

White lives in Louisville, Colo., and, at age 39, is preparing for his life after wrestling, in the movies and as a business entrepreneur.

When knee injuries forced a career change, Leon White stepped into the world of professional wrestling and became a star, first as "Bull Power" and then as "Vader."

Mark Haynes was such a good cornerback for CU between 1976-79, he doesn't even rank among the school's top 33 interception leaders. Opponents simply didn't throw the ball in his direction. Haynes was named to the 1979 Associated Press All-American team in 1979, giving him the chance to appear on television with Bob Hope.

0-49 Oklahoma parlay in 1981. If selecting a single low-water mark during 1979-80-81 was too difficult to determine, there was no doubt about this: that 3-year period was, by a figurative mile, the worst in CU's first 100 seasons."

THE END Despite all the failures and troubles, Fairbanks' resignation actually caught some people by surprise, although ultimately both parties, CU and Fairbanks, were glad to move on. Fairbanks stepped into a promising endeavor as a main player in the formation of a new pro football league, the USFL. He became president and head coach of the New Jersey Generals.

Meanwhile, brighter days were ahead.

Remember Walter Stanley? He's CU's 85th-ranked rusher with 399 yards and no touchdowns between 1980-81. Stanley played for four NFL teams between 1985-92.

Bill McCartney
1982-1994

Overall Record: 93-55-5 (.624 winning percentage)
Conference Championships: 1989 (11-1), 1990 (11-1-1), 1991 (tie, 8-3-1).
Worst Seasons: 1982 (2-8-1), 1983 (4-7), 1984 (1-10).

In 1982, the Colorado Buffaloes didn't need a coach as much as they needed a savior. In Bill McCartney, they found both.

In the 13 seasons to follow, they had also found their first win over Nebraska in 19 years, their first undefeated regular season since 1937, their first No. 1 ranking, their first national championship, three consecutive Big Eight titles, a Miracle in Michigan, a Heisman Trophy winner and a 47-10-4 (.770) record in the 1990s.

A 41-year-old veteran assistant on Bo Schembechler's Michigan staff as defensive coordinator, McCartney came to Boulder in June of 1982 relatively unknown. He retired in 1995 as CU's winningest coach and the most recognizable figure in Boulder.

"I promise you we will have a program built on integrity, honesty and character," McCartney said the day he was hired, June 9, 1982. "Our top priority will be the graduation of the student athlete. That's how you're going to measure us. That's not going to be as glamorous as that scoreboard in the end zone. Maybe they won't keep a tally as pronounced. And yet, that's how we're going to measure success here."

Born in Michigan, McCartney took his three-sport talents to the University of Missouri, where he played in two Orange Bowls and was a second-team All-Big Eight linebacker as a senior in 1961. Ten years of high school coaching back in Michigan was highlighted by McCartney leading Divine Child High to the state football and basketball titles in the same season in 1973.

He joined the Michigan staff the next year and became Schembechler's defensive coordinator in 1977 until CU came calling in 1982.

> "Not since another Michigan native, Sonny Grandelius, swept CU committees off their feet 24 years ago, has a coaching candidate made as favorable an impression here as McCartney did."
>
> Dan Creedon column, Daily Camera, June 10, 1982

While serving as Bo Schembechler's defensive coordinator, McCartney was named the Big Ten's "Player" of the Week for devising a zone defensive scheme to befuddle Purdue and quarterback Mark Herrmann in 1980.

McCartney played linebacker and center for Missouri and lettered three times.

CU QUIZ

26. On his way to winning the 1994 Heisman Trophy, CU's Rashaan Salaam rushed for 317 yards in a 34-31 victory at Texas. It wasn't a CU record, however. Who holds the CU record for most yards rushing in a game?

THE SEARCH Here are the circumstances leading up to McCartney being hired, as recalled by Creedon in a "10-year anniversary" Daily Camera column on June 9, 1992:

Chuck Fairbanks turned in his surprise resignation Tuesday following Memorial Day in 1982. Drake coach Chuck Shelton, who had beaten Fairbanks' teams in back-to-back years, spent four days in Boulder with athletic director Eddie Crowder and appeared to have the job locked up. Shelton even spent Saturday morning interviewing prospective assistants, but by dinner time Crowder coyly dropped Shelton off at his restaurant (Eddie's Mexican Cafe) with two reporters (keeping both parties occupied) while he ran off to meet with BYU's LaVell Edwards.

But by Sunday morning, Edwards had decided he didn't want any part of CU's problems. Crowder apparently ditched his "If you can't beat 'em, hire 'em" notion and Shelton was history. McCartney, a darkhorse candidate, arrived Monday, took 24 hours to dazzle Crowder, the Board of Regents and media alike, and was offered the job by Crowder on his way back to the airport Tuesday morning. After talking it over with his wife, Lyndi, back in Ann Arbor, McCartney accepted later that evening and was back in Boulder on Wednesday morning for the press conference.

Bill McCartney, with his wife Lyndi by his side, meets the Colorado media for the first time on June 9, 1982. Twelve years later on Nov. 19, 1994, McCartney announced his resignation with Lyndi at his side.

LATE START The first time McCartney met the majority of his team was the first day of fall drills. McCartney tried to prepare the returning players for what was in store by mailing each of them a summer training regimen that included weight lifting and running. As a motivating force, he let them know that on the day before the first practice, there would be a 1 1/2-mile run around the track at Potts Field.

In a 1987 Daily Camera story on McCartney's five-year coaching anniversary, McCartney recalled the scene:

> "Guys were laying all over the track, throwing up," he said. "It was sickening. I couldn't even believe these were Division I athletes. ... Several guys couldn't finish the run. Some couldn't finish half the run. That was my first real indication of what I had walked into."

HUMBLE BEGINNINGS What McCartney had walked into was a mess. His first three teams were 2-8-1, 4-7 and 1-10. He challenged CU fans to "stand up and be counted" and fill Folsom Field in support of his first team in the home finale against Kansas. He didn't get a sellout (only 35,114 braved the cold), but he got his first win, a 28-3 triumph over Kansas. McCartney was carried off the field and fans tore down the goalposts.

Inside Sports magazine tabbed Bill McCartney as one of the nation's top five recruiters in 1982

McCartney was carried off the field after his first win in Folsom Field, a 28-3 home-finale victory over Kansas on Nov. 13, 1982.

CU lost to its new "rival" Nebraska, 40-14, which was pretty good compared to the 69-19 whipping Mike Rozier, Turner Gill and Irving Fryar put on them the next season. Nebraska scored 48 points in the third quarter alone. But McCartney remained steadfast in his declaration that neighboring Nebraska was the team the Buffs would judge themselves against each year.

TRAGEDY In the 1984 season-opening 24-21 loss at Michigan State, sophomore tight end Ed Reinhardt caught a CU single-game record 10 passes for 142 yards and went into CU's next game at Oregon as the nation's leading receiver.

With 1:53 left, Reinhardt caught a 19-yard pass and was tackled by two Oregon players. He remained on the field for a few minutes before walking off under his own power. But once on the sidelines, he collapsed. Within a half hour, a blood clot in Reinhardt's brain was being removed by Dr. Arthur Hockey, who was in attendance that day.

Reinhardt remained in a coma for 62 days. That's

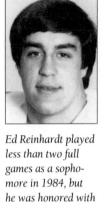

Ed Reinhardt played less than two full games as a sophomore in 1984, but he was honored with a letter. Reinhardt's miraculous recovery continues today, but it reached an emotional peak in 1994 when he sang the National Anthem before CU's season opener.

when his remarkable recovery began. At first he couldn't speak and his entire right side was paralyzed. On the 10-year anniversary of his injury, Reinhardt, 29, walked into a packed Folsom Field and sang the National Anthem.

GOD AND THE GRIDIRON
Headline in the Daily Camera, Dec. 16, 1984

It was often difficult to separate McCartney the football coach and McCartney the man. McCartney's strong religious faith surfaced in the personality of the coach many times, winning him respect from some and making enemies of others.

Although his team was to face and lose to powerhouse Notre Dame the following week after Reinhardt's injury, McCartney stayed in Oregon to pray over his fallen player for several days, putting game preparations aside.

McCartney told the Catholic Register, "That scoreboard in the endzone is very important to me, but not nearly so important as the scoreboard of life."

The Daily Camera, in an article titled "God and the Gridiron," described McCartney's religious zeal:

> "Regardless of the professional demands on his time during the football season, and the Herculean travel regimen he maintains recruiting players nationwide during the off-season, McCartney also abides by a strict spiritual schedule. Whether at his home near the Boulder Country Club or in a hotel room, McCartney spends an hour each morning at dawn, alone on his knees studying the Scriptures. He also attends Mass three times a week at Sacred Heart of Jesus Church, regularly attends the Fellowship of Christian Athletes' early morning prayer and the Bible study groups Wednesdays and Fridays on campus, and makes time during the day for additional prayer and Bible discussions with players and staff members.
>
> " 'When you don't take time on your knees to be purged, to really repent, things get out of whack in your life real fast,' says the coach. 'I shudder to think of a day without prayer and the Scriptures.' "

McCartney, raised Catholic, was "born again" in 1974, his first year as a Michigan assistant coach. "Before 1974, I would drive 300 to 500 miles to hear a coach speak," he said. "After, I would drive 300 to 500 miles to hear a man of God speak. Before, it was Bear Bryant. Then, Billy Graham."

In 1989, McCartney received some mild criticism for speaking at a rally for Operation Rescue, an anti-abortion

27. True or false. CU never has beaten a No. 1-ranked team in football.

One of the first changes McCartney made was abolishing the athletic dorm in 1982. Brackett Hall, filled almost exclusively by football players, had earned the name "Animal House."

In the first few years of his coaching career, McCartney led the team in a pre-game prayer, a practice he later abolished due to outside opposition.

group. Three years later McCartney denounced homosexuality at a press conference as "an abomination in the eyes of almighty God," causing CU president Judith Albino to publically reprimand the coach.

McCartney learned and survived. He reserved his evangelical talents to pre-game pep talks and Promise Keepers, the all-male Christian organization that was born in his head in 1990 and fills up football stadiums across the country today.

When he resigned in 1994, McCartney cited his need to uphold the standards he had been preaching as the founder of the Promise Keepers and said he intended to spend more time with his family and especially his wife, Lyndi.

When several people were calling for McCartney to be fired in 1984, new athletic director Bill Marolt gave the coach a contract extension.

AD SWITCH After nearly 30 years as CU's athletic director, Crowder retired in the summer of 1984 and was replaced by young Bill Marolt, a former CU skier who graduated onto the 1964 United States ski team, which he later coached to five gold medals in 1984. Marolt also coached CU's ski team for 10 years from 1969-78, and he guided the Buffs to seven straight national championships.

A change in the AD post usually makes for a nervous

head football coach.

"(Former school president) Arnold Weber brought me here," McCartney said in a 1987 Daily Camera article. "And so I didn't know necessarily whether President (Gordon) Gee or Bill Marolt would want to bring in their own man, which occasionally happens."

After a 52-7 loss to Missouri, McCartney's fears were assailed. Despite his team's 0-5 record at the time, McCartney had his contract extended by Marolt.

"There were a couple of reasons I did that," Marolt said. "My experience as coach of the U.S. Ski Team taught me that you build top programs with consistency and leadership. Secondly, I felt he had inherited a program that philosophically was headed in another direction. Thirdly, I thought he was a good guy and that the program needed stability."

McCartney rewarded the faithful the next week with a 23-21 win against Iowa State when a late Cyclone field-goal attempt went wide. It turned out to be the difference between a winless season and the 1-10 campaign CU endured.

In a note sent to CU season-ticket holders in 1984, McCartney pleaded with fans not to sell their tickets to Nebraska fans, a practice which had resulted in Folsom Field looking a lot like Memorial Stadium on game days. "We need the stadium for home games to be filled with Buff fans," McCartney wrote.

WISHBONE WONDERS The Buffs finished dead last in Division I-A rushing in 1984, so there was room for improvement. Fairbanks' passing attack was grounded, and his baby blue uniforms were closeted in favor of black jerseys. After a two-week love affair with the run-oriented Veer-T, McCartney settled on the wishbone as CU's offense of the future.

"If there was one key thing that turned the program around," McCartney said in 1987, "that was the one."

CU was the nation's most improved team with a 7-5

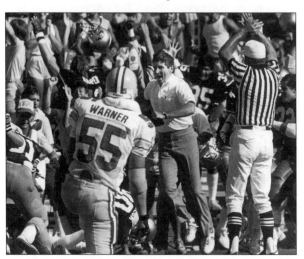

McCartney reacts to Mickey Pruitt's game-saving sack against Oregon in 1985.

record and went from last in rushing to ninth (259.8) and last in net punting to first (43.6). Punter Barry Helton, from tiny Simla, Colo., enjoyed the first of two All-American seasons.

McCartney was named the Big Eight's Coach of the Year.

MIGHTY MICKEY Three-time All-Big Eight safety Mickey Pruitt made a lot of tackles in his CU career (340 actually), but he's remembered for one. It came on the final play of CU's second game in 1985 against Oregon at Folsom Field. With the Ducks looking for the winning score at the CU 3-yard line, Pruitt, a sophomore, blitzed and sacked quarterback Chris Miller to preserve a 21-17 win, the biggest to that point in the McCartney era.

"It seemed like a thousand people jumped on me," Pruitt said on Sept. 14, 1985. Halfback Ron Brown added, "Everyone made that last tackle: the bench, the stands, everyone."

Pruitt joined Helton, also a three-time All-Big Eight player, on the conference's All-Decade Team in 1989.

TURNAROUND One of McCartney's most satisfying wins came on Oct. 12, 1985, when the 4-1 Buffs clobbered his alma mater, Missouri, 38-7, to gain revenge for a 52-7 shellacking the year before in Columbia.

Mark Hatcher, who ran for 151 yards and three touchdowns and passed for 110 yards and one touchdown, quarterbacked the CU wishbone to season highs in total offense (505) and rushing (390).

"In the chronological year," McCartney said, "young kids can accomplish some significant things, particularly if they stick together as a team. After last year's game, the Missouri players said we were paper thin. We were. They didn't flaunt it; just put 500 yards on us."

The Buffs finished 7-4 and a Tennessee win over Vanderbilt gave CU a berth in the Freedom Bowl, its first bowl appearance in 10 years.

"I don't think there'll be a team in a bowl game that will be more excited than we are," McCartney told Freedom Bowl executive director Tom Starr. "I can't think of a bowl that's more ideally suited for us. I'd rather be there than any other besides a New Year's Day (bowl)."

Helton, a quarterback in high school, hit tight end Jon Embree with a 31-yard touchdown pass on a fake punt to rally CU to a 20-17 deficit. But a Mike Marquez questionable fumble on the Washington 2-yard line as the Buffs were driving for the winning score left CU with an empty feeling and a 20-17 loss.

Linebacker Mickey Pruitt was just one of many "difference-makers" in McCartney's first recruiting class.

28. *The Buffs have played 953 games in 105 seasons, dating to 1890. What is their overall record?*

29. *How many Big Eight titles has CU won?*

1986: TURNING THE CORNER

The Buffs hoped to use the Freedom Bowl as a springboard into 1986. They should have checked if there was any water in the pool.

CU fell flat with an 0-4 opening month in 1986. The bad start had a bad start as CU was soundly trounced in the opener, 23-7, by Colorado State, the only loss to their in-state rival in the McCartney era.

"A bitter defeat, I'll tell you that," McCartney said. "Bitter."

But somehow CU discovered itself when the Big Eight season arrived. The Buffs rolled through the conference 6-1, losing to Oklahoma, 28-0, and beating Nebraska for the first time in 19 years.

The 20-10 win on Oct. 25, 1986, at Folsom Field, is generally accepted as "The Turning Point" in the CU program. Freshman walk-on Jeff Campbell scored on a 39-yard end-around, freshman running back O.C. Oliver threw a 52-yard TD pass to Lance Carl and the CU defense held Nebraska, averaging 335.2 yards per game, to just 123 rushing yards.

And CU fans brought down the goalposts.

"I didn't even coach," McCartney said. "I was just along for the ride."

"It's the best thing to happen in Boulder in a long time," Carl said. "I've had people I don't even know come up and say, 'Thank you. Thank you.'"

Bolstered by the Nebraska win, a 6-5 CU team was invited to the Bluebonnet Bowl, where Baylor shut down the wishbone and won, 21-9.

SECOND FIDDLE It was huge sports news in every other paper in the nation, but the New York Mets' 10-inning, 6-5 win over the Boston Red Sox in Game 6 of the 1986 World Series barely crept onto the front pages of Colorado newspapers on Oct. 26.

Bill Buckner wishes he had it so lucky in Boston.

NO LOYALTY On Feb. 11, 1987, the day the Buffs signed seven future NFL players, including Eric Bieniemy, Mike Pritchard, and the H-Boys, Kanavis McGhee and Alfred Williams out of Houston, McCartney spent most of his press conference complaining about the lack of loyalty among Colorado's prep stars.

CU signed just one in-state player, Aurora Hinkley's Joel Steed (although Longmont's Greg Biekert was added later). In-staters Brian Boerboom and Tahaun Lewis picked Nebraska and Boulder's Scott Lockwood, a super-talented running back from Fairview High, ignored a

Under McCartney, the Buffs lost 15 of their first 20 games and won 15 of their last 16.

30. The first player in school history to catch 50 passes in a season has been a CU assistant coach since March, 1993. Who is he?

Eric Bieniemy is CU's all-time leading rusher with 3,940 career yards.

ERIC McCARTY

Bill McCartney had to climb a mountain to sign Eric McCarty in 1983.

Literally.

When he signed three days after the national signing date, the Boulder High star was considered the crowning jewel in McCartney's first recruiting class. McCarty did the honors on top of Flagstaff Mountain, his training ground where he built his 6-2, 225-pound frame.

"I am the mountain," he said that day.

McCarty chose CU over Michigan, Stanford and Southern California. It was the first of many recruiting battles McCartney would win against the big boys.

"It's like Bobby Anderson told me," McCarty said in the Daily Camera, Feb. 13, 1983. "He said that growing up here you always want to go to CU, but once you get in high school and all those schools are looking at you, you think it might not be too bad. But when it comes right down to it, this place is the best."

A knee injury sidelined McCarty in 1983. He didn't realize the huge expectations at CU until he switched from fullback to linebacker as a junior in 1986. McCarty earned All-Big Eight and Academic All-America honors in 1987.

A 3.7 pre-med student at CU, McCarty, a doctor, represented the players from the "Mac Era" at McCartney's 1995 going away tribute.

petition signed by over 5,000 CU students asking him to attend CU and chose Taiback U., Southern Cal, instead.

"The issue is not what's wrong with Colorado," McCartney grumbled. "The issue is where is the state loyalty of the kids? Why don't they want to come and make this state university great? That's the issue. Why don't they develop loyalty, take sides, take pride in what's going on up here and push this program over the top?"

QUOTABLE From the Daily Camera, McCartney on his 1-9 record against Nebraska and Oklahoma heading into the 1987 season:

> "Nebraska still has the greatest program in the country, in my opinion. Oklahoma has the greatest athletes. They just both happen to be in our con-

ference. All we have is the prettiest campus in the conference.

"... We're not on par with them, but we're moving in that direction. That would be absurd to think that we're on a par with them, because we're not. But that doesn't mean we can't beat them. Those two teams will be ranked in the top five this year. In all the years I've been in college football, Oklahoma is the most prohibitive favorite to win the national championship that I've ever seen. Oklahoma is the most overwhelming choice to win it all.

"They have the greatest array of experienced talent I've seen since I've been coaching and in a position to evaluate it.

"I went through a publication last week that had Oklahoma with six guys on offense and six on defense who deserve All-America consideration. That's with Boz (Brian Bosworth) gone. This is the year Oklahoma has pointed toward. They have a bevy of All-America players. It's the greatest talent assembled in a long time.

"But it doesn't mean we can't beat them."

CU lost to No. 1 Oklahoma 24-6 in Norman and lost 24-7 at home to fifth-ranked Nebraska in the season-finale. McCartney was now 1-11 against the Big Two.

BIG PLANS When McCartney brought in his first recruiting class in 1983, it was seen as a major building block to

CU's defensive fortunes turned in 1987 with the signing of the "H-Boys." The trio of Houston products included (from left) Alfred Williams, Arthur Walker and Kanavis McGhee.

31. In the 1985 season, CU made a stunning 5 1/2-game improvement to match Fresno State that year as the NCAA's most-improved team from the previous season. What were CU's records in 1984 and '85?

the future. Eric McCarty, Mickey Pruitt, Morris Copeland and Curt Koch would grow with CU. Twenty-two of the 24 members of the class were redshirted their first year, meaning the 1987 team would be dominated with fifth-year seniors. The plan was to suffer now, reap the benefits later.

"This is the year we've looked forward to. Any judgment made on our program is premature until now," McCartney told visiting Big Eight Skywriters in August, 1987. "We have our heart set on playing Jan. 1, 1988, and winning."

Instead, the Buffs slumbered through a good, but not great, 7-4 season, losing to all three ranked teams they faced. When it was time to pass out bowl invitations, the Buffs were left waiting by the phone.

SMU SAGA The Buffs, quietly going about their business, didn't figure to make too many off-season headlines going into a promising 1988 season.

But that all changed in early January with news that McCartney was in Dallas to interview with SMU athletic director Doug Single. SMU wanted McCartney to revive its literally dead program in the wake of the pay-for-play recruiting scandal and subsequent NCAA "death penalty."

Almost everyone, including McCartney, believed he was gone. CU assistants, out on the road recruiting, started sending out feelers for job opportunities. Marolt was ready to begin a new coaching search, and the press was busy lambasting McCartney for his "lack of loyalty" to the university.

On Saturday afternoon, Jan. 9, Single was actually in the process of assembling a press conference to announce the hiring when McCartney phoned to turn the job down. A 15-minute meeting with Marolt and President Gordon Gee completely reversed McCartney, who was "leaning heavily" toward SMU the night before.

32. Wheat Ridge's Dave Logan was named to CU's All-Century football team and might be the best athlete in Buffs history. He was a standout player in CU basketball as well as football. But he only played in one bowl game. Name that bowl game.

" 'I realized today when I walked out of the president's office that I had made a commitment that I wasn't following through on,' McCartney said at the hastily arranged press conference. 'Why I didn't come to grips with that sooner would be a fair question. And when I did, it was very obvious to me what I had to do.

" 'I had shook hands, signed a contract and made a commitment. The very thing I was asking of others, I was in jeopardy of turning away from myself. I could not in good conscience consider it any further.' "

Daily Camera, Jan. 10, 1988

McCartney described his mood as "very humble. I want to say to the people here whose lives I have disrupted that I am very sorry. I truly, genuinely apologize for what I have done. I am determined to make amends by doing a good job and fulfilling my contract to the hilt."

BUILDING THE FOUNDATION McCartney's consistent recruiting was about to pay off. The fabulous 1987 class – Bieniemy, McGhee, Pritchard and Co. – grew up as sophomores in 1988. To the mix, the Buffs added one of their most prestigious signees ever in quarterback Darian Hagan of Los Angeles' Locke High in February of 1988.

CU beat out Notre Dame, Washington and Nebraska for the services of the talented and confident 5-foot-9, 190-pound All-American.

"CU is just a couple of players away," Hagan told the Daily Camera. "If we don't make a run at them next year, we're definitely Big Eight champs my sophomore year. I think one of the things Colorado needs is a breakaway

Quarterback Darian Hagan, considered by many to be the most exciting player in CU history, eclipsed the 1,000-yard mark in both rushing and passing as a sophomore in 1989.

Headphones or no headphones? McCartney's critics felt he did his best coaching when he took off the headphones and left the detailed work to his assistants.

runner at quarterback."

What CU had was a pretty solid returning junior. On a hot and muggy mid-September afternoon in Iowa City, Iowa, Sal Aunese took the Buffs on an 85-yard touchdown drive in the final minutes of the fourth quarter to upset No. 19 Iowa, 24-21. It was the first of many clutch performances by the emerging Aunese, who led CU to a Top 20 ranking for the first time in 10 years and an 8-4 record.

Hagan occasionally saw playing time as a freshman, although not enough to earn a letter. His first three carries of his career went for 11, 63 and 10 yards, the last a touchdown against Fresno State.

SWITCH HITTER Buff fans witnessed many incredible exploits from Hagan, but they never got to see his most unique talent.

In high school, Hagan was a pitcher for the baseball team. A left-handed pitcher and right-handed pitcher. He would switch in the middle of an inning if necessary.

He took his ambidextrous talents to the football field, where he estimated he threw 40 percent of his passes with his left hand, his natural side. Hagan wrote, ate and played other sports left-handed, but he threw a football a little more accurately with his right hand. McCartney made it clear early in Hagan's freshman year that he didn't want a switch-hitting quarterback.

"You will never see Darian throw left-handed in a game here, period," McCartney said.

"We have sophisticated rules about where and when he can pitch the ball," offensive coordinator Gary Barnett told Sports Illustrated. "Darian never breaks the rules. He expands them."

33. Name the Missouri Valley Conference school that beat CU in back-to-back trips (1979-80) to Boulder and later dropped football.

UNDER THE LIGHTS The Buffs just missed finding the spotlight in the first night game ever at Folsom Field on Oct. 23, 1988. Eighth-ranked OU nipped CU, 17-14 before 49,716 fans and an ESPN national audience. Ken Culbertson's 62-yard field-goal attempt to tie fell just a few feet short and a little wide with 29 seconds remaining.

The Buffs turned the ball over three times in Nebraska territory in a disheartening 7-0 loss at Lincoln, including J.J. Flannigan's fumble in the open field on the way to what should have been a 43-yard TD run. The Buffs accepted a return trip to the Freedom Bowl to play Brigham Young, believing that they were good enough to play on New Year's Day.

FREEDOM FIASCO For the second time in the brief five-year existence of the Freedom Bowl, Colorado lost 20-17. CU had many chances to put the game away early

34. Other than the records, what was identical about the 1-10 seasons suffered by the Buffs in 1980 and 1984?

When Sal Aunese suffered through a dreadful performance in the Buffs' 20-17 loss to BYU in the 1988 Freedom Bowl, no one knew it would be his last game.

35. When the 1988 Buffs opened 4-0, it marked CU's best start since what season?

and then completely tripped over itself in the fourth quarter to let BYU escape with the win.

Hagan relieved an ineffective Aunese (4-for-13, 1 INT) in the fourth quarter and immediately threw an interception to set up BYU's winning field goal. McCartney rushed Aunese back in the game, but it was too late. The Buffs were befuddled and beaten.

"It will be a tough off-season," said Bieniemy, who ran for 144 yards on 33 carries. "But we'll come out and work hard."

The performance inspired Hagan to request a position change to tailback. CU coaches told him to think about it. Circumstances soon made the issue moot.

SHOCKING NEWS The disappointment of the Freedom Bowl and embarrassment of the off-field troubles were quickly overshadowed. Aunese, complaining of chest pains and having difficulty breathing, checked into the student health center in March. He was first diagnosed with pneumonia, then a respiratory ailment, but by the end of the month more tests at University Hospital in Denver produced much worse news.

At a quiet, grim press conference on March 30, 1989, CU team physician Dr. Wayne Gersoff reported that Aunese had a rare form of inoperable stomach cancer, which affects only eight of every 100,000 Americans. The prognosis was not good and chemotherapy was started immediately. Aunese chose to undergo treatment in Denver rather than at home in Oceanside, Calif., because he wanted to "stay close to his teammates."

INSPIRATION Less than a month after the diagnosis, Aunese attended CU's spring game at Folsom Field.

Afterwards, Aunese spoke privately to his teammates and coaches who surrounded him. He then addressed the record spring game crowd of 13,642, who remained in the cold drizzle.

"I'd like to thank God, the city of Boulder and my teammates," Aunese said softly over a microphone. "God Bless you. See you next year."

"This is something you don't experience but we are," McCartney said. "Each one of us is living through this. We're together to see Sal fight this incredible battle. He said, 'See you next year.' That's Sal; he's planning on being here."

His teammates called Aunese their leader until his death.

1989: TRIUMPH AND TRAGEDY

In their 100th anniversary 1989 season, the Buffs experienced a century's worth of incredible highs and agonizing lows.

Fall practice opened with great expectations as 37 lettermen, including 16 starters, returned. But it was the one that wasn't there – Aunese – who everyone was thinking about. Aunese, weak and sick from radiation treatments, missed all but a few practices. Still, he was voted an honorary captain along with four of his senior classmates – Bill Coleman, Erich Kissick, Michael Jones and Bruce Young.

Without Aunese, the biggest, and really the only, question facing a very talented CU team was at quarterback. Aunese, who showed a flair for the dramatic in leading comeback wins over CSU and Iowa a year earlier, figured to shine in his senior campaign. But instead, the exciting little sophomore Hagan was thrust onto the scene in Aunese's fading light.

A tough non-conference schedule, which included Texas, Illinois and Washington, awaited.

ANSWERING QUESTIONS With Aunese watching from a private box high above the field, Hagan quickly put any doubts about his ability to lead his team to rest in the

CU was ranked 14th in the AP and UPI polls before the 1989 season, marking the Buffs' first preseason ranking since 1977. The team finished the regular season undefeated for the first time since 1937.

Running back J.J. Flannigan stops at Aunese's locker following CU's 27-21 win over Nebraska at Folsom Field in the "Game of the Century."

Labor Day opener against Texas.

On the second play of the game, Hagan hopped through the Longhorns' line and juked his way to a 75-yard run to the Texas 2-yard line. The longest non-scoring running play in CU history set up Bieniemy's 1-yard dive and the Buffs were on their way to a 27-6 rout.

Hagan accounted for 211 yards of total offense and threw for one TD and ran for another.

"I didn't expect to go out and do as much as I did," Hagan said. "But I'm glad it happened. ... I've always believed I'm a leader. I believe I can lead this team to a Big Eight championship."

36. Name the two former Colorado assistant coaches who became NFL head coaches.

'A PEACEFUL DEATH' Hagan and CU swept to a 3-0 start. Despite only five days of preparation, the Buffs broke open a close game against rival CSU and won 45-20 at home.

A national television audience and a soldout crowd at Folsom Field then witnessed one of the most emotional and impressive CU victories ever, 38-7 over No. 10 Illinois and highly-touted quarterback Jeff George.

Backed up in the closed end of the stadium filled mostly by CU students, George repeatedly backed away from center, claiming it was too loud to run a play. Linebacker Alfred Williams sent George temporarily to the sideline in the second quarter with a vicious 16-yard sack.

Meanwhile, Hagan passed for 175 yards, including a 74-yard bomb to Jeff Campbell, to set up CU's first touchdown. Campbell hopped off the turf and pointed to Aunese in his now familiar location below the press box, a salute which was repeated throughout the sunny afternoon.

It was Aunese's last public appearance. One week later, on CU's off Saturday of the season, Aunese died at 8:47 p.m., Sept. 23, 1989, at University Hospital. He was 21.

"He died a peaceful death, without suffering any pain," Gersoff said.

37. Name the former CU assistant (1968-70) who later coached a Pacific-10 school to the national championship.

"Ah, Sal. I'm sorry. For us.

"It was such a valiant struggle, and one that was so blatantly unwinnable from the start. And you still fought it. We're the losers and the winners. We lose because we can't watch you demonstrate the human spirit at its best any longer, and we win because of what you leave us as a model."

Dick Connor, The Denver Post, Sept. 24, 1989

MEMORIAL SERVICE Over 2,000 friends, family and fans packed the University's Macky Auditorium the following

Monday for Aunese's memorial service, which featured a rich feel for Aunese's Samoan heritage and a public revelation from McCartney.

Aunese's brothers and cousins dressed in white shirts, black ties and knee-length skirts.

> " 'Pass on Sal's legend,' CU co-captain Michael Jones told fellow Samoan teammates Oakland Salavea and Tamasi Amituani. Aunese helped recruit Salavea, and they both helped persuade Amituanai. 'Down through the ages,' said Jones.
>
> " 'Let it live. He'll live longer than any one in this room.' "
>
> *The Denver Post, Sept. 26, 1989*

For CU's 1989 game at Oklahoma, the Buffs traveling squad consisted of only 59 players, one short of the limit. A seat on the airplane, a bed at the hotel, and a place at the team dinner was reserved for the late Sal Aunese.

McCartney said publicly for the first time that his daughter, Kristyn, was the mother of Aunese's 6-month-old son, Timothy Chase McCartney. It was hardly a secret. A Denver area newspaper printed the details of the story a month prior to Aunese's death and Kristy and son were frequent visitors to CU practices in the fall.

McCartney, in an emotional voice, concluded his comments about Sal with a message for his daughter:

"Kristy McCartney. You've been a trooper. You could have had an abortion, or gone away and had the baby someplace else to avoid the shame. But you didn't. You stayed here. You're gonna raise that little guy, and all of us are going to watch him. It looks like we've got another left-hander coming up in the ranks.

"Kristy, I admire you. I respect you. I love you so much."

Aunese's casket is carried away by O.C. Oliver, Joe Garten, Jeff Campbell, Erich Kissick, Bruce Young, Oakland Salavea and J.J. Flannigan.

TRIBUTE FROM AFAR Southern California linebacker Junior Seau dedicated his junior season to his late cousin, Sal Aunese.

"It's heavy on my mind," said Seau, who wore a towel with the name "SAL" printed on it. "But what helps me deal with it is that he went out as a winner. Sal Aunese is a true warrior, and that's how I'd like to go on in my life thinking about him. ... He's looking down with a smile. I'm going to go on and try to achieve the goals that Sal and I both had. I'm going to live the dream. He's always going to live through me."

38. Bill Mallory was the last coach to take CU to the Orange Bowl before Bill McCartney came to the Flatirons. What other three schools has Mallory coached to bowl games?

LETTER FROM SAL Aunese left a final message to his teammates in the form of a letter, which was handed out to each player before a Week 4 showdown at Washington on Sept. 30:

"My dearest teammates, coaches, and brothers, whom apart from my family do I hold so close. I come to you all with love and encouragement, to continue to do what we all have been doing when our season first started, only to excel and better ourselves mentally, physically and spirtually. Unity is our strength and love is our guide from here on in!

"Don't be saddened that you no longer see me in the flesh, because, I assure you I'll always be with you in spirit. Hold me dear to your hearts as you know I do all of you. Strive only for victory each time we play and trust in the Lord, for He truly is the way! I love you all. Go get 'em and bring home the Orange Bowl."

Love, Sal

BACK ON THE FIELD After a couple of early mistakes, an emotional Colorado team crushed No. 21 Washington 45-28 behind tailback tandem Flannigan and Bieniemy, who combined for 167 yards rushing and two touchdowns.

THIS IS FOR YOU, SAL

Headline in Sports Illustrated, Oct. 2, 1989

"It may well have been the most deafening moment of silence in the history of college football. Just before the kickoff of their game last Saturday with Washington in Seattle, Colorado's players dropped to their knees, pointed to the weepy sky that spread like a bruise above Husky Stadium and, as opposing players and more then

69,000 spectators looked on in silence, bade a wordless farewell to quarterback Sal Aunese, who had died a week earlier of stomach and lung cancer at age 21.

"That this silent salute looked a lot like 60 guys signaling 'We're No. 1' may have been the purest of coincidences. Then again, judging by the 45-28 defeat the Buffaloes dealt the Huskies to raise their record to 4-0, maybe it wasn't.

" 'We pointed to the sky to let Sal know we were thinking about him,' said Darian Hagan, a sophomore who replaced Aunese as the starting quarterback. 'And to say the sky's the limit for this team.' "

SMELLING ORANGES CU cruised through its early portion of the Big Eight schedule 3-0, although Bieniemy suffered a broken leg against Iowa State and didn't return until the Orange Bowl.

The first real test for the Buffs, clad in "Things Have Changed" T-shirts, came at Oklahoma, also missing its top runner in Mike Gaddis. An acrobatic and extremely risky Hagan pitch over two OU defenders to a waiting Flannigan at the goal line sparked CU to a 10-0 lead on the way to a 20-3 win, setting up a Nov. 4, 1989, showdown between No. 2 CU and No. 3 Nebraska in Boulder. It was billed locally as the "Game of the Century."

The Buffs answered a touchdown by Nebraska on its first play from scrimmage when Hagan broke loose

39. In their 105-year history, the Buffs have scored 38 points or more in 130 games. What is their record in those games?

Until Kordell Stewart surpassed him, Darian Hagan owned CU's single season record for passing yardage with 1,538 in 1990.

around the left side and 30 yards downfield flipped a lateral to Flannigan, who completed the 70-yard tying touchdown run.

Jeff Campbell, he of the 1986 reverse fame, burned the Huskers again. The senior set up two scores with 47- and 55-yard punt returns and Dave McCloughan knocked down Nebraska quarterback Gerry Gdowski's last-second desparation heave into the end zone to preserve a 27-21 win and give the Buffs, for all intents and purposes, their first trip to the Orange Bowl since 1976.

Two expected wins over Oklahoma State and Kansas State finalized CU's Miami travel plans. And a late-season loss by Notre Dame, the Buffs' Orange Bowl opponent, gave 11-0 CU its first-ever No. 1 national ranking.

Hagan ran for 156 yards and passed for 69 more in a season-ending 59-11 blowout of Kansas State to become the fifth player in college history to eclipse 1,000 yards rushing and passing in the same season. Hagan finished with 1,004 rushing and 1,002 passing despite sitting out the third quarter twice and fourth quarter eight times in CU routs.

RIVALRY? WHAT RIVALRY? Probably nothing has fueled the Nebraska-Colorado rivalry, in the view of CU fans, more than Nebraska coach Tom Osborne's refusal to attach special significance to the game.

While McCartney printed the yearly date in red on CU schedules, Osborne wondered what all the fuss was about.

"Sure, it's a big game, but they're all big games," Osborne was quoted as saying in the Rocky Mountain News on Nov. 1, 1989. "Iowa State's a big game for us. Oklahoma State's a big game for us.

40. *Larry Zimmer of Denver's KOA radio has been the play-by-by voice of Colorado football for 21 years. Zimmer graduated from what Big Eight school?*

"The downside of risk is so tremendous at this school. If this team loses to Iowa State, people in Nebraska think the sky is falling. So to me, there's a football team out there in Colorado with some good players, and let's go play 'em. I just try to play football teams. It doesn't matter to me what color a team wears or which state it's from."

"ST. SAL" Following CU's win, an editorial in the Nov. 7, 1989, Omaha World-Herald questioned Aunese's "moral character" and accused Colorado officials of canonizing Aunese. It read, in part:

"No post-game comment would be complete without a reference to Sal Aunese, and, in our judgment, the unseemly effort to hype his death into a sort of 12th-man presence on the Colorado team.

"What claims to secular canonization – St. Sal, as it were – could be made for Aunese?

"Apparently Aunese, quarterback of the 1988 Buffs, was a likable young man, respected by his teammates. But so are several hundred other college football players across the country.

"The continual talk about the sainted Aunese and the teary visits to his locker after the big game not only represent a questionable tribute to what the young man actually was. But these things also detract from the performance of the talented football players whom Colorado put on the field this year. The Buffaloes might be good enough to have earned an Orange Bowl bid without their coaches' exploiting the Aunese tragedy. The way coach McCartney has played out this season, however, it will be hard for anyone to really know."

HEISMAN VOTE In the Rocky Mountain News' Heisman Trophy poll to gauge the favorites for college football's most prestigious award, Aunese received one first-place vote posthumanously.

"Aren't we supposed to give the Heisman to someone who means a lot to his team?" asked John Rohde, sportswriter for the Daily Oklahoman in Oklahoma City. "I can't imagine anyone who has meant more to his team than Sal Aunese."

LIVING A LIE Preparations in Miami for the Orange Bowl were interrupted by controversy when a Denver television station (KCNC) taped Notre Dame coach Lou Holtz speaking to his team before a practice three days before the game.

The camera caught Holtz saying:

"Let me tell you what, they're living a lie. They've been living a lie all year. ... They're going to see the best Notre Dame's been, and we're going to whip them. ... No. 1, (Colorado's) used to scoring a lot of points. They ain't playing any Kansas State.

"We've got to be patient on defense, just play our football game. On offense, we want to control the football. All we want is a first down, a first down. (Then) frustration will set in on Colorado's offense. By the middle of the third quarter, they will leave the game plan completely and start grab-bagging.

"Remember me telling you that – they are not patient. The quarterback will want to make plays and we aren't gonna let him."

41. Name the CU staffer who carries a diploma from the Lenin Institute for Physical Culture in Moscow, from the German Institute of Physical Culture and Sports Science in Leipzig and from the Institute of Physical Culture and Sports in Bulgaria.

Notre Dame coach Lou Holtz is 1-2 against Colorado in bowl games.

42. When the Buffs won three consecutive Big Eight titles from 1989-91, what was their record for those 21 league games?

It made for great television and the huge throng of media jumped on the story and began looking for reaction. McCartney refused to fuel the fire by saying, "From what I've been able to gather, he didn't say those things for anyone to hear other than his squad, so I don't feel I should comment on it."

Holtz, who said he had no idea his pep talk was being taped, did speak to McCartney about the incident. "I told him if we had offended the Colorado football team, I apologize."

Said CU defensive tackle Arthur Walker: "All I can say is talk is cheap. All season teams have popped off on us, and we've been coming out on top all year long. So let them keep doing it."

After failing to convert several scoring chances in the first half, the Buffs went into halftime tied 0-0 but looked beaten. It turns out they were. The Irish scored on their first two possessions of the second half, withstood a 39-yard TD scamper from Hagan and held on for a 21-6 victory to deny CU the national championship.

Bieniemy fumbled at the Notre Dame 15-yard line when he appeared headed for the end zone in the first quarter. Late in the second quarter, CU failed to convert a first-and-goal from the Irish 1-yard line, although television replays appeared to show Bieniemy scored on a first-down dive. Failing to get into the end zone, the Buffs botched a fake field-goal attempt when holder Campbell couldn't find a receiver.

The play was designed for fullback George Hemmingway to receive the throw, but McCartney had suspended Hemmingway for breaking a team rule earlier in the week. In his place, freshman linebacker Chad Brown couldn't get open.

Bieniemy pointed the finger of blame at himself, the Daily Camera reported:

43. What is Folsom Field's listed seating capacity?

"I blew it, plain and simple. I blew two scoring opportunities I should've converted. Basically, I blew the game. When people look back, they'll see my mistakes and I can't blame them. Whatever people think, I deserve. I should've scored twice and I didn't."

CU, 11-1, finished fourth in the polls. Miami, which had defeated Notre Dame 27-10, won the national championship.

MOVING ON McCartney said getting back to work and hitting the recruiting trail right away helped him deal with the disappointment of the loss.

"I was in a kid's home on Jan. 3," McCartney said in the Rocky Mountain News, "and Tom Osborne had already visited him at his school. (Osborne) had a tough loss, too (in the Fiesta Bowl), and it didn't take him long to get back after it.

"I think as soon as you divert your thinking, it serves to energize you. It's the best antidote for the depression of defeat. I found (recruiting) was the ideal scenario for me."

LIFETIME CONTRACT McCartney received quite a "going away" present from CU President Gordon Gee, who was on his way to Ohio State in July of 1990. Before he left, he signed McCartney to a 15-year contract through the year 2005, an unprecedented deal in college sports.

> "Fi ... fif ... fifteen?
> "Fifteen years. Is that a contract or a sentence?
> "If Bill McCartney lives out his new contract as head football coach at the University of Colorado, the Buffs won't need a new search committee until the year 2005. There is a 3-year-old out there somewhere whom McCartney will actually wind up coaching."
> Dick Connor column, The Denver Post, July 27, 1990

It went basically unnoticed at the time, but Paragraph 10 in the contract ultimately would be the most important of the entire document. The clause stipulated that after fulfilling five years of the deal, McCartney could resign. In an Aug. 14, 1994, Rocky Mountain News story, McCartney, just three months from quitting, said it was an out he didn't intend to use.

44. *In their national championship season of 1990, the Buffs had three unanimous All-America players. Name them.*

CU President Gordon Gee (right) gave McCartney an unprecedented 15-year contract extension in 1990.

Chapter 7: Bill McCartney 1982-1994

Referee J.C. Louderback, who worked CU's 33-31 "Fifth Down" win over Missouri in 1990, only moonlighted as a Big Eight official. His regular job in Arkansas City, Kan., was as a math teacher.

Lost in the "Fifth Down" aftermath: Eric Bieniemy ran for 217 yards to pass Charlie Davis as CU's all-time leading rusher.

"God willing, and if I'm physically and mentally capable, my plans at this point are to fill out the contract," he said.

SEEING RED During McCartney's tenure, it was an unwritten law, but a well-enforced one, that the color red, symbolizing hated Nebraska, was strictly forbidden.

McCartney threatened to boycott the 1988 Fiesta Bowl dinner if it had red table cloths and turned down a courtesy car because it was red, according to an Oct. 27, 1990, Denver Post story:

"He doesn't allow any red at work," said his secretary, Judy Wolf. "If you wear red, you get it from the time you arrive to the time you leave. ... We had one girl, a receptionist, who had a red dress on and, waiting for coach Mac, she hid under her desk.

"He caught her."

McCartney's son, Tom, said the idiosyncrasy wasn't limited to work: "He doesn't buy anthing red. Nothing in our home is red. He doesn't own anything red."

1990: A CHAMPIONSHIP SEASON

CU's national championship season never quite had a feel like a championship year until the Buffs were handed the trophy on Jan. 2, 1991.

Ranked No. 5 in the preseason poll, the Buffs started 1-1-1 and slipped to 20th before starting a slow, improbable climb back to the top ranking. McCartney suspended Bieniemy, a senior, for disciplinary reasons for the first annual Disneyland Pigskin Classic matchup with Tennessee. Mike Pritchard, a multi-talented but under-appreciated wingback, moved to tailback and had the game of his life.

In a wild, mistake-filled 31-31 tie, Pritchard ran for 217 yards, including touchdown bursts of 55 and 78 yards. His career totals before the game were nine carries for 23 yards. "Eric can keep the tailback position," Pritchard said. "I just stepped in for him today."

Bieniemy returned for a Sept. 6 night game against Stanford at Folsom Field and scored the winning touchdown in the 21-17 victory on a fourth-down 1-yard dive. This time, unlike the Orange Bowl, it didn't look like Bieniemy crossed the goal line.

It appeared CU's luck ran out the next week when No. 21 Illinois gained some revenge and held on for a 23-22 win, but the Buffs were just on their way to

45. Bill McCartney is CU's all-time winningest coach, with an 93-55-5 (.624) record over 13 seasons. What was Mac's record after 33 games and three years?

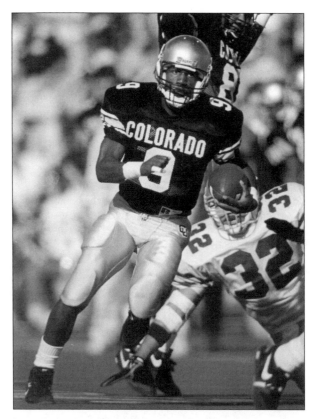

Mike Pritchard averaged 26.4 yards per catch over his career (1987-90). He ranks fourth on the all-time charts with 1,241 yards and 10 touchdowns.

becoming "the luckiest team in college football," as their critics liked to refer to them.

NAIL BITER Facing 12th-ranked Washington, a team that in one year would win a share of the national championship, CU turned its season with a dramatic goal-line stand at Folsom Field.

The Huskies attempted four passes from first-and-goal at the 7, which failed. Sophomore cornerback Deon Figures, the Big Eight's Freshman of the Year in 1988 but suspended for the 1989 season, outjumped Washington's Mario Bailey in the corner of the end zone for an interception to preserve the 20-14 win.

"Nine times out of 10 a receiver can't outjump Deon for the ball," said CU strong safety Tim James, who also made an interception. "When I saw the ball floating to Deon's side, I wasn't worried. Deon's got big-time hops."

The victory was costly. Hagan sprained his left shoulder, beginning a season-long list of injury troubles, and he didn't start 3-1-1 CU's Big Eight opener at Missouri.

46. In the second game of the 1982 season, Bill McCartney notched the first victory of his CU career. Name the Pac-10 Conference school those Buffs beat.

Chapter 7: Bill McCartney 1982-1994 **121**

CU 'TAKES THE FIFTH' AT MISSOURI

Headline in the Daily Camera, Oct. 7, 1990

CU's season erupted in controversy on Oct. 6, 1990, at Faurot Field when backup quarterback Charles S. Johnson scored a 1-yard touchdown on the final play of a 33-31 win.

In one of the most bizarre finishes in college football history, Johnson's winning score came on CU's fifth down inside the Missouri 5-yard line, as both teams were oblivious to the situation. Furthermore, the actual touchdown signal came late as Johnson dived to the goal line on his back and reached the ball over his head in between players to score.

47. *The Buffs had consensus All-America punters in 1988 and '89. Name them.*

"On Saturday, a young man named Charles Johnson advanced the football 3 feet to score the winning touchdown on the last play of the game as Colorado beat Missouri, 33-31.

"It was the greatest blow to 'lower education' since half of America's students and most of America's parents went down for the count against something academic social tinkers called new math.

"Well, the math can't get any newer than it got Saturday afternoon on the 1-yard line out in Columbia, Mo."

New York Post, Oct. 8, 1990

Here's the sequence:

:30, 1st-and-goal, MU 4, Johnson spikes ball to stop clock.
:28, 2nd-and-goal, MU 4, Bieniemy runs up middle for 3 yards, CU timeout, down marker still reads second down.
:18, 3rd-and-goal, MU 1, Bieniemy stopped for no gain, clocked stopped by referees to unpile players.
:04, 4th-and-goal, MU 1, Johnson spikes ball to stop clock.
:02, 5th-and-goal, MU 1, Johnson runs right, dives, and scores winning touchdown as clock expires.

48. *When the Buffs and Notre Dame met in the 1995 Fiesta Bowl at Tempe, Ariz., CU won by a 41-24 score. Why is that score noteworthy?*

Sports Illustrated called for CU to forfeit the win. McCartney scoffed at the notion, instead choosing to focus on what he called a "treacherous" playing field. After reviewing the game films, McCartney said his players slipped on Mizzou's old Omniturf surface 92 times.

The Big Eight Conference agreed that the result would not be overturned, but the officiating crew, led by referee J.C. Louderback, was suspended.

WHAT'S GOING ON? The confusion wasn't reserved for

Charles S. Johnson (left) scored the most controversial touchdown in CU history on fifth down to beat Missouri, 33-31, in 1990. Above, McCartney holds a copy of the Oct. 7, 1990, Kansas City Star. Although several newspapers called for McCartney to forfeit the tainted win, he never considered it.

49. What must happen before CU will consider retiring a football player's jersey number?

the participants on the field, where angry Missouri fans tore down one goalpost. They had to be cleared so the teams could come back on the field 15 minutes later for the conversion attempt, because it was possible had Missouri somehow returned the ball for a 2-point conversion, the Tigers could have tied the game. But Johnson simply took the snap and dropped on the ball. Up in the broadcast booth, both radio and television announcers were in the dark as well. Dave Logan, the ex-CU star working color for the television broadcast, said during the crazy sequence, "The yardage and down markers seem mixed up," but left it at that.

PARTING THE BIG RED SEA Before the Nov. 3, 1990, showdown against No. 3 Nebraska, McCartney calmly stated, "Everything we've done is in preparation for this. Everything."

Bieniemy fumbled five times in the first three quarters in the chilling rain at Nebraska's Memorial Stadium, but the CU senior more than made up for it by scoring four touchdowns in the fourth quarter to give CU a 27-12 win over the Huskers.

"We're going back to the beach," Hagan yelled as CU fans rushed the field to celebrate CU's first win in Lincoln since 1967.

The 27 points scored against Nebraska in a fourth

Eric Bieniemy celebrates one of his four fourth-quarter touchdowns to beat Nebraska, 27-12, in 1990.

quarter were the most ever surrendered by the "Blackshirts" in a conference game. McCartney kept with his T-shirt tradition by handing out ones reading "The Real Blackshirts" to CU's defense.

"When they put their minds to it," said Nebraska defensive coordinator and former Buff Charlie McBride, the Buffs "can beat anybody they want to."

It marked the first and only time the Buffs beat Nebraska and Oklahoma in the same season in consecutive seasons. "It should've happened my sophomore year," linebacker Alfred Williams said. "It should've been a clean, three-year sweep.

"But I'll take two."

CU earned another nice double. They became the first team other than Nebraska or Oklahoma to play in back-to-back Orange Bowls since Missouri in 1941-42.

THE COLORADO ROCKET Once again, the Buffs' preparations for the Orange Bowl revolved around the talents of Notre Dame's do-everything star Raghib Ismail, the Rocket.

But in Mike Pritchard, the Buffs' had a multi-dimensional threat of their own to rival the Rocket. "He's just flat-out a big-play person," Pritchard said. "I have that capability, too, but I'd never compare myself to him."

Others did. McCartney called the two the best big-play makers in college football. Pritchard's tight-rope catch along the sideline against Nebraska set up CU's comeback in the fourth quarter. It was a play that epitomized Pritchard's career at CU: Clutch, spectacular but usually overlooked.

Pritchard was one of a school-record 12 All-Big Eight performers in 1990, joining Bieniemy, Joe Garten, Hagan, Gerry Howe, James, Jay Leeuwenburg, McCloughan, McGhee, Steed, Mark Vander Poel and Williams.

Bieniemy, Williams and Garten, a guard who started a school-record 44 straight games, were unanimous All-American picks.

Pritchard's talents were appreciated by the pros. He was the 13th overall pick by the Atlanta Falcons in the 1991 NFL Draft before being traded to the Denver Broncos in 1994.

CU IN MIAMI The 10-1-1 Buffs, ranked No. 1 in the nation, returned to the Orange Bowl hoping to claim their first national title with a second chance against Notre Dame.

Down 6-3 at halftime and with Hagan sidelined with a ruptured knee tendon, backup quarterback Charles S. Johnson once again stepped into the spotlight. There was

One week after he led CU to a 10-9 Orange Bowl victory over Notre Dame and a share of the national championship, quarterback Charles S. Johnson became the first CU athlete to ever appear on the Tonight Show on Jan. 8, 1991. Appropriately, Johnny Carson didn't host the show, but his backup, Jay Leno, did.

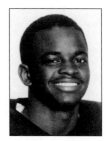

Charles S. Johnson was named MVP of the final game he played.

McCartney is escorted off a crazed Orange Bowl field after the Buffs captured their first and only national championship with a 10-9 win over Notre Dame.

no controversy, only celebration this time. Johnson completed all three of his passes on CU's lone TD drive and 5 of 6 for 80 yards for the game. The performance allowed him to replace the label of "Fifth Down QB" with "Orange Bowl MVP."

"Maybe this will put all that stuff to rest. I spent all last week talking about that to everyone, and I don't want to talk about it anymore."

He didn't have to. Johnson bypassed his senior year of eligibility, went to law school, and now works as a sports agent.

As he did in the key victory over Washington, Figures sealed the win with an interception of Rick Mirer. Cornerback Ronnie Bradford's blocked extra point after Notre Dame's second-quarter touchdown proved to be the difference.

Oh, there was one more difference. Ismail's apparent 91-yard punt return for a touchdown with 35 seconds left was called back because of a clipping penalty on Notre Dame's Greg Davis against CU's Tim James.

THINK AGAIN McCartney on punting to the Rocket: "I could have used a little better strategy in that situation. I would probably have never forgiven myself if there hadn't been a clip on the play."

SPLIT VOTE The AP poll, voted on by media members, tabbed CU the No. 1 team in the land, but the UPI poll, voted on by coaches, gave the national title to Georgia

Tech by the slimmest of margins, 847 points to 846. The 11-0-1 Yellow Jackets had routed Nebraska, 45-21, in the Citrus Bowl.

"I'm a coach and I have to respect my peers," McCartney said. "But it's kind of unprecedented to have the No. 1 team in the country play a schedule judged the most difficult in the nation, then beat the No. 2 team and not retain its ranking."

SPEAKING OF PUNT RETURNERS McCartney slightly shocked the Big Eight world when he agreed to let Hagan, the team's starting quarterback who was recovering from major off-season knee surgery, return punts his senior year in 1991.

Hagan went to McCartney with the request.

"I said, 'Hagan, do you want to get me fired?'" McCartney said. "Do you realize what everybody will say if you go out there and get hurt? They'll all say I'm the dumbest coach in America. But then I said, 'OK.'"

In the fourth quarter of the season opener against Wyoming, Hagan had returns of 37 yards and 30 yards to help break open a close game, which CU won 30-13. On the season, Hagan averaged 11.5 yards on 25 punt returns.

HUSKER BASHING Although there's been an effort to downplay it recently, radio talk shows in Denver served as battlegrounds during "Nebraska Week" in the early 1990s.

Husker Jokes, which seemed awfully similar to Aggie jokes or blonde jokes or just about any other type of jokes, dominated the Denver radio airwaves, to the delight of the on-air personalities and the pro-CU listening audience.

"They don't pay me to be fair," Joe Williams, who teams with Irv Brown on KYBG's afternoon show, said in the Nov. 1, 1991, Daily Camera. "I make no bones about it, I have no compassion for them. Nebraska week is different. I've always been blessed with having at least one neighbor who was a diehard Nebraska fan. For that week, we don't speak. The rest of the time they're great people, but business comes first."

Unruly behavior, bordering on violence, toward visiting fans at both Folsom Field and Memorial Stadium eventually led both coaches and the local radio stations and newspapers to temper the pre-game extracurriculars.

SNOWBRAWL CU and Nebraska gave the radio shows plenty to talk about with a brutal 19-19 tie in the freez-

50. Colorado won its only national championship in 1990. Who was the preseason No. 1 team that year?

CU has produced five unanimous All-Americans in the 1990s: running back Eric Bieniemy (1990), guard Joe Garten ('90), linebacker Alfred Williams ('90), center Jay Leeuwenburg ('91) and running back Rashaan Salaam ('94)

Safety Greg Thomas preserved a 19-19 tie with Nebraska on a freezing November night in Folsom Field in 1991 with this blocked field goal on the game's final play. Thomas blocked a CU record six kicks in his career.

51. What member of the CU coaching staff played in Super Bowl XX with the Chicago Bears?

ing snow in Boulder in 1991. The tie gave CU a share of its third-straight Big Eight title, but it sent Nebraska to Miami. Safety Greg Thomas blocked his sixth career kick (a CU record) on the final play of the game to preserve the tie. Linebacker Greg Biekert, CU's second all-time leading tackler, zigzagged through the snowflakes with a blocked PAT attempt for a key and rare defensive two-point conversion.

Early season losses to Baylor and Stanford put a damper on CU's accomplishments over the season but the Buffs did march through their third-straight Big Eight season unbeaten and posted three-year records of 20-0-1 in the conference, 30-5-2 overall and 16-1-1 at home with "The Magician" Hagan at quarterback.

UNDER WRAPS McCartney closed all of the Buffs' bowl practices in Miami as he prepared his team for Alabama in the Dec. 28 Blockbuster Bowl and for the future.

Deon Figures, fifth all-time at CU with 12 interceptions, won the 1992 Thorpe Award as the nation's premier defensive back.

In a move nearly as bold as switching to the wishbone back in 1985, McCartney ditched CU's effective I-bone attack in favor of a one-back, pass-oriented offense.

The debut produced mixed results. Hagan, an option quarterback, misfired on his first seven passes and completed just 11 of 30 passes for 210 yards and one interception. The Buffs did, however, roll up 25 points against a good Alabama defense in the 30-25 loss, McCartney's fifth in six bowl trips.

McCartney was widely criticized for "ruining" Hagan's career finale by thrusting him into an offense he clearly wasn't suited to play. McCartney defended the decision by saying his team needed the extra two weeks of practice and he needed to show recruits he was serious about rebuilding the offense.

"It's his program, and he does what he wants to do. I had a good career. It didn't end with a great game for me, but that doesn't matter. I've had good games and bad games. I had fun with what they were trying to do. It's going to be a good offense for them," Hagan said.

AIRBORNE McCartney's recruiting pipeline pumped out the key pieces to make Air McCartney fly in 1992. Wide receivers Michael Westbrook, who caught a 62-yard TD pass from Hagan in the Blockbuster Bowl, and Charles E. Johnson supplied all kinds of speed and talent outside.

At quarterback, sophomore Kordell Stewart was

52. Ben Gregory and Charlie McBride know the Nebraska-Colorado rivalry inside and out. Where did they play, and where do they coach?

Kordell Stewart was recruited to CU as an option quarterback and left the most prolific passer in school history.

53. Who was the last defending Rose Bowl champion to play CU in Boulder?

groomed to take over the offense and a freshman from Texas, named Koy Detmer, arrived to supply relief help. Sophomore running back Lamont Warren shared time with senior James Hill, a fullback, and freshman Rashaan Salaam, an 8-man high school legend from California who rushed for nearly 5,000 yards and 112 touchdowns.

In his first career start, Stewart set school records for passing yardage (409) and total offense (430) and tied Hagan's school mark of four touchdown passes in a 37-17 win over Colorado State. It's not only a cliche, but a fact, that Stewart and Co. rewrote the Colorado passing record book in 1992. In CU's 57-38 blowout of Baylor in Waco the following week, Stewart completed 16 of 17 passes for 251 yards in the first half before leaving with an injury.

FIT TO BE TIED Detmer, little brother of BYU's Heisman Trophy winner Ty Detmer, came off the bench to spark CU comeback wins over Minnesota (21-20) and Iowa (28-12) before earning his first career start against Oklahoma on Oct. 17, 1992.

Detmer threw five interceptions and lost two fumbles, but also set new school records with 33 completions for 418 yards, including a record 92-yard TD pass to Johnson. Still, CU needed Mitch Berger's 53-yard field goal to knuckball through the uprights as time expired to earn a 24-24 tie.

HALLOWEEN MASSACRE CU's 25-game unbeaten streak in the Big Eight came to a definite halt on Oct. 31, 1992, in the rain at Lincoln. The Huskers dominated the matchup between a pair of No. 8 teams in the nation quarterbacked by freshmen (Detmer and Tommie Frazier). The 52-7 thrashing was the worst in the McCartney era in 10 years.

"That's the worst I've been beaten in my life," CU strong safety Dwayne Davis said.

DYNAMIC DUO CU never had a pair of receivers as good as Westbrook and Johnson, No. 1 and 2 on its all-time charts, and it's unlikely many other schools have either.

Both became NFL first-round draft picks. Until he made "The Catch" to beat Michigan in 1994, Westbrook was known mainly for his consistent routes, devastating blocking and physical potential. Johnson made the spec-

CHARLES E. JOHNSON

Four years after attempting suicide by swallowing a fistfull of pills in his home in California, Charles Johnson graduated from college with a degree in marketing and left CU as the school's all-time leading receiver.

Coach Bill McCartney said in Sports Illustrated in 1993, "You can coach a lifetime and not get someone like Charles. He is an extraordinary youngster and a sweet kid."

Johnson, whose mother was addicted to cocaine, forcing him to live in 11 different homes and often sleep under a tree outside his high school, failed at suicide. His little sister, Christine, found him on his bed and made him live.

At CU, Johnson emerged as a player and a student. Somehow between his duties as All-Big Eight receiver on the football team and sprinter on the track squad, Johnson found time to graduate in just three years.

That same year (1993), he enjoyed his second-straight 1,000-yard receiving season, scored nine touchdowns to match his uniform number and was named the Big Eight's Offensive Player of the Year, making him the first receiver to win the award since Nebraska's Johnny Rodgers in 1972.

He ranks second with 2,447 career receiving yards behind good friend Michael Westbrook (2,548), who had the luxury of playing in the Buffs' one-back offense one more year.

The Pittsburgh Steelers made Johnson the 17th overall NFL Draft pick in 1994.

Chapter 7: Bill McCartney 1982-1994

Michael Westbrook (right) and Charles E. Johnson (left) rank 1-2 as CU's all-time receiving leaders. They caught a combined 294 passes for 4,995 yards and 34 touchdowns.

tacular catch look easy, occasionally tipping the ball away from defenders before grabbing it himself. He once described how he simply caught the shadow of the ball on a sliding, backwards reception.

In 1992, they made history together:
"What's 2,209 yards between friends?

"For Colorado's receiving tandem and best friend twosome, Charles Johnson and Michael Westbrook, the yardage means a place in the NCAA record book.

"Westbrook's 24-yard touchdown reception in the second quarter Saturday not only helped the Buffs to their 31-10 victory over Iowa State, but also put Westbrook over the 1,000-yard receiving plateau for the season – joining Johnson, who achieved the feat last week against Kansas.

"The two finished the season with the spoils of Bill McCartney's off-season offensive restructuring and made a little history on the way. The Westbrook-Johnson combination became the fourth receiving pair to go over the 1,000-yard mark in the same season."

Daily Camera, Nov. 22, 1992

The Buffs set a Big Eight record by allowing Kansas State just 16 yards of offense in a 54-7 blowout win in 1992. The Wildcats, however, tied CU, 16-16, in 1993.

I CHOOSE ME When offensive coordinator Les Steckel moved down the road to work for the Denver Broncos in

Koy Detmer ended up on the deck in his 1992 matchup with the Big Eight's other premier freshman quarterback, Nebraska's Tommie Frazier, in Lincoln.

1993, the Buffs were in need of their third offensive coordinator in four years. McCartney hired Elliot Uzelac. The two had worked together on Schembechler's staff at Michigan in 1974. But the Buffs still needed a quarterbacks coach.

McCartney gave himself the job.

"The reason I started coaching the quarterbacks is we've had turnover there," McCartney said. "What we're doing right now, I don't want anymore turnover. I want to do it myself. I look forward to it."

The experiment was, at best, a wash. In 1993 as a junior, Stewart put up respectable passing numbers: 157 of 294 (53.4 percent), 2,299 yards, 11 TDs and seven interceptions. But he came nowhere close to the production he would deliver the following fall as a senior with his fourth quarterbacks coach in four years, Rick Neuheisel.

MIAMI PUNCHES OUT CU, 35-29

Headline in the Daily Camera, Sept. 26, 1993

"Colorado lost 35-29 to No. 3 Miami on Saturday at Folsom Field, but the Buffs didn't go down without a fight.

"Or two, or three."

A bench-clearing brawl between the No. 3-ranked Hurricanes and No. 13 Buffs erupted in the second quarter and delayed the game for nearly 15 minutes. Twelve players (seven Hurricanes, five Buffs) were ejected in the ugly scene, which sent cheerleaders scurrying for cover and turned linebackers into karate kickers.

The wild afternoon, which ended with CU inside the Miami 15-yard line driving for a winning touchdown, included CU athletic director Bill Marolt chastising the all-Big East officiating crew from the Miami sidelines.

After the game, Marolt, who later received a reprimand from the Big Eight conference, told the Daily Camera, "This is an embarrassment. It was an embarrassment to college football, and it was an embarrassment to the integrity of the game."

The Buffs never really got going after their 2-2 start and capped a tumultuous 1993 season (8-3-1) with a 41-30 Aloha Bowl win over Trent Dilfer and Fresno State. Salaam, on the verge of a breakthrough season, scored three times and ran for 135 yards to earn game MVP honors.

1994: THE END OF AN ERA

The McCartney era spanned four CU presidents, two athletic directors and two buffalo mascots.

McCartney, as they say, went out in style. His 1994 squad, possibly his most talented with apologies to the 1990 national champions, cruised to an 11-1 record in spectacular and history-making fashion.

The season featured CU's first Heisman Trophy winner in Salaam, a Play of the Decade candidate courtesy of Stewart and Westbrook, and was capped by McCartney's farewell dismantling of Notre Dame in the Fiesta Bowl.

CU boasts two of the last three Thorpe Award winners, given to the top defensive back in the country, in Deon Figures (1992) and Chris Hudson (1994).

Ten Buffs moved on to the NFL via the downsized, seven-round draft, and McCartney was suddenly gone as well.

A MIRACLE IN MICHIGAN

"There are sports moments that become the property of time, improbable, magical, indelible.

"One moment will last as long as there is a Colorado, certainly as long as college football endorses the passions of full stadiums and scattered alumni, as long as Michigan can feel grief.

"... There, reaching for a clattering and fateful forward pass, amid the ill-will and flailing arms of Michigan defenders, a Colorado senior named Michael Westbrook secures himself a piece of legend, and, not incidentally, the football.

"Back up the field, some 70 yards away, the man who has thrown the football, quarterback Kordell Stewart, is already racing to join the pile of joy that heaps upon Westbrook, while most of the

Christian Fauria, noted for his pass-catching concentration and soft hands, collected 98 receptions, the most ever for a Big Eight tight end.

106,427 witnesses freeze in silence as the end zone scoreboards blink the truth, Colorado 27, Michigan 26."

    Bernie Lincicome, Chicago Tribune, Sept. 25, 1994

In the CU playbook, it's called Rocket Left. Trailing 26-21 with six seconds left, with the ball on their own 36-yard line, that's the play Stewart called in the huddle. As Westbrook, Blake Anderson and Rae Carruth lined up wide left, Westbrook turned to his fellow receivers and said, "I'm going to catch it."

On the CU sideline, junior defensive tackle Shannon Clavelle turned his back to the field, put his arms straight over his head and mouthed the word "Touchdown" over and over to the biggest crowd ever to see CU play.

Stewart faded back, stepped forward to his left and launched a perfect spiral nearly 70 yards. Michigan defensive back Chuck Winters was the first to get his hands on it, but before he came down with the ball, Anderson, the son of All-American and NFL All-Pro Dick Anderson, tipped the ball back into the air.

Westbrook, who grew up in Detroit, came down with

54. Name the three Heisman Trophy winners to play in the Fiesta Bowl.

Rashaan Salaam breaks free on his record-setting 67-yard run against Iowa State in 1994, which put him over the 2,000-yard rushing plateau.

the ball and a place in history. Still clutching the football to his chest, all Westbrook could say was "I got it, I got it" over and over before his teammates buried him.

McCartney, the former Michigan assistant, called it "the ultimate victory." Michigan coach Gary Moeller said afterward, "We practice against that play all the time. That's no miracle."

IT'S JUST A TROPHY Salaam may have made history as the first player to campaign for not winning the Heisman Trophy. As the season progressed and it became apparent he was a favorite for the award, the CU junior championed the qualifications of Washington's Napoleon Kaufman or Penn State's Ki-Jana Carter.

"It's just a trophy," Salaam said after scoring four touchdowns against Wisconsin on ESPN to vault into the national spotlight on Sept. 17.

Meanwhile, after Salaam's grueling 317-yard performance through the heat and Longhorns of Texas in Week 4, fans and media began wondering if Salaam could reach the 2,000-yard mark and if he would go pro.

In beating Wisconsin, Michigan, and Texas, CU defeated three nationally ranked teams in a row in 1994, including two on the road. The last team to win two of three on the road against Top 20 competition was UCLA in 1952.

NO CONTEST Colorado's national title hopes were buried in a familiar site: Nebraska's Memorial Stadium on Oct. 30, 1994. The third-ranked Huskers, without ailing quarterback Frazier, used a thorough 24-7 domination of No. 2 CU to vault into the No. 1 spot in the country past Penn State.

"I'm shocked really," Salaam said. "We came here confident that we were going to win. We just didn't answer the call. When I work out, I think about Nebraska. I feel bad for our fans, the coaching staff, everybody. Right now, (the loss) is stuck in my throat and I can't swallow it."

A BUSY DAY A less-than-capacity crowd of 41,293 attended CU's victorious regular-season finale over Iowa State, 41-20, at Folsom Field on Nov. 19, 1994.

Those who weren't there missed a chance to witness history.

On his final and longest carry of the season, Salaam broke free along the east sideline for a 67-yard touchdown and became the fourth runner in history to eclipse the 2,000-yard rushing plateau. He joined Oklahoma State's Barry Sanders, USC's Marcus Allen and Nebraska's Mike Rozier, all Heisman Trophy winners. He finished with a school-record 2,055 yards.

In addition, Stewart set a Big Eight record for total offense in a career (7,770 yards) and Christian Fauria became the most prolific receiving tight end in Big Eight history (98 catches).

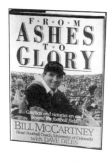

McCartney updated his 1990 book, "From Ashes to Glory," in 1995.

Salaam poses with the 1994 Heisman Trophy. The running back from San Diego, Calif., is CU's only winner of college football's most prestigious award.

In three years, Rashaan Salaam ran for 3,057 career yards (second best all-time) and produced 3,482 all-purpose yards (third best).

55. Where does CU rank among Big Eight members in bowl victories?

They all quickly became a footnote on the day the winningest and most controversial coach in CU history resigned.

"It's time," McCartney told the assembled press with his wife at his side in the basement of the Dal Ward Center. "This chapter has ended."

McCartney's reasons for leaving were vague, but he had a desire to spend more time with his family, and his role as founder of Promise Keepers continued to expand with the movement.

McCartney informed his assistant coaches before the game, but the players did not learn of his intentions until afterward. A victorious locker room suddenly turned somber.

In his revised autobiography, "From Ashes to Glory," McCartney said only his wife Lyndi and pastor James Ryle knew of his plans to resign before game day. CU president Judith Albino, one of the last people to hear of the news, tried to convince McCartney to delay the decision or take a sabbatical. "I thought he was going to be here forever," linebacker Mike Phillips said. "I thought he was immortal."

56. What was Bill McCartney's bowl record as CU's head coach?

STRIKE THE POSE After winning the Walter Camp Player of the Year and Doak Walker Award as the nation's best running back, Salaam appeared to be a sure thing to win the Heisman Trophy.

He was. Despite his apparent apathy, Salaam easily outdistanced Carter, 1,743 votes to 901, to become CU's first winner of college football's most prestigious award on Dec. 10, 1994, at New York's Dowtown Athletic Club. "Whizzer" White finished second in 1937.

The All-American promised winning the Heisman wouldn't change him.

"It feels good, but it's just an award," he said. "No more, no less. It's a piece of wood and brass to me. I'm excited for the whole program, especially my teammates."

The trophy resides in the California home of Khalada Salaam, Rashaan's mother. "This is for her," Salaam said. Khalada said: "I don't know where we're going to put it, but we'll put it somewhere and bolt it down."

BIG 'MAC' ATTACK CU proved two head coaches were better than one in a Fiesta Bowl blowout of Notre Dame, 41-24, in Tempe, Ariz. The Buffs gave McCartney a resounding going-away win while welcoming new head coach Rick Neuheisel, who was hired on Nov. 28. It added up to a helpless season-ender for Notre Dame's Lou Holtz, who said later that it was the best performance he'd seen against one of his teams.

"I just have never seen a football team be that sharp, that crisp and that effective overall," Holtz said.

CU rolled to a 31-10 halftime lead while outgaining the Irish 332 yards to 161. The 11-1 Buffs finished the season ranked third behind undefeated Nebraska and Penn State, their highest final ranking since 1990.

McCartney's final season was highlighted by beating the four winningest teams in college football history: Michigan, Notre Dame, Oklahoma and Texas. He was carried off the field after putting the final touches on a 93-55-5 career record.

Salaam, who scored three touchdowns, said goodbye with "Mac" and announced his intention to turn pro after the game.

Stewart accounted for a CU bowl record 348 yards of total offense and two touchdowns to earn game MVP

57. Name the six schools the Buffs have beaten in bowl games.

Chapter 7: Bill McCartney 1982-1994 **139**

honors. In April, he was a second-round draft pick of the Pittsburgh Steelers, culminating a career which began with doubts about his ability to be a passing quarterback.

THE FUTURE McCartney's first summer as a civilian was spent in part the same way his previous few were. He was the culminating speaker at Promise Keepers 1995, which moved from Folsom Field in Boulder to Denver's 75,000-seat Mile High Stadium.

His biggest challenge as CU's former coach was dodging rumors about his future. In his revised book, McCartney addressed his plans this way: "A lot of people seem to be wondering about my future, if I ever plan to return to coaching. Though I'm hesitant to bring the sub-

ALL-CENTURY TEAM

The star of stars in the CU galaxy proved to be Byron "Whizzer" White, CU's first All-American in 1937 and top vote getter some 52 years later when CU named its "All-Century Team" during its centennial football 1989 season. White, then an active Justice on the U.S. Supreme Court, led a 25-member class of the best of the Buffs by receiving 5,812 of a possible 6,265 votes. Bobby Anderson, the star of the 1969 Liberty Bowl, received 5,636 and Rhodes Scholar and two-time All-American Joe Romig finished third at 5,145. They are the only three players in CU history to have their numbers retired.

Electrifying kick returner Cliff Branch, a fixture on CU's No. 3- ranked 1971 squad, also eclipsed 5,000 votes while Eric Bieniemy, the only active player at the time to make the top 25, finished fifth with 3,989 votes.

A total of 11 All-Americans made the team, including the aforementioned five and Dick Anderson ('67), Pete Brock ('75), Mark Haynes ('79), Dave Logan ('75), Herb Orvis ('71) and Bob Stransky ('57).

While Bieniemy was the most current All-Century Teamer, Walt Franklin, a playing star between 1917-21 and a fixture in the program for the next two decades as team manager and assistant coach, was well remembered.

The team was formally announced during halftime of the 1989 Nebraska game at Folsom Field, capping a three-month process to select the squad. All the

ject up, the truth is I haven't ruled out the possibility of coaching. For right now, I'm committed to my family and I'm not making any long-range plans."

When the Michigan job opened up in May of 1995, McCartney quickly squelched speculation that he would replace Moeller, again stressing his commitment to his family and wife. "That'll probably preclude any coaching. If I were to coach, I would have stayed here at Colorado. I don't have any regrets."

players still living, including Justice White, were on hand for the ceremony.

Former CU players pared a list of 881 lettermen (at the time) down to 118 players. The public then voted for the team, which is listed here:

Bobby Anderson, QB/TB (1967-68-69)
Dick Anderson, DB (1965-66-67)
Eric Bieniemy, RB (1987-88-89-90)
Cliff Branch, WR/KR (1970-71)
Pete Brock, C (1973-74-75)
Hatfield Chilson, B (1923-24-25)
Boyd Dowler, QB (1956-57-58)
Walt Franklin, C/E (1917-18-19-20)
Carroll Hardy, HB (1951-52-53-54)
Mark Haynes, CB (1976-77-78-79)
Hale Irwin, DB (1964-65-66)
Zack Jordan, HB/P (1950-51-52)
William "Kayo" Lam, B (1933-34-35)
Dave Logan, WR (1972-73-74-75)
Bill McGlone, G (1923-24-25-26)
Herb Orvis, DE (1969-70-71)
Mickey Pruitt, DB (1984-85-86-87)
Joe Romig, G/LB (1959-60-61)
John Stearns, DB/P (1969-70-71)
Bob Stransky, HB (1955-56-57)
Billy Waddy, RB (1973-74-75-76)
Gale Weidner, QB (1959-60-61)
Byron "Whizzer" White (1935-36-37)
Lee Willard, B (1918-19-20-21)
John Wooten, G (1956-57-58)

Rick Neuheisel 1995-

Rick Neuheisel accepted his first head coaching position at any level on Nov. 28, 1994.

In the festive locker room following Colorado's 41-24 win over Notre Dame in the Fiesta Bowl, someone asked Rick Neuheisel whether he now officially felt like the head football coach.

"I guess so. I guess this is where they give me the keys. Now, I've just got to find out where they parked the sonofagun."

And so began the "Neu" era.

As a fifth-year senior at UCLA in 1984, Neuheisel passed for four touchdowns to lead the Bruins to a Rose Bowl victory over Illinois. He was named the game's MVP.

The CU coaching torch was passed in the aftermath of CU's 1995 Fiesta Bowl win over Notre Dame from McCartney to Neuheisel. Below, Neuheisel meets the media for the first time as head coach.

HATS IN A RING Bill McCartney's resignation on Nov. 19, 1994, floored everybody, assistant coaches included. Almost nobody saw it coming.

When McCartney made the announcement, you could feel the shockwaves emanating through the locker room. Almost instantly, the question that arose was, "Who's going to be the next coach?"

There were several candidates on the current staff. Defensive line coach Bob Simmons, 46, was in his seventh season at CU. McCartney had promoted him to assistant head coach two years earlier in order to increase his visibility as a head coaching candidate. McCartney was that confident in Simmons. Elliot Uzelac, 53, was the man credited with fine-tuning CU's offensive machine, which ran out of control for the first year after the 1992 switch until Uzelac arrived as offensive coordinator in '93. Uzelac also received McCartney's support.

Defensive coordinator Mike Hankwitz, 46, a loyal

58. What year's NFL draft was CU's most productive?

Neuheisel, escorting his wife Susan, arrived at the Dal Ward Center late on the evening of Nov. 28, 1994, to formally accept the head coaching post.

59. Just four drafts later, in 1980, the Buffs had two first-round picks. Name them.

CU's 11-1 season in 1994 marked its 10th straight winning season and seventh straight with at least eight wins, a school record.

McCartney servant for 10 years, deserved a chance at the big job. And then there was the quarterbacks coach, Neuheisel, who everyone agreed would make a fine head coach someday, but at age 33 when it was still hard to pick him out of a group of ballboys?

When talking to reporters, each "candidate" tried to walk the fine line of showing proper deference for McCartney while still hinting an interest in the job. They agreed on two things: They all felt the job should go to someone from the staff and they all wanted to be that someone.

"I feel strong that somebody from within the program will get the job," Uzelac said the following Monday. "If they feel the program's good and built on a solid foundation, why should they go outside?"

Athletic director Bill Marolt agreed. Within days, Marolt indicated that the coaching search would be restricted to assistant coaching offices in the Dal Ward Center. Within a few more days, the search was over.

A YOUNG GUN Neuheisel, a high school quarterback, led McClintock High in Tempe to the 1978 Arizona state championship. Unable to secure a scholarship to a Pac-10 school, he walked on at UCLA in 1979. Five years later, he was named the 1984 Rose Bowl MVP after passing for 248 yards and four touchdowns in UCLA's 45-9 win over Illinois.

Neuheisel bounced around the USFL and NFL briefly. He was 3-0 as a replacement starter for the San Diego Chargers during the NFL strike in 1987, and his name still appears above Dan Fouts in the Chargers' record book for single-game pass efficiency. Neuheisel completed 18 of 22 in a comeback win over Tampa Bay.

He returned to UCLA in 1988 on Terry Donahue's staff, where two years earlier as a volunteer assistant, he coached Dallas Cowboys star Troy Aikman. After Donahue passed on Neuheisel for UCLA's offensive coordinator post, Neuheisel got a call from McCartney before the 1994 season.

"When I brought Rick in to replace me as quarterbacks coach," McCartney joked, "That's all I had in mind. But Rick moves quickly."

Rick Neuheisel, 34, enters his first season as the second-youngest Division I-A head coach. Louisville's Ron Cooper is four days younger than Neuheisel.

BRAINS, TOO The son of Dick and Jane Neuheisel was brought up to obey the law. His dad runs a law firm in Tempe, while two of his three sisters pursued law degrees. Rick was no different. He earned his law degree from Southern California and has passed the bar exam in Arizona and Washington, D.C.

RICK NEUHEISEL BOLD CU CHOICE

Headline in Daily Camera, Neill Woelk column, Nov. 22, 1994

"... Instead of trying to protect a lead and watching it slowly disappear, as is the case with

Chapter 8: Rick Neuheisel 1995- **145**

Neuheisel enthusiastically participates at "50s Night" at Eisenhower Elementary.

College football records since 1989:
1. Miami (Fla.)
63-9-0 (.875)
2. Florida St.
64-9-1 (.872)
3. Nebraska
61-11-1 (.842)
4. Alabama
62-12-1 (.833)
5. Colorado
58-11-4 (.822)
5. Texas A&M
59-12-2 (.822)
7. Notre Dame
58-14-2 (.797)
8. Penn St.
57-15-1 (.788)
9. Florida
56-17-1 (.764)
10. Tennessee
55-15-3 (.774)

any prevent defense, Marolt can attempt to widen the gap. Marolt can take a chance with a young, relatively unproven assistant who might have the vision and charisma to take the CU program up another notch. Marolt can do what his predecessor did in 1982 when (Eddie Crowder) hired a young, idealistic dreamer out of Michigan.

"Marolt can hire Rick Neuheisel."

In less than a week, Neuheisel had gone from paper boy to people's choice. President Judith Albino, who reportedly began the process in support of Simmons, was eventually won over. Marolt dropped his conservatism and began taking Neuheisel seriously. The CU Board of Regents was heavily in favor of CU's "Young Gun."

A NEW LEADER On Nov. 28, 1994, Marolt reached Neuheisel on a recruiting trip in a California high school and told him he had been chosen to succeed McCartney.

"From there on, watching the film, I was a little distracted," Neuheisel said.

Neuheisel and his wife, Susan, arrived at the Dal Ward Center just before the evening press conference. Neuheisel was welcomed privately by Marolt, the Regents and Albino before meeting the media.

"There at the table, surrounded by the stuffy and veritable, the CU Regents and royalty, men and women twice his age – shoot, twice with plenty to spare – was a kid.

"A blond-haired, blue-eyed kid, looking like he was ready for the prom. Even had his date with him.

"But the folks in charge at the Dal Ward Center didn't hand Rick Neuheisel the keys to the car. The powers that be handed Rick Neuheisel the keys to the University of Colorado football program, one of the most powerful, well-built, finely tuned machines in the land. They handed Rick Neuheisel the keys to one of their most prized possessions.

"And what did they say?"

"Here ya go, Rick. Enjoy the ride.

"Oh, try to bring it back with a full tank, OK? Somewhere along the lines of a Big Eight title? Maybe top it off with a national championship? And don't forget to check the graduation rate. Make sure that baby's running smooth.

"As for a curfew? The contract said five years.

"Don't worry, we'll be waiting up for you."

Neill Woelk column, Daily Camera, Nov. 29, 1994

Marolt explained his choice by saying, "Rick Neuheisel is energetic and full of enthusiasm. I think right now that, more than anything, the youth of our

60. Koy Detmer was a freshman when he made his first start for CU in an October, 1992, game against Oklahoma. What school records did Detmer set or match in that game?

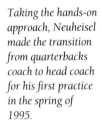

Taking the hands-on approach, Neuheisel made the transition from quarterbacks coach to head coach for his first practice in the spring of 1995.

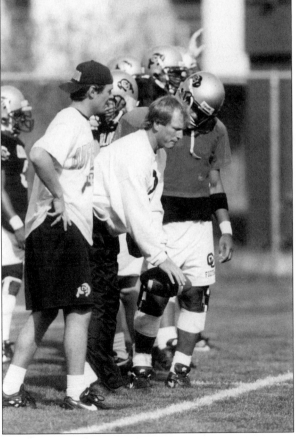

Neuheisel hired former UCLA teammate Karl Dorrell, 31, as his offensive coordinator, meaning CU will be led by one of the youngest offensive duos in the nation.

Heading into the 1995 season, the Buffs have been ranked among the nation's Top 25 teams for 100 straight weeks and in the Top 10 for 17 straight.

country needs to look to leaders who are full of life and have that spark and enthusiasm that makes a difference."

Neuheisel told the assembly, which included many of his future players, "I want to thank my parents. They taught me to dream with my feet on the ground. Thanks, Mom and Dad."

CONTROVERSY Almost out of nowhere, Neuheisel was blindsided during his first week on the job by the Rev. Jesse Jackson, speaking on behalf of the Rainbow Coalition. Jackson threatened to organize a boycott and charged CU with "a blatant example of racism" for hiring the younger, less experienced Neuheisel, who is white, over the older, more experienced Simmons, who is black.

In a letter to Albino, Jackson wrote that the hiring is "proof that the good ole boy system continues to thrive. Only this time the system was aided and abetted by you, a woman who must know what it is like to try and succeed in a white, male-dominated environment."

Since 1988, the Buffs have been on national or regional television 36 times, most of any Big Eight school.

Running back Rashaan Salaam, who would later meet Jackson personally in Boulder to discuss the situation, said Jackson was wrong. "For him to make remarks like that, he didn't do his research very well. What he said is not correct at all."

In the end, it appeared Jackson may have been misled, in part, by false newspaper reports that said Simmons was McCartney's hand-picked successor when, in fact, McCartney gave his support to both Simmons and Uzelac, who is white.

For the defensive coordinator post, Neuheisel sought experience and found it with A. J. Christoff from UCLA.

STAFF SWITCHES Simmons was named head coach at Big Eight rival Oklahoma State. Hankwitz moved to Kansas as the Jayhawks' defensive coordinator and Uzelac accepted a coaching position at Kentucky.

Filling both coordinator spots became Neuheisel's No. 1 task in the off-season. He brought former CU assistant Karl Dorrell, 31, back to Boulder from Arizona State to run the offense and hired experienced defensive mind A.J. Christoff from UCLA.

While Dorrell, a UCLA teammate, will coordinate the offense, Neuheisel will call the plays. When asked if he found it strange that two young guys from UCLA suddenly had control of CU's offensive future, Neuheisel said, "We've got the keys to the car. And we're going to drive really fast."

One of the alterations promised is putting quarterback Koy Detmer in a shotgun formation on occasion.

HE'S EVERYWHERE Neuheisel didn't barricade himself in his new office in the Dal Ward Center the moment he became head coach. In fact, friends and co-workers say Neuheisel's greatest fault is his inability to turn down a request for his time. In his first month as coach, Neuheisel could be found playing the guitar and singing songs for a "50s Rock 'n Roll Party" at Boulder's Eisenhower Elementary School, reading "Paul Bunyan and Babe the Blue Ox" for fifth graders at Ryan Elementary or making one of his frequent surprise visits to an area senior citizens center.

"The youngsters looked like statues sitting on

61. During his Heisman Trophy-winning season, CU's Rashaan Salaam failed to rush for 100 yards in only one regular-season game. Name that opponent.

The new sheriff in town for the CU offense is quarterback Koy Detmer, who already ranks 17th among CU's all-time passing leaders.

62. *In what Big Ten Conference town was CU head coach Rick Neuheisel born?*

the carpet and seemed in awe of the coach. Neuheisel stopped every once in a while to show the pictures and gently ask the children questions. 'Paul was a pretty big guy, wasn't he? He would have been a great Buffalo.' "

Daily Camera, Feb. 3, 1995

Two days before the 1994 Nebraska game, Neuheisel brought his guitar along to a weekly meeting of the Buffalo Belles, a female booster group at CU some 300 strong. Included in an article in the Rocky Mountain News on Dec. 4, 1994, was this transcription of lyrics sung by Neuheisel, a Jimmy Buffett fan, to the tune of, well, you'll recognize the tune. It was Buffett's song that, as the News said, "urges full disdain for sobriety and puritanical behavior."

> "I really do appreciate the fact that you've invited me here
> "I also love the way you ladies all stand up and cheer
> "But this week's a little different, it requires a different mind-frame. So ...
> "Why don't we kick butt and take names
> "The folks up in Nebraska don't think this is a big game.
> "They believe they will win just upon their name
> "But they don't know the Buffs Belles are not that tame. So ...
> "Why don't we all kick butt and take names
> "Michigan, Texas and now Nebraska, too, will all remember our games
> "They say Colorado's no rival, well, let's just see what they say after ...
> "We all kick butt and take names."

CAPTAIN SUNSHINE The new coach had little trouble brightening CU's first spring practice despite the gray and cold conditions.

Neuheisel spiced his first on-field day as head coach on April 6, 1995, with a running commentary of the action. Just after a pass was completed during a drill utilizing kickers, punters and ball boys as defenders, Neuheisel shouted, "We're killin' ya Mitchell! We're killin' ya out there!" to punter Andy Mitchell.

"You've got to have a little fun," Neuheisel said. "Two and a half hours is too long not to laugh once in a while."

"I think you saw the excitement of a new era," holdover assistant coach Terry Lewis told the Daily Camera. "Rick was their choice for the coach and the players are excited about getting everything off on the right start. I don't think they wanted to let Rick down when he took the field. Enthusiasm starts at the top, from the guy who's running the ship."

Rick Neuheisel, the 21st coach in school history, now steers CU's ship toward the 21st century.

CU head coaches are 8-11-1 in their debuts, including 10 consecutive losses. Neuheisel's Buffs open Sept. 2 at Wisconsin.

As a member of the San Diego Chargers in 1987, Neuheisel scored on a muffed PAT attempt, making him the last player to rush for a one-point conversion. The NFL now uses the two-point conversion.

63. Colorado head coach Rick Neuheisel graduated from UCLA with a degree in political science. From which law school did Neuheisel graduate?

By the Numbers

The statistics, lists and records that appear in this chapter are taken from the University of Colorado media guide, which is produced by the CU Sports Information Office. The text was updated through the 1994 season.

RECORD BY SEASON

Season	Coach	Conference						Overall					
		W	L	T	Pct.	Pts.	Opp.	Rk	W	L	T	Pct.	Pts.	Opp.
1890	None	0	4	0	.000	4	217	6	0	4	0	.000	4	217
1891	None	1	4	0	.200	30	106	5	1	4	0	.200	30	106
1892	None	2	1	0	.667	102	16	2	3	2	0	.600	178	64
1893	None	1	1	0	.500	54	30	3	2	3	0	.400	62	76
1894	Harry Heller	5	0	0	1.000	198	4	1	8	1	0	.839	283	32
1895	Fred Folsom	3	0	0	1.000	80	10	1	5	1	0	.833	158	32
1896	Fred Folsom	2	0	0	1.000	80	0	1	5	0	0	1.000	171	6
1897	Fred Folsom	2	0	0	1.000	44	2	t1	7	1	0	.875	188	10
1898	Fred Folsom	0	2	0	.000	0	34	4	4	4	0	.500	150	73
1899	Fred Folsom	2	2	0	.500	99	34	t2	7	2	0	.778	210	34
1900	T.W. Mortimer	1	2	0	.333	29	32	3	6	4	0	.600	150	78
1901	Fred Folsom	2	0	0	1.000	34	2	t1	5	1	1	.786	56	31
1902	Fred Folsom	4	0	0	1.000	75	12	1	5	1	0	.833	87	22
1903	Dave Cropp	4	0	0	1.000	63	6	1	8	2	0	.800	197	54
1904	Dave Cropp	3	1	0	.750	136	13	t1	6	2	1	.722	187	58
1905	Willis Keinholtz	–	–	–	–	–	–	–	8	1	0	.889	359	28
1906	Frank Castleman	1	1	2	.500	6	6	3	2	3	4	.444	28	32
1907	Frank Castlemarn	2	2	0	.500	50	32	3	5	3	0	.714	127	64
1908	Fred Folsom	3	0	0	1.000	37	0	1	1	5	20	.714	96	35
1909	Fred Folsom	3	0	0	1.000	82	0	1	6	0	0	1.000	141	0
1910	Fred Folsom	3	0	0	1.000	74	0	2	6	0	0	1.000	121	3
1911	Fred Folsom	4	0	0	1.000	59	2	1	6	0	0	1.000	83	5
1912	Fred Folsom	2	2	0	.500	16	52	t3	6	3	0	.667	147	81
1913	Fred Folsom	3	0	1	.875	66	19	1	5	1	1	.786	82	33
1914	Fred Folsom	4	1	0	.800	84	19	2	5	1	0	.833	111	22
1915	Fred Folsom	0	5	0	.000	15	122	6	1	6	0	.143	45	168
1916	Bob Evans	1	5	0	.167	40	162	6	1	5	1	.214	40	162
1917	Bob Evans	4	2	0	.667	54	56	3	6	2	0	.750	114	56
1918	Joe Mills	1	2	0	.333	23	27	t3	2	3	0	.400	43	42
1919	Joe Mills	2	3	1	.417	87	96	5	2	3	1	.417	87	96
1920	Myron Witham	3	1	2	.667	59	21	t3	4	1	2	.714	99	28
1921	Myron Witham	4	0	1	.900	65	28	2	4	1	1	.750	65	63
1922	Myron Witham	3	2	0	.600	33	40	5	4	4	0	.500	56	79
1923	Myron Witham	7	0	0	1.000	169	27	1	9	0	0	1.000	280	27
1924	Myron Witham	5	0	1	.917	124	0	1	8	1	1	.850	237	13
1925	Myron Witham	5	2	0	.714	142	36	4	6	3	0	.667	156	45
1926	Myron Witham	2	5	1	.313	52	103	8	3	5	1	.389	77	103
1927	Myron Witham	4	4	0	.500	129	149	t5	4	5	0	.444	136	195
1928	Myron Witham	5	1	0	.833	110	51	2	5	1	0	.833	110	57
1929	Myron Witham	4	1	1	.750	51	56	t2	5	1	1	.786	78	69
1930	Myron Witham	5	1	1	.786	111	68	2	6	1	1	.813	120	68
1931	Myron Witham	3	2	0	.600	75	64	t4	5	3	0	.625	111	94
1932	William Saunders	2	4	0	.333	63	46	8	2	4	0	.333	63	46
1933	William Saunders	5	2	0	.714	158	51	4	7	2	0	.778	183	51
1934	William Saunders	6	1	0	.857	167	40	11	1	6	12	.778	167	40
1935	Bunnie Oakes	5	1	0	.833	128	12	t1	5	4	0	.556	140	47
1936	Bunnie Oakes	4	2	0	.667	99	35	4	4	3	0	.571	99	43
1937	Bunnie Oakes	5	0	0	1.000	145	14	1	8	1	0	.889	262	54
1938	Bunnie Oakes	3	2	1	.583	71	51	t2	3	4	1	.438	78	78
1939	Bunnie Oakes	5	1	0	.833	106	60	1	5	3	0	.625	106	110
1940	Frank Potts	4	1	1	.750	162	50	t2	5	3	1	.611	182	106
1941	Jim Yeager	3	2	1	.583	85	106	t4	3	4	1	.438	97	161
1942	Jim Yeager	5	1	0	.833	178	47	t1	7	2	0	.778	251	73
1943	Jim Yeager	2	0	0	1.000	57	14	–	5	2	0	.714	134	47
1944	Frank Potts	2	0	0	1.000	66	6	–	6	2	0	.750	201	72
1945	Frank Potts	3	1	0	.750	61	40	–	5	3	0	.625	111	58
1946	Jim Yeager	3	2	1	.583	64	30	t4	5	4	1	.550	91	147
1947	Jim Yeager	3	3	0	.500	83	94	t3	4	5	0	.444	90	162
1948	Dallas Ward	2	3	0	.400	97	98	4	3	6	0	.333	168	164
1949	Dallas Ward	1	4	0	.200	59	97	6	3	7	0	.300	129	184
1950	Dallas Ward	2	4	0	.333	127	114	6	5	4	1	.550	227	172

Season	Coach	Conference							Overall					
		W	L	T	Pct.	Pts.	Opp.	Rk	W	L	T	Pct.	Pts.	Opp.
1951	Dallas Ward	5	1	0	.833	186	136	2	7	3	0	.700	289	229
1952	Dallas Ward	2	2	2	.500	111	111	t4	6	2	2	.700	246	158
1953	Dallas Ward	2	4	0	.333	126	153	t4	6	4	0	.600	201	194
1954	Dallas Ward	3	2	1	.583	116	66	t3	7	2	1	.750	283	91
1955	Dallas Ward	3	3	0	.500	139	126	t3	6	4	0	.600	203	149
1956	Dallas Ward	4	1	1	.750	161	66	2	8	2	1	.773	294	143
1957	Dallas Ward	3	3	0	.500	160	93	t3	6	3	1	.650	250	137
1958	Dallas Ward	4	2	0	.667	107	75	3	6	4	0	.600	207	122
1959	Sonny Grandelius	3	3	0	.500	92	134	t3	5	5	0	.500	144	177
1960	Sonny Grandelius	5	2	0	.714	99	75	2	6	4	0	.600	140	133
1961	Sonny Grandelius	7	0	0	1.000	127	39	1	9	2	0	.818	184	104
1962	Bud Davis	1	6	0	.143	55	278	7	2	8	0	.200	122	346
1963	Eddie Crowder	2	5	0	.286	80	173	6	2	8	0	.200	100	245
1964	Eddie Crowder	1	6	0	.143	66	98	7	2	8	0	.200	101	156
1965	Eddie Crowder	4	2	1	.643	134	93	3	6	2	2	.700	163	106
1966	Eddie Crowder	5	2	0	.714	165	92	2	7	3	0	.700	191	132
1967	Eddie Crowder	5	2	0	.714	137	72	t2	9	2	0	.818	245	113
1968	Eddie Crowder	3	4	0	.429	157	169	t4	4	6	0	.400	220	244
1969	Eddie Crowder	5	2	0	.714	161	143	3	8	3	0	.727	276	227
1970	Eddie Crowder	3	4	0	.429	200	148	4	6	5	0	.545	309	206
1971	Eddie Crowder	5	2	0	.714	181	138	3	10	2	0	.833	370	220
1972	Eddie Crowder	4	3	0	.571	158	145	t3	8	4	0	.667	313	206
1973	Eddie Crowder	2	5	0	.286	116	163	t6	5	6	0	.455	240	250
1974	Bill Mallory	3	4	0	.429	160	186	5	5	6	0	.455	226	307
1975	Bill Mallory	5	2	0	.714	174	166	3	9	3	0	.750	331	251
1976	Bill Mallory	5	2	0	.714	189	140	t1	8	4	0	.667	305	225
1977	Bill Mallory	3	3	1	.500	124	146	4	7	3	1	.682	266	174
1978	Bill Mallory	2	5	0	.286	112	178	7	6	5	0	.545	230	206
1979	Chuck Fairbanks	2	5	0	.286	123	168	t5	3	8	0	.273	168	274
1980	Chuck Fairbanks	1	6	0	.143	97	282	t7	1	10	0	.091	160	451
1981	Chuck Fairbanks	2	5	0	.286	59	213	7	3	8	0	.273	141	322
1982	Bill McCartney	1	5	1	.214	115	212	t6	2	8	1	.227	160	301
1983	Bill McCartney	2	5	0	.286	163	275	6	4	7	0	.364	252	342
1984	Bill McCartney	1	6	0	.143	101	225	7	1	10	0	.091	172	364
1985	Bill McCartney	4	3	0	.571	140	78	t3	7	5	0	.583	228	174
1986	Bill McCartney	6	1	0	.857	165	80	2	6	6	0	.500	242	193
1987	Bill McCartney	4	3	0	.571	175	120	4	7	4	0	.636	268	180
1988	Bill McCartney	4	3	0	.571	181	108	4	8	4	0	.667	322	196
1989	Bill McCartney	7	0	0	1.000	297	89	1	11	1	0	.917	458	171
1990	Bill McCartney	7	0	0	1.000	266	113	1	11	1	1	.885	399	229
1991	Bill McCartney	6	0	1	.929	181	93	t1	8	3	1	.708	329	180
1992	Bill McCartney	5	1	1	.786	175	111	2	9	2	1	.792	340	224
1993	Bill McCartney	5	1	1	.786	180	109	2	8	3	1	.708	368	250
1994	Bill McCartney	6	1	0	.857	234	124	2	11	1	0	.917	439	235

CU's Conference Affiliations – Colorado Football Association, 1890-1909; Rocky Mountain Faculty Athletic Conference, 1910-1936; Mountain States Conference (Skyline), 1931-1941; Big Seven/Eight, 1948-present.

COACHING RECORDS

Coach	Seasons	Games	W	L	T	Pct.	Pts.	Opp.
Harry Heller	1	9	8	1	0	.889	288	32
Willis Keinholtz	1	9	8	1	0	.889	359	28
Fred Folsom	15	102	77	23	2	.765	1,815	555
Dave Cropp	2	19	14	4	1	.763	384	112
Myron Witham	12	96	63	26	7	.693	1,525	841
William Saunders	3	24	15	7	2	.667	413	137
Bunnie Oakes	5	41	25	15	1	.662	685	332
Frank Potts	3	25	16	8	1	.660	494	236
Sonny Grandelius	3	31	20	11	0	.645	468	414
Bill McCartney	13	153	93	55	5	.624	3,977	3,039
Bill Mallory	5	57	35	21	1	.623	1,358	1,163
Dallas Ward	11	110	63	41	6	.600	2,497	1,743
T.W. Mortimer	1	10	6	4	0	.600	150	78
Jim Yeager	5	43	24	17	2	.581	663	590
Eddie Crowder	11	118	67	49	2	.571	2,528	2,105
Frank Castleman	2	17	7	6	4	.529	155	96
Bob Evans	2	15	7	7	1	.500	154	218
Joe Mills	2	11	4	6	1	.409	130	138
Chuck Fairbanks	3	33	7	26	0	.212	469	1,047
Bud Davis	1	10	2	8	0	.200	122	346
*None	4	20	7	13	0	.350	310	463
Totals	105	953	568	349	36	.615	18,942	13,713

*Folsom's first game as a coach was the second game of the 1895 season. The first game is included under the "None" category.

TEAM RECORDS

TOTAL OFFENSE

Plays/Game – 105 (for 514 yards) vs. Kansas State in Boulder, Oct. 24, 1992.
Plays/Season – 858 (for 4,471 yards), in 1975.
Yards Gained/Quarter – 337, vs. Oklahoma State in Boulder, Nov. 13, 1971 (2nd).
Yards Gained/Half – 512, vs. Oklahoma State in Boulder, Nov. 13, 1971 (lst).
Yards Gained/Game – 676 (89 plays) vs. Oklahoma State in Boulder, Nov. 13, 1971.
Yards Gained/Season – 5,448 (773 plays), in 1994.
Average Per Play/Game – 9.41 (69 plays for 649 yards) vs. NE Louisiana in Boulder, Sept. 3, 1994.
Average Per Play/Season – 7.05 (773 plays for 5,448 yards), 1994.
Most Yards Gained, Colorado and Opponent/Game – 1,205, CU (330) vs. Oklahoma (875) in Boulder, Oct. 4, 1980.
Most Yards Gained, Colorado and Opponent/Season – 9,237, CU (5,175), Opponents (4,062), 1993.
Most Yards Gained in Losing a Game – 551, vs. Stanford at Palo Alto, Sept. 18, 1993; 442, vs. Nebraska in Boulder, Oct. 9, 1982.
Most Yards Gained, Two Consecutive Games – 1,257 (595 vs. Missouri, 662 at Iowa State), Oct. 7-14, 1989.
Fewest Yards Gained/Game – 23, vs. Texas at Dallas, Sept. 28, 1946.
Fewest Yards Gained/Season – 2,189, in 1964.
Most Touchdowns, Rushing and Passing/Game – 9 (8 rush, 1 pass), vs. Arizona at Tucson, Oct. 11, 1958.
Most Touchdowns, Rushing and Passing/Season – 59 (54 rush, 5 pass), in 1989.
Highest Average Per Game/Season – 495.3 (5,448 yards in 11 games), 1994.

COLORADO'S TOP OFFENSIVE EFFORTS (600+ YARDS)

Yds	Opponent, Site, Date	Yds	Opponent, Site, Date
676	Oklahoma State in Boulder, Nov. 13, 1971.	639	Kansas at Lawrence, Nov. 12, 1994.
675	Air Force in Boulder, Nov. 21, 1970.	634	Kansas State in Boulder, Nov. 17, 1990.
662	Iowa State at Ames, Oct. 14, 1989.	627	Utah in Boulder, Nov. 10, 1951.
656	Missouri in Boulder, Oct. 12, 1991.	625	Arizona at Tucson, Oct. 11, 1958.
649	NE Louisiana in Boulder, Sept. 3, 1994.	612	Minnesota in Boulder, Sept. 21, 1991.
647	Kansas State in Boulder, Oct. 19, 1957.		

RUSHING

Most Rushes/Game – 83 (for 482 yards), vs. Air Force at USAFA, Nov. 21, 1970.
Most Rushes/Season – 666 (for 4,090 yards), in 1989.
Yards Gained/Game – 551 (69 attempts), vs. Arizona in Tucson, Oct. 11, 1958.
Yards Gained/Season – 4,090 in 1989.
Average Per Game/Season – 371.8 (4,090 yards in 11 games), 1989.
Average Per Rush/Game – 14.28 (36 for 514 yards) vs. Kansas State in Boulder, Nov. 20, 1954
Average Per Rush/Season – 6.42 (492 for 3,160 yards), 1954.
Touchdowns/Game – 8, vs. Arizona at Tucson, Oct. 11, 1958; vs. Northwestern in Boulder, Sept. 30, 1978; vs. Kansas State at Manhattan, Nov. 18, 1989.
Touchdowns/Season – 54, in 1989.

PASSING

Attempts/Game – 52, vs. Kansas State at Manhattan, Nov. 20, 1982.
Attempts/Season – 398 (232 completions) in 1992.
Fewest Attempts/Game – 4, vs. Arizona at Tucson, Sept. 28, 1985; vs. Kansas State at Manhattan, Nov. 22, 1986; vs. Kansas at Lawrence, Oct. 15, 1988.
Fewest Attempts/Season – 72 (33 completions), in 1954.
Completions/Game – 33, vs. Oklahoma in Boulder, Oct. 17, 1992.
Completions/Season – 232 (of 398 attempts) in 1992.
Fewest Completions/Game – 0, vs. Missouri at Columbia, Nov. 5, 1966 (of 5 attempts).
Fewest Completions/Season – 29 (of 76), in 1956.
Yards/Game – 418, vs. Oklahoma in Boulder, Oct. 17, 1992.
Yards/Season – 3,271, in 1992.
Highest Completion Percentage/Game (minimum 25 att.) – .813 (26 of 32), vs. Baylor at Waco, Sept. 12, 1992.
Highest Completion Percentage/Season – .613 (157 of 256), in 1994.
Passes Had Intercepted/Game – 5, vs. Texas Tech at Lubbock, Sept. 11, 1976; vs. Oklahoma in Boulder, Oct. 17, 1992.
Passes Had Intercepted/Season – 22, in 1982.
Fewest Passes Had Intercepted/Season – 4, in 1994.
Touchdowns/Game – 4, vs. Oklahoma State in Boulder, Nov. 10, 1990; vs. Colorado State in Boulder, Sept. 5, 1992; vs. Baylor at Waco, Sept. 12, 1992.
Touchdowns/Season – 22, in 1992.
Lowest Interception Percentage/Season – 1.6 in 1994 (4 interceptions in 256 attempts).
Highest Average Per Game/Season – 297.4, in 1992.

SCORING

Points Scored/Quarter – 35, vs. Iowa State at Ames, Oct. 14, 1989 (2nd quarter).
Points Scored/Half – 45, vs. Iowa State at Ames, Oct. 14, 1989 (lst half).
Points Scored/Game – 65, vs. Arizona at Tucson, Oct. 11, 1958.
Points Scored/Season – 452, in 1989.
Most Points Scored in Losing a Game – 42 vs. Oklahoma (82) in Boulder, Oct. 4, 1980.
Touchdowns Scored/Game – 10, vs. Arizona at Tucson, Oct. 11, 1958.
Touchdowns Scored/Season – 59, in 1989 (54 rush, 5 pass).
Field Goals Made/Game – 4, vs. Washington State at Spokane, Sept. 18, 1982; vs. Oklahoma State at Stillwater, Oct. 16,

1982; vs. Kansas State in Boulder, Oct. 24, 1992.
Field Goals Made/Season – 15, in 1972; 1990.
Field Goals Attempted/Game – 5, seven times. Last: vs. Washington State at Spokane, Sept. 18, 1982.
Field Goals Attempted/Season – 34, in 1972.
Extra Points Attempted/Game – 10 vs. Arizona at Tucson, Oct. 11, 1958.
Extra Points Attempted/Season – 59 (made 59), in 1989.
Scoring Average/Season – 41.1 (452 points in 11 games), 1989.

TOTAL DEFENSE

Fewest Plays Allowed/Game – 35, vs. Nebraska at Lincoln, Nov. 18, 1961.
Fewest Plays Allowed/Season – 509, in 1946.
Most Plays Allowed/Game – 101, by Oklahoma State in Boulder, Oct. 29, 1983.
Most Plays Allowed/Season – 896, in 1983.
Fewest Rushes Allowed/Game – 21, vs. Stanford in Boulder, Sept. 19, 1987.
Fewest Rushes Allowed/Season – 336, in 1946.
Most Rushes Allowed/Game – 77, by Nebraska in Boulder, Oct. 20, 1984; Nebraska at Lincoln, Oct. 31, 1992.
Most Rushes Allowed/Season – 645, in 1973.
Fewest Passing Attempts Allowed/Game – 0, vs. Oklahoma in Boulder, Nov. 15, 1986.
Fewest Passing Attempts Allowed/Season – 101, in 1948.
Most Passing Attempts Allowed/Game – 61, vs. Kansas State in Boulder, Nov. 22, 1969.
Most Passing Attempts Allowed/Season – 349, in 1990.
Fewest Completions Allowed/Game – 0 (of 12) vs. Nebraska at Lincoln, Nov. 18, 1961; (of 3, at LSU, Sept. 14, 1974); (of 1) vs. Oklahoma at Norman, Oct. 4, 1975; (of 0) vs. Oklahoma in Boulder, Nov. 15, 1986.
Fewest Completions Allowed/Season – 39 (of 107), in 1947
Most Completions Allowed/Game – 30, vs. Colorado State at Fort Collins, Oct. 3, 1987.
Most Completions Allowed/Season – 199, in 1994.
Fewest Yards Allowed/Game – 16 (47 plays) vs. Kansas State in Boulder, Oct. 24, 1992.
Fewest Yards Allowed/Season – 1,796, in 1946.
Most Yards Allowed/Game – 875 (758 rush, 117 pass) vs. Oklahoma in Boulder, Oct. 4, 1980.
Most Yards Allowed/Season – 5,108, in 1980.
Fewest Rushing Yards Allowed/Game – minus 40 (31 attempts), vs. Wichita State in Boulder, Sept. 27,
Fewest Rushing Yards Allowed/Season – 799 (10 games), in 1946.
Most Rushing Yards Allowed/Game – 758 (73 attempts), vs. Oklahoma in Boulder, Oct. 4, 1980.
Most Rushing Yards Allowed/Season – 3,493, in 1980.
Fewest Passing Yards Allowed/Game – 0, vs. Nebraska at Lincoln, Nov. 18, 1961; vs. Louisiana State at Baton Rouge, Sept. 14, 1974; vs. Oklahoma at Norman, Oct. 4, 1975; vs. Oklahoma in Boulder, Nov. 15, 1986.
Fewest Passing Yards Allowed/Season – 557, in 1960.
Most Passing Yards Allowed/Game – 439, vs. Kansas State in Boulder, Nov. 22, 1969.
Most Passing Yards Allowed/Season – 2,525, in 1994.
Fewest Points Allowed/Game – 0, 220 times. Last: vs. Kansas State at Manhattan, Oct. 26, 1991.
Fewest Points Allowed/Season – 13 (10 games), in 1924.
Most Points Allowed/Game – 82, vs. Oklahoma in Boulder, Oct. 4, 1980.
Most Points Allowed/Season – 451, in 1980.
Fewest First Downs Allowed/Game – 0, vs. Nebraska at Lincoln, Nov. 18, 1961.
Fewest First Downs Allowed/Season – 102, in 1958.
Most First Downs Allowed/Game – 42, vs. Nebraska in Lincoln, Oct. 10, 1981.
Most First Downs Allowed/Season – 266, in 1983.
Most Turnovers Forced/Game – 10, Kansas in Boulder, Nov. 13, 1976 (six fumbles, four interceptions).
Most Turnovers Forced/Season – 49 (30 fumbles, 19 interceptions), in 1976.
Most Quarterback Sacks/Game – 11 (for 70 yards), vs. Wichita State in Boulder, Sept. 27, 1975.
Most Quarterback Sacks/Season – 41 (for 231 yards), in 1990; (for 311 yards), in 1992.
Most Safeties/Game – 1, on several occasions.
Most Safeties/Season – 3, in 1990.
Most Defensive Extra Points/Game – 1, vs. Nebraska in Boulder, Nov. 2, 1991.
Most Defensive Extra Points/Season – 1, in 1991.

MISCELLANEOUS

Highest Scoring Game, Colorado and Opponent – 124, Colorado (42) vs. Oklahoma (82) in Boulder, Oct. 4, 1980.
Highest Scoring Tie Game, Colorado and Opponent – 31-31, Colorado vs. Tennessee at Anaheim, Aug. 26, 1990.
Most Consecutive Victories – 21 (Nov. 15, 1908 to Oct. 5, 1912).
Most Consecutive Victories at Home – 15 (Nov. 15, 1908 to Oct. 19, 1912; Oct. 29, 1988 to Sept. 7, 1991).
Most Consecutive Victories on the Road – 8 (Nov. 23, 1922 to Oct. 25, 1924).
Most Consecutive Games Without a Loss – 21 (Nov. 15, 1908 to Oct. 5, 1912).
Most Consecutive Games Without a Tie – 133 (Oct. 23, 1965 to Oct. 8, 1977).
Most Consecutive Losses – 10 (Oct. 19, 1963 to Oct. 10, 1964).
Most Consecutive Shutouts – 9, in 1924.
Most Consecutive Games Without Being Shutout – 84 (Oct. 18, 1947 to Nov. 19, 1955).
Most Consecutive Quarters Scored In – 23 – Oct. 31, 1970 to Sept. 25, 1971 (seven games; record in one season: 22, Sept. 4 to Oct. 16, 1993).
Most Consecutive Quarters Opponent Shutout In – 37 – Oct. 4, 1924 to Jan. 1, 1925 (modern record: 14, Nov. 28, 1953 to Oct. 2, 1954).
Most Consecutive Winning Seasons in Conference Play – 10 (Big Eight; 1985 through 1994)
Most Consecutive Victories in Conference Play – 18 (Big Eight; Nov. 19, 1988 to Oct. 26, 1991).
Most Consecutive Games in Conference Play Without a Loss – 25 (Big Eight; Nov. 19, 1988 to Oct. 24, 1992; 23-0-2).
Most Consecutive Victories at Home in Conference Play – 10 (Big Eight; Oct. 31, 1959 to Sept. 29, 1962; and Oct. 29, 1988 to Oct. 12, 1991).

Most Consecutive Victories on Road in Conference Play – 12 (Big Eight; Oct. 14, 1989 to Oct. 8, 1992).
Most Consecutive Losses in Conference Play – 8 (Colorado Football Assn.; Nov. 15, 1890 to Nov. 7, 1891); 8 (Big Eight; Nov. 4, 1978 to Nov. 10, 1979).

INDIVIDUAL RECORDS

(NOTE: Bowl games not included in career totals.)

SERVICE

Most Games Played/Career – 45, Tom Field, 1979-83; Terry Johnson, 1987-90; Alfred Williams, 1987-90.
Most Games Started/Career – 44, Joe Garten, 1987-90.

RUSHING

Attempts/Game – 40 (for 174 yards), James Mayberry vs. Kansas State in Boulder, Nov. 19, 1977.
Attempts/Season – 298 (for 2,055 yards), Rashaan Salaam, 1994.
Attempts/Career – 699 (for 3,940 yards), Eric Bieniemy, 1990.
Net Yards/Quarter – 131, Eric Bieniemy vs. Oregon State in Boulder, Sept. 24, 1988 (on nine carries, fourth quarter).
Net Yards/Half – 206, Charlie Davis vs. Oklahoma State in Boulder, Nov. 13, 1971.
Net Yards/Game – 342, Charlie Davis vs. Oklahoma State in Boulder, Nov. 13, 1971.
Net Yards/Season – 2,055, Rashaan Salaam, 1994.
Net Yards/Career – 3,940, Eric Bieniemy, 1987-90.
Average Per Play/Game (10 minimum) – 23.8 (10 for 238), Carroll Hardy vs. Kansas State in Boulder, Nov. 20, 1954.
Average Per Play/Season (30 minimum) – 9.17 (70 for 642), Carroll Hardy, 1954.
Average Per Play/Season (100 minimum) – 7.24 (164 for 1187), J.J. Flannigan, 1989.
Average Per Play/Career (100 minimum per season) – 6.39 (328 for 2096), J.J. Flannigan, 1987-89.
Average Per Game/Season – 186.8 (2,055 yards in 11 games), Rashaan Salaam, 1994.
Average Per Game/Career – 113.2 (3,057 yards in 27 games), Rashaan Salaam, 1992-94.
Touchdowns/Game – 4, on 11 occasions. Last time: Rashaan Salaam vs. Oklahoma in Boulder, Oct. 15, 1994.
Touchdowns/Season – 24, Rashaan Salaam, 1994.
Touchdowns/Career – 41, Eric Bieniemy, 1987-90.
Longest Play from Scrimmage/Scoring – 95, Emerson Wilson vs. Kansas State in Boulder, Nov. 20, 1954.
Longest Play from Scrimmage/Non-scoring – 75, Darian Hagan vs. Texas in Boulder, Sept. 4, 1989.
Yards, by Class/Season – Freshman, 830, Lamont Warren, 1991; Sophomore, 1,386, Charlie Davis, 1971; Junior, 2,055, Rashaan Salaam, 1994; Senior, 1,628, Eric Bieniemy, 1990.
Yards by Class/Game – Freshman, 202, Billy Waddy vs. Wisconsin at Madison, Sept. 22, 1973; Sophomore, 342, Charlie Davis vs. Oklahoma State in Boulder, Nov. 13, 1971; Junior, 317, Rashaan Salaam vs. Texas at Austin, Oct. 1, 1994; Senior, 246, J.J. Flannigan vs. Kansas State at Manhattan, Nov. 18, 1989.
Most 100-Yard Rushing Games/Season – 10, Eric Bieniemy, 1990, and Rashaan Salaam, 1994.
Most 100-Yard Rushing Games/Career – 21, Eric Bieniemy, 1987-90 (13 home, eight road).
Most Players Gaining 100 Yards/Game – 3, twice (Carroll Hardy 238, Emerson Wilson 124, Frank Bernardi 113 vs. Kansas State in Boulder, Nov. 20, 1954; and Jon Keyworth 124, Paul Arendt 116, Ward Walsh 101 at Air Force, Nov. 21, 1970).
Most Players Gaining 100 Yards/Season – 13 in 1989 (Darian Hagan 6, J.J. Flannigan 4, Eric Bieniemy 3).
Most 200-Yard Rushing Games/Season – 4, Rashaan Salaam, 1994.
Most 200-Yard Rushing Games/Career – 4, Rashaan Salaam, 1992-94.
Most Consecutive Games Gaining 100 Yards or More/Career – 9, Rashaan Salaam, 1994.
Most Seasons Gaining 1,000 Yards or More – 2, Eric Bieniemy (1,243 in 1988; 1,628 in 1990).
Most Yards Gained by Two Players, Same Team/Game – 402 (J.J. Flannigan 246, Darian Hagan 156) vs. Kansas State at Manhattan, Nov. 18, 1989.
Most Yards Gained by Two Players, Same Team/Season – 2,694 (Rashaan Salaam 2,055, Kordell Stewart 639), in 1994.

RUSHING SINGLE-SEASON YARDS

2,055 Rashaan Salaam, 1994.
1,628 Eric Bieniemy, 1990.
1,386 Charlie Davis, 1971.
1,299 James Mayberry, 1977.
1,243 Eric Bieniemy, 1988.
1,210 Tony Reed, 1976.
1,187 J.J. Flannigan, 1989.
1,121 Byron White, 1937.
1,097 Bob Stransky, 1957.
1,043 Kayo Lam, 1935.
1,004 Darian Hagan, 1989.

PASSING

Attempts/Game – 51, Randy Essington (24 completions) vs. Nebraska at Boulder, Oct. 9, 1982; Steve Vogel (25 completions) vs. Kansas State at Manhattan, Nov. 20, 1982.
Attempts/Season – 294 (157 completed), Kordell Stewart, 1993.
Attempts/Career – 785 (456 completed), Kordell Stewart, 1991-94.
Completions/Game – 33, Koy Detmer (50 attempts) vs. Oklahoma in Boulder, Oct. 17, 1992.
Completions/Season – 157 (of 294), Kordell Stewart, 1993.
Completions/Career – 456 (of 785), Kordell Stewart, 1991-94.
Most Yards Gained/Quarter – 192, Koy Detmer vs. Oklahoma in Boulder, Oct. 17, 1992 (fourth).
Most Yards Gained/Half – 307, Koy Detmer vs. Oklahoma in Boulder, Oct. 17, 1992 (second).
Most Yards Gained/Game – 418, Koy Detmer vs. Oklahoma in Boulder, Oct. 17, 1992.
Most Yards Gained/Season – 2,229, Kordell Stewart, 1993.
Most Yards Gained/Career – 6,481, Kordell Stewart, 1991-94.
Yards Gained by Class – Freshman, 962, Koy Detmer, 1992; Sophomore, 2,109, Kordell Stewart, 1992; Junior, 2,299, Kordell Stewart, 1993; Senior, 2,071, Kordell Stewart, 1994.
Most Touchdown Passes Thrown/Quarter – 3, Darian Hagan, vs. Oklahoma at Norman, Oct. 19, 1991
Most Touchdown Passes Thrown/Game – 4, Darian Hagan, vs. Oklahoma State in Boulder, Nov. 10, 1990; Kordell Stewart, vs. Colorado State in Boulder, Sept. 5, 1992.
Most Touchdown Passes Thrown/Season – 12, Steve Vogel, 1983; Darian Hagan, 1991; Kordell Stewart, 1992.

Most Touchdown Passes Thrown/Career – 33, Kordell Stewart, 1991-94.
Most Touchdown Passes, Duo/Season – 7, Kordell Stewart to Charles Johnson, 1993.
Most Touchdown Passes, Duo/Career – 11, Kordell Stewart to Michael Westbrook, 1992-94.
Most Interceptions Thrown/Game – 5, Jeff Austin vs. Texas Tech at Lubbock, Sept. 11, 1976; Koy Detmer vs. Oklahoma in Boulder, Oct. 17, 1992.
Most Interceptions Thrown/Season – 13, Gale Weidner (1959), Bernie McCall (1965), Jeff Knapple (1977), Bill Solomon (1979), Randy Essington (1982).
Most Interceptions Thrown/Career – 33, Steve Vogel, 1981-84.
Consecutive Pass Completions – 12, Kordell Stewart (2 games; vs. Colorado State in Boulder, Sept. 5, 1992; Baylor at Waco, Sept. 12, 1992).
Completions Per Game/Season – 16.8 (151 in 9 games), Kordell Stewart, 1992.
Completions Per Game/Career – 13.8 (456 in 33 games), Kordell Stewart, 1991-94.
Highest Completion Percentage/Game – 1.000 (7 for 7), Dane Craves vs. Colorado A&M at Fort Collins, Nov. 21, 1950.
Highest Completion Percentage/Game (minimum 15 att.) – .941 (16 of 17), Kordell Stewart vs. Baylor at Waco, Sept. 12, 1992.
Highest Completion Percentage/Season – .620 (147 of 237), Kordell Stewart, 1994.
Highest Completion Percentage/Career – .581 (456 of 785), Kordell Stewart, 1991-94.
Lowest Interception Percentage/Season (100 attempts minimum) – .013 (237 attempts, 3 intercepted), Kordell Stewart, 1994.
Lowest Interception Percentage/Career (100 attempts per season) – .024 (785 attempts, 19 intercepted), Kordell Stewart, 1991-94.
Most Consecutive Attempts Without An Interception/Game – 40, Kordell Stewart vs. Miami, Fla. in Boulder, Sept. 25, 1993.
Most Consecutive Attempts Without An Interception/Career – 99, Darian Hagan (Sept. 21, 1991 to Nov. 2, 1991; six games); 98, Kordell Stewart (Oct. 22, 1994 to Nov. 19, 1994; four games).
Longest Play/Scoring – 92 yards, Koy Detmer to Charles E. Johnson, vs. Oklahoma in Boulder, Oct. 17, 1992.
Longest Play/Non-Scoring – 77 yards, Woody Shelton to Ronnie Johnson, vs. Northwestern at Evanston, Sept. 29, 1951.

PASSING SINGLE-SEASON YARDS

2,299 Kordell Stewart, 1993.
2,109 Kordell Stewart, 1992.
2,071 Kordell Stewart, 1994.
1,538 Darian Hagan, 1990.
1,432 Steve Vogel, 1984.
1,385 Steve Vogel, 1983.
1,341 Bobby Anderson, 1968.
1,282 David Williams, 1975.
1,228 Darian Hagan, 1991.
1,203 Jeff Knapple, 1977.
1,200 Cale Weidner, 1959.
1,199 Randy Essington, 1981.
1,175 Bernie McCall, 1965.
1,174 Bill Solomon, 1979.
1,126 Ken Johnson, 1971.
1,121 Randy Essington, 1982.
1,101 Cale Weidner, 1960.

TOTAL OFFENSE

Plays/Half – 36 (5 rush, 31 pass), Koy Detmer vs. Oklahoma in Boulder, Oct. 17, 1992.
Plays/Game – 59 (9 rush, 50 pass), Koy Detmer vs. Oklahoma in Boulder, Oct. 17, 1992.
Plays/Season – 405 (183 rush, 222 pass), Bobby Anderson, 1968.
Plays/Career – 1,087 (302 rush, 785 pass), Kordell Stewart, 1991-94.
Yards Gained/Quarter – 188 (92 pass, -4 rush), Koy Detmer vs. Oklahoma in Boulder, Oct. 17, 1992.
Yards Gained/Half – 296 (307 pass, -11 rush), Koy Detmer vs. Oklahoma in Boulder, Oct. 17, 1992.
Yards Gained/Game – 430 (409 pass, 21 rush), Kordell Stewart vs. Colorado State in Boulder, Sept. 5, 1992.
Yards Gained/Season – 2,823 (524 rush, 2,299 pass), Kordell Stewart, 1993.
Yards Gained/Career – 7,770 (1,289 rush, 6,481 pass), Kordell Stewart, 1991-94.
Average Per Game/Season – 256.6 (2,823 yards in 11 games), Kordell Stewart, 1993.
Average Per Game/Career – 235.5 (7,770 yards in 33 games), Kordell Stewart, 1991-94.
Yards Gained by Class/Season – Freshman, 957 (962 pass, -5 rush), Koy Detmer, 1992; Sophomore, 2,091 (2,109 pass, -18 rush), Kordell Stewart, 1992; Junior, 2,823 (524 rush, 2,299 pass), Kordell Stewart, 1993; Senior, 2,710 (639 rush, 2,071 pass), Kordell Stewart, 1994.
Highest Average Per Play/Game (minimum 30 plays) – 10.1, Charlie Davis vs. Oklahoma State in Boulder, Nov. 13, 1971.
Highest Average Per Play/Season (minimum 1,000 yards) – 7.55 (259 plays, 2,710 yards), Kordell Stewart, 1994.
Highest Average Per Play/Career (minimum 2,000 yards) – 7.15 (1,087 plays, 7,770 yards), Kordell Stewart, 1991-94.
Touchdowns Responsible For/Game – 5, Paul McClung vs. Wyoming in Boulder, Oct. 26, 1940 (3 passing, 2 rushing).
Touchdowns Responsible For/Season – 24, Rashaan Salaam, 1994 (24 rushing, 0 passing).
Touchdowns Responsible For/Career – 54, Darian Hagan, 1988-91 (27 rushing, 27 passing).
Points Responsible For/Game – 30, Paul McClung vs. Wyoming in Boulder, Oct. 26, 1940.
Points Responsible For/Season – 144, Rashaan Salaam, 1994.
Points Responsible For/Career – 324, Darian Hagan, 1988-91.

SINGLE-GAME TOTAL OFFENSE BESTS

430 Kordell Stewart vs. Colorado State in Boulder, Sept. 5, 1992.
396 Koy Detmer vs. Oklahoma in Boulder, Oct. 17, 1992.
379 Kordell Stewart vs. Michigan at Ann Arbor, Sept. 24, 1994.
353 Bobby Anderson vs. Oklahoma State at Stillwater, Nov. 9, 1968.
352 Randy Essington vs. Nebraska in Boulder, Oct. 9, 1982.
348 Kordell Stewart vs. Missouri at Columbia, Oct. 8, 1992.
348 Kordell Stewart vs. Oklahoma State at Stillwater, Nov. 6, 1993.
348 Kordell Stewart vs. Notre Dame (Fiesta Bowl) at Tempe, Jan. 2, 1995.
344 Randy Essington vs. Texas Tech in Boulder, Sept. 12, 1981.
342 Charlie Davis vs. Oklahoma State in Boulder, Nov. 13, 1971.
332 Ken Johnson vs. Kansas State in Boulder, Oct. 2, 1971.
325 Kordell Stewart vs. Stanford at Palo Alto, Sept. 18, 1993.

310 Jim Bratten vs. Kansas State in Boulder, Nov. 22, 1969.
308 Craig Keenan vs. Kansas in Boulder, Nov. 3, 1984.
301 Kordell Stewart vs. Wisconsin in Boulder, Sept. 17, 1994.

OFFENSIVE SINGLE-SEASON YARDS

2,823 Kordell Stewart, 1993.	1,980 Darian Hagan, 1990.	1,475 Ken Johnson, 1971.
2,710 Kordell Stewart, 1994.	1,854 David Williams, 1975.	1,428 Bernie McCall, 1965.
2,129 Bobby Anderson, 1968.	1,643 Eric Bieniemy, 1990.	1,387 Bob Stransky, 1957.
2,091 Kordell Stewart, 1992.	1,614 Darian Hagan, 1991.	1,386 Charlie Davis, 1971.
2,055 Rashaan Salaam, 1994.	1,596 Byron White, 1937.	
2,006 Darian Hagan, 1989.	1,515 Bobby Anderson, 1967.	

OFFENSIVE CAREER YARDS

7,770 Kordell Stewart, 1991-94.	3,501 Steve Vogel, 1981-84.	3,057 Rashaan Salaam, 1991-94.
5,808 Darian Hagan, 1988-91.	3,408 David Williams, 1973-75.	3,025 Zack Jordan, 1950-52.
4,565 Bobby Anderson, 1967-69.	3,091 Cale Weidner, 1959-61.	
4,003 Eric Bieniemy, 1987-90.	3,057 Bernie McCall, 1964-66.	

RECEIVING

Receptions/Game – 11 (for 186 yards), Michael Westbrook vs. Baylor at Waco, Sept. 12, 1992; (for 168 yards), Charles Johnson vs. Missouri at Columbia, Oct. 8, 1992.
Receptions/Season – 76 (for 1,060 yards), Michael Westbrook, 1992.
Receptions/Career – 167 (for 2,548 yards), Michael Westbrook, 1991-94.
Receptions Per Game/Season – 6.9 (76 receptions in 11 games), Michael Westbrook, 1992.
Receptions Per Game/Career – 4.1 (167 receptions in 41 games), Michael Westbrook, 1991-94.
Consecutive Games Catching One Pass – 27, Charles E. Johnson, 1991-93.
Consecutive Games Catching Two Passes – 20, Charles E. Johnson, 1992-93.
Receptions by Class/Season – Freshman, 39 (for 337 yards), Chris McLemore, 1982; Sophomore, 76 (for 1,060 yards), Michael Westbrook, 1992; Junior, 57 (for 1,149 yards), Charles E. Johnson, 1992; Senior, 57 (for 1,082 yards), Charles E. Johnson, 1993.
Yards Gained/Game – 222 (5 receptions), Walter Stanley vs. Texas Tech in Boulder, Sept. 12, 1981.
Yards Gained/Season – 1,149 (57 receptions), Charles E. Johnson, 1992.
Yards Gained/Career – 2,548 (167 receptions), Michael Westbrook, 1991-94.
Yards Gained Per Game/Season – 104.5 (1,149 yards in 11 games), Charles E. Johnson, 1992.
Yards Gained Per Game/Career – 69.9 (2,447 yards in 35 games), Charles E. Johnson, 1990-93.
Average Gain Per Reception/Game (5 minimum) – 44.4 (5 for 222), Walter Stanley vs. Texas Tech in Boulder, Sept. 12, 1981.
Average Gain Per Reception/Season (20 minimum) – 26.2 (28 for 733 yards), Mike Pritchard, 1990.
Average Gain Per Reception/Career (50 minimum) – 21.4 (57 for 1,217), Ron Brown, 1981-1985.
Yards by Class/Season – Freshman, 337 (39 receptions), Chris McLemore, 1982; Sophomore, 1,060 (76 receptions), Michael Westbrook, 1992; Junior, 1,149 (57 receptions), Charles E. Johnson, 1992; Senior, 1,082 (57 receptions), Charles E. Johnson, 1993.
Most 100-Yard Receiving Games/Season – 6, Charles E. Johnson, 1992 and 1993.
Most 100-Yard Receiving Games/Career – 12, Charles E. Johnson, 1990-93.
Touchdown Passes Caught/Game – 3, Richard Johnson vs. Kansas in Boulder, Nov. 1982.
Touchdown Passes Caught/Season – 9, Charles E. Johnson, 1993.
Touchdown Passes Caught/Career – 19, Michael Westbrook, 1991-94.
Touchdown Receptions by a Freshman/Season – 5, Michael Westbrook, 1991.

SINGLE-GAME RECEPTION BESTS

11 Michael Westbrook vs. Baylor at Waco, Sept. 12, 1992.
11 Charles E. Johnson vs. Missouri at Columbia, Oct. 8, 1992.
10 Ed Reinhardt vs. Michigan State in Boulder, Sept. 8, 1984.
9 Monte Huber vs. California at Berkeley, Sept. 28, 1968.
9 Michael Westbrook vs. Oklahoma in Boulder, Oct. 17, 1992.
9 Michael Westbrook vs. Kansas at Lawrence, Nov. 14, 1992.
9 Christian Fauria vs. Texas in Boulder, Sept. 4, 1993.

CAREER RECEPTIONS

167 Michael Westbrook, 1991-94.	80 Jon Embree, 1983-86.	52 Chris McLemore, 1982-83.
127 Charles E. Johnson, 1990-93.	78 Loy Alexander, 1982-85.	51 Don Hasselbeck, 1973-76.
111 Monte Huber, 1967-69.	67 Dave Logan, 1972-75.	49 Bob Niziolek, 1977-80.
98 Christian Fauria, 1991-94.	61 J.V. Cain, 1971-73.	48 Merwin Hodel, 1949-51.
91 Dave Hestera, 1981-83.	57 Ron Brown, 1981-85.	47 Mike Pritchard, 1987-90.
86 Lee Rouson, 1981-84.	52 Bill Symons, 1962-64.	

SINGLE-SEASON RECEPTIONS

76 Michael Westbrook, 1992.	39 Loy Alexander, 1983.	35 Loy Alexander, 1984.
57 Charles E. Johnson, 1992.	39 Chris McLemore, 1982.	35 Christian Fauria, 1994.
57 Charles E. Johnson, 1993.	38 Monte Huber, 1968.	33 Michael Westbrook, 1993.
51 Jon Embree, 1984.	36 John McGuire, 1962.	31 Christian Fauria, 1992.
45 Monte Huber, 1967.	36 Michael Westbrook, 1994.	30 J.V. Cain, 1972.
41 Dave Hestera, 1982.	35 Ken Blair, 1962.	30 Christian Fauria, 1993.

SINGLE-SEASON YARDS

1,149 Charles E. Johnson, 1992.
1,082 Charles E. Johnson, 1993.
1,060 Michael Westbrook, 1992.
733 Mike Pritchard, 1990.
689 Michael Westbrook, 1994.
680 Jon Embree, 1984.
673 Ron Brown, 1984.

557 Loy Alexander, 1983.
515 Ron Brown, 1983.
496 Loy Alexander, 1984.
490 Michael Westbrook, 1993.
489 Dave Hestera, 1982.
488 Monte Huber, 1969.
486 Monte Huber, 1967.

466 Jeff Campbell, 1988.
462 Monte Huber, 1968.
451 Gary Knafelc, 1953.
416 Bob Niziolek, 1977.
407 Frank Clarke, 1955.
407 J.V. Cain, 1972.

PUNT RETURNS

Number of Returns/Game – 10 (for 167 yards), Deon Figures vs. Kansas State in Boulder, Oct. 24, 1992.
Number of Returns/Season – 47 (for 587 yards), Byron White, 1937.
Number of Returns/Career – 84 (for 632 yards), Mike E. Davis, 1976-79; (for 904 yards), Jeff Campbell, 1986-89.
Punt Return Yards/Game – 167 (10 returns), Deon Figures vs. Kansas State in Boulder, Oct. 24, 1992.
Punt Return Yards/Season – 587 (47 returns), Byron White, 1937.
Punt Return Yards/Career – 904 (84 returns), Jeff Campbell, 1986-89.
Punt Return Average/Game – 53.0 (3 returns for 159 yards), Byron White vs. Utah in Boulder, Nov. 7, 1936.
Punt Return Average/Season – 16.6 (26 returns for 431 yards), Charlie Greer, 1965.
Punt Return Average/Career – 10.8 (84 returns for 904 yards), Jeff Campbell, 1986-89.
Punt Return Touchdowns/Game – 1, on 23 occasions. Last: Dave McCloughan vs. Kansas at Lawrence, Oct. 20, 1990.
Punt Return Touchdowns/Season – 4, Cliff Branch, 1971.
Punt Return Touchdowns/Career – 6, Cliff Branch, 1970-71.
Most Consecutive Games, Touchdown Scored on Punt Return – 2, Cliff Branch, Sept. 25, 1971 to Oct. 2, 1971.
Longest Punt Return – 98, Bob West vs. Colorado College at Colorado Springs, Nov. 18, 1944.

KICKOFF RETURNS

Kickoff Returns/Game – 8, Walter Stanley vs. Nebraska at Lincoln, Oct. 10, 1981 (123 yards); and Shelby Nash vs. Missouri in Boulder, Oct. 8, 1983 (151 yards).
Kickoff Returns/Season – 30 (for 704 yards), Walter Stanley, 1981.
Kickoff Returns/Career – 51 (for 1,198 yards), M.J. Nelson, 1986-89.
Kickoff Return Yards/Game – 184 (5 returns), Howard Ballage vs. Nebraska in Boulder, Oct. 21, 1978.
Kickoff Return Yards/Season – 704 (30 returns), Walter Stanley, 1981.
Kickoff Return Yards/Career – 1,198 yards (51 returns), M.J. Nelson, 1986-89.
Kickoff Return Average/Game – 53.3 (3 for 160 yards), Walter Stanley vs. Oklahoma in Boulder, Oct. 4, 1980.
Kickoff Return Average/Season – 29.4 (18 for 530 yards), Howard Ballage, 1978.
Kickoff Return Average/Career – 26.5 (32 for 849 yards), Billy Waddy, 1973-76.
Kickoff Return Touchdowns/Season – 2, Cliff Branch, 1971.
Kickoff Return Touchdowns/Career – 2, Cliff Branch (1970-71), Billy Waddy (1973-76), Howard Ballage (1976-78).
Longest Kickoff Return – 102, Byron White vs. Denver at Denver, Nov. 26 1936 (old record); 100, Cliff Branch vs. Kansas in Boulder, Nov. 7, 1970; Billy Waddy vs. Kansas State in Boulder, Nov. 22, 1975; Howard Ballage vs. Nebraska in Boulder, Oct. 21, 1978, Walter Stanley vs. Oklahoma in Boulder Oct. 4, 1980.

INTERCEPTIONS

Passes Intercepted/Game – 3, Roy Shepherd vs. Colorado A&M in Boulder, Nov. 29, 1952; Frank Bernardi and Carroll Hardy vs. Utah in Boulder, Nov. 7, 1953; Dick Anderson vs. Oregon at Eugene, Sept. 23, 1967; Rich Bland vs. Air Force in Boulder, Oct. 13, 1973; Victor Scott vs. Oklahoma State at Stillwater, Okla., Oct. 16, 1982.
Passes Intercepted/Season – 7, DickAnderson (1967), and Cullen Bryant (1972).
Passes Intercepted/Career – 16, John Steams, 1970-72.
Interception Return Yards/Game – 120 (2 retuns), Dick Keams vs. Denver at Denver, Nov. 24, 1938.
Interception Return Yards/Season – 158 (5 retums), John Steams, 1971.
Interception Return Yards/Career – 339 (16 returns), John Steams, 1970-72.
Interception Return Average/Season (5 minimum) – 31.6 (5 retums for 158 yards), John Steams, 1971.
Interception Return Average/Career (10 minimum) – 21.2 (16 retums for 339 yards), John Steams, 1970-72.
Longest Interception Return – 102, Dick Keams vs. Denver in Denver, Nov. 24, 1938.
Interception Return Touchdowns/Game – 2, Victor Scott vs. Oklahoma State at Stillwater, Oct. 16, 1982.
Interception Return Touchdowns/Season – 2, Victor Scott, 1982.
Interception Return Touchdowns/Career – 3, Victor Scott, 1980-83.

PUNTING

Punts/Game – 11, Don Evans vs. Iowa State at Ames, Oct. 16, 1948.
Punts/Season – 76, Art Woods, 1981.
Punts/Career – 199, Art Woods, 1979-82.
Yards/Game – 441 (10 punts), Lance Olander vs. Louisiana State, Sept. 15, 1979.
Yards/Season – 3,004 (76 punts), Art Woods, 1981.
Yards/Career – 8,038 (199 punts), Art Woods, 1979-82.
Highest Average Per Punt/Game (5 minimum) – 59.8 (5 for 299), Keith English vs. Oregon State Boulder, Sept. 24, 1988.
Highest Average Per Punt/Season (30 minimum) – 48.2 (38 for 1,830), Zack Jordan, 1950.
Highest Average Per Punt/Career (75 minimum) – 44.9 (153 for 6,873), Barry Helton, 1984-87.
Longest Punt – 84, Byron White vs. Missouri in Boulder, Oct. 2, 1937 (without roll).

SCORING

Points Scored/Game – 25, Byron White vs. Utah in Boulder, Nov. 7, 1936 (4 TDs, 1 PAT); Howard Cook vs. Arizona at Tucson, Oct. 11, 1958 (4 TDs, 1 PAT).
Points Scored/Season – 144, Rashaan Salaam, 1994 (24 TDs).

Points Scored/Career – 254, Eric Bieniemy, 1987-90 (42 TDs, 1 PAT).
Touchdowns Scored/Game – 4, on 12 occasions. Last: Rashaan Salaam vs. Oklahoma in Boulder, Oct. 15, 1994.
Touchdowns Scored/Season – 24, Rashaan Salaam, 1994.
Touchdowns Scored/Career – 42, Eric Bieniemy, 1987-90.
Points Accounted For/Game – 34, Byron White vs. Denver at Denver, Nov. 25, 1937. (Rushed for two TDs, passed for two, returned interception for one, and converted 4 of 5 PATs).
Points Accounted For/Season – 134, Byron White, 1937.
Field Goals Attempted/Game – 5, seven times. Last: Tom Field vs. Washington State at Spokane, Sept. 18, 1982.
Field Goals Attempted/Season – 34, Fred Lima, 1972.
Field Goals Attempted/Career – 55, Tom Feld, 1979-83.
Field Goals Made/Game – 4, Tom Field vs. Washington State at Spokane, Sept. 18, 1982; Tom Field vs. Oklahoma State at Stillwater, Oct. 16, 1982; Mitch Berger vs. Kansas State in Boulder, Oct. 24, 1992.
Field Goals Made/Season – 15 (of 34), Fred Lima, 1972.
Field Goals Made/Career – 36 (of 55), Tom Field, 1979-83.
Field Goal Percentage/Game (minimum 4) – 1.000 (4 of 4), Tom Field vs. Oklahoma State at Stillwater, Oct. 16, 1982; Mitch Berger vs. Kansas State in Boulder, Oct. 24, 1992.
Field Goal Percentage/Season (minimum 12) – .765 (13 of 17), Frank Rogers, 1967, and Ken Culbertson, 1989.
Field Goal Percentage/Career (minimum 25) – .654 (36 of 55), Tom Field, 1979-83.
Consecutive Field Goals Made – 8, Ken Culbertson, Oct. 14, 1989 to Nov. 18, 1989; and Mitch Berger, Sept. 25, 1993 to Oct. 23, 1993.
Longest Field Goals Made – 58, Jerry Hamilton, vs. Iowa State in Ames, Oct. 24, 1981; 57, Dave DeLine, vs. Nebraska in Boulder, Oct. 25, 1986; 57, Fred Lima, vs. Iowa State in Boulder, Oct. 14, 1972; 54, Jerry Hillebrand, vs. Oklahoma State in Boulder, Sept. 30, 1991; 54, Jim Harper, vs. Illinois at Champaign, Sept. 15, 1990; 54, Mitch Berger, vs. Miami, Fla. in Boulder, Sept. 25, 1993.
Longest Field Goal Attempted – 62, Ken Culbertson, vs. Oklahoma in Boulder, Oct. 22, 1988.
Two-Point Conversions Attempted/Season – 4, Darian Hagan, 1990.
Two-Point Conversions Made/Season – 2 (of 2), Clyde Crutchmer, 1973.
Two-Point Conversions Made/Career – 3 (of 3), Clyde Crutchmer, 1973-74.
Most Players Scoring in One Game – 10, vs. Wyoming in Boulder, Oct. 26, 1940. (Touchdowns scored by: Paul McClung (2), Leo Stasica (2), Vern Miller, Vern Lockard, Harold Carver, Leonard Scott and Hugh Gardner. Conversions scored by: Ray Jenkins (3), John Pudlik (3), Bob Barnes and Paul McClung).

SINGLE-SEASON POINTS

144 Rashaan Salaam, 1994.
122 Byron White, 1937.
114 Bob Anderson, 1969.
108 J.J. Flannigan, 1989.
102 Darian Hagan, 1989.

102 Eric Bieniemy, 1990.
98 Ken Culbertson, 1989.
90 Merwin Hodel, 1950.
90 Jim Kelleher, 1976.
84 Charlie Davis, 1972.

83 Jim Harper, 1990.
80 Fred Lima, 1972.
80 Neil Voskeritchian, 1994.

SINGLE-SEASON TOUCHDOWNS

24 Rashaan Salaam, 1994.
19 Bobby Anderson, 1969.
18 J.J. Flannigan, 1989.

17 Darian Hagan, 1989.
17 Eric Bieniemy, 1990.
16 Byron White, 1937.

15 Merwin Hodel, 1950.
15 Jim Kelleher, 1976.
14 Charlie Davis, 1972.

CAREER TOUCHDOWNS

42 Eric Bieniemy, 1987-90.
35 BobbyAnderson, 1967-69.
33 Rashaan Salaam, 1994.
28 Merwin Hodel, 1949-51.

27 J.J. Flannigan, 1987-89.
27 Darian Hagan, 1988-91.
26 Charlie Davis, 1971-73.
25 James Mayberry, 1975-78.

24 Byron White, 1935-37.
24 John Bayuk, 1954-56.
23 Carroll Hardy, 1951-54.
23 Lamont Warren, 1991-93.

DEFENSIVE

Total Tackles/Game – 30 (5 UT, 25 AT), Jeff Geiser vs. Kansas State in Boulder, Nov. 24, 1973.
Total Tackles/Season – 183 (102 UT, 81 AT), Ray Cone, 1982.
Total Tackles/Career – 493 (245 UT, 248 AT), Barry Remington, 1982-86.
Tackles By Position – Lineman, Season, 136, Laval Short, 1979; Lineman, Career, 372, Laval Short, 1976-79; Linebacker, Season, 183, Ray Cone, 1982; Linebacker, Career, 493, Barry Remington, 1982-86; Back, Season, 116, Mickey Pruitt, 1987; Back, Career, 340, Mickey Pruitt, 1984-87.
Unassisted Tackles/Game – 19, Greg Biekert vs. Illinois at Champaign, Sept. 15, 1990.
Unassisted Tackles/Season – 105, Greg Biekert, 1990.
Unassisted Tackles/Career – 280, Greg Biekert, 1989-92.
Assisted Tackles/Game – 25, Jeff Geiser vs. Kansas State in Boulder, Nov. 24, 1973.
Assisted Tackles/Season – 100, Jeff Geiser, 1973.
Assisted Tackles/Career – 248, Barry Remington, 1982-86.
Tackles for Loss/Game – 7 (for 56 yards), Ron Woolfork vs. Iowa in Boulder, Sept. 26, 1992.
Tackles for Loss/Season – 24 (for 123 yards), Bill Brundige, 1969.
Tackles for Loss/Career – 59 (for 303 yards), Alfred Williams, 1987-90.
Quarterback Sacks/Game – 5 (for 36 yards), Dan McMillen vs. Kansas at Lawrence, Nov. 2, 1985.
Quarterback Sacks/Season – 14 (for 86 yards), Dan McMillen, 1985.
Quarterback Sacks/Career – 35 (for 242 yards), Alfred Williams, 1987-90.
Pass Deflections/Game – 5, Eric Harris vs. Tulsa in Boulder, Sept. 20, 1969.
Pass Deflections/Season – 17, Eric Harris, 1969.
Pass Deflections/Career – 32, Mickey Pruitt, 1984-87.
Fumble Recoveries/Game – 2, on several occasions.
Fumble Recoveries/Season – 5, Stuart Walker, 1978; Mark Haynes, 1979; George Smith, 1983.
Fumble Recoveries/Career – 10, Stuart Walker, 1976-78; Mark Haynes, 1976-79.
Forced Fumbles/Game – 2, on several occasions.

Forced Fumbles/Season – 6, Barry Remington, 1985.
Forced Fumbles/Career – 11, Brian Cabral, 1975-77.
Quarterback Hurries/Game – 8, Curt Koch vs. Kansas State at Manhattan, Nov. 22, 1986.
Quarterback Hurries/Season – 30, Curt Koch, 1986.
Quarterback Hurries/Career – 56, Curt Koch, 1984-87.
Blocked Kicks/Game – 1, on several occasions.
Blocked Kicks/Season – 4, Greg Thomas, 1991.
Blocked Kicks/Career – 6, Greg Thomas, 1988-91.
Defensive Extra Points/Game – 1, Greg Biekert, vs. Nebraska in Boulder, Nov. 2, 1991.
Defensive Extra Points/Season – 1, Greg Biekert, 1991.
Defensive Extra Points/Career – 1, Greg Biekert, 1989-92.

SINGLE-SEASON TACKLES (OVERALL)

Player		
Ray Cone (LB, 1982)	102	81 – 183
Bill Roe (LB, 1979)	73	89 – 162
Barry Remington (LB, 1985)	83	79 – 162
Greg Biekert (LB, 1990)	105	45 – 150
Eric McCarty (LB, 1987)	88	60 – 148
Ted Johnson (LB, 1994)	92	55 – 147
Jeff Geiser (LB, 1973)	46	100 – 146
Don DeLuzio (LB, 1986)	77	64 – 141
Greg Biekert (LB, 1991)	78	61 – 139
Greg Biekert (LB, 1992)	87	50 – 137
Laval Short (LM, 1979)	66	70 – 136

ALL-TIME CAREER RUSHING LEADERS

Player (Seasons)	Att.	Net Yards	TD
Eric Bieniemy (87-90)	699	3,940	41
Rashaan Salaam (92-94)	486	3,057	33
Charlie Davis (71-73)	538	2,958	24
James Mayberry (75-78)	546	2,548	25
Bob Anderson (67-69)	568	2,367	34
Lee Rouson (81-84)	581	2,296	10
Lamont Warren (91-93)	488	2,242	22
Kayo Lam (33-35)	433	2,140	18
Merwin Hodel (49-51)	502	2,102	24
J.J. Flannigan (87-89)	328	2,096	27
Darian Hagan (88-91)	489	2,007	27
Carroll Hardy (51-54)	291	1,999	23
John Bayuk (54-56)	367	1,943	23
Tony Reed (75-76)	421	1,932	10
Bob Stransky (55-57)	328	1,868	21
Byron White (35-37)	342	1,864	22
Eddie Dove (56-58)	239	1,612	15
William Harris (65-67)	330	1,585	4
Terry Kunz (74-75)	312	1,575	17
Ward Walsh (68-70)	334	1,565	8

ALL-TIME CAREER PASSING LEADERS

Player (Seasons)	Att-Com-Int	Pct.	Yards	TD
Kordell Stewart (91-94)	785-456-19	58.1	6,481	33
Steve Vogel (81-84)	688-309-33	44.9	3,912	27
Darian Hagan (88-91)	424-213-19	50.2	3,801	27
Gale Weidner (59-61)	480-218-32	45.4	3,033	18
Randy Essington (80-82)	496-247-26	49.8	2,773	10
David Williams (73-75)	366-198-19	54.1	2,449	13
Bernie McCall (64-66)	361-177-23	49	2,332	4
Zack Jordan (50-52)	311-160-22	51.4	2,287	14
Bobby Anderson (67-69)	375-188-21	50.1	2,198	9
Ken Johnson (71-73)	348-148-24	42.5	2,175	13
Bill Solomon (77-79)	343-168-22	49	2,115	13
Jeff Knapple (76-77)	316-139-23	44	2,107	7
Sal Aunese (87-88)	157- 67- 6	42.7	1,526	5
Jim Bratten (68-70)	247-105-14	42.5	1,416	6
Frank Cesarek (62-63)	262-123-14	46.9	1,398	7
Mark Hatcher (84-87)	170- 66-18	38.8	1,148	9
Koy Detmer (92-94)	136- 77-11	56.6	1,133	10
Craig Keenan (84-85)	177- 92- 7	52	1,128	3
Clyde Crutchmer (73-74)	150- 74-11	49.3	1,081	7
Paul Arendt (69-70)	137- 57- 7	41.6	1,007	4

ALL-TIME CAREER RECEIVING LEADERS

Player (Seasons)	No.	Yards	Avg.	TD
Michael Westbrook (91-94)	167	2,548	15.3	19
Charles E. Johnson (90-93)	127	2,447	19.3	15
Monte Huber (67-69)	111	1,436	12.9	5
Mike Pritchard (87-90)	47	1,241	26.4	10
Ron Brown (81-85)	57	1,217	21.4	8
Jon Embree (83-86)	80	1,166	14.6	5
Loy Alexander (83-85)	78	1,107	14.2	8
Christian Fauria (91-94)	98	1,058	10.8	11
Dave Logan (72-75)	67	1,078	16.1	4
Dave Hestera (81-83)	91	1,057	11.6	2
J.V. Cain (71-73)	61	873	14.3	3
Jeff Campbell (86-89)	28	802	28.6	1
Emery Moorehead (74-76)	40	751	18.8	2
Steve Gaunty (75-77)	33	715	21.7	3
Kazell Pugh (77-79)	42	709	16.9	4
Lee Rouson (81-84)	86	699	8.1	4
Jerry Hillebrand (59-61)	40	696	17.4	6
Cliff Branch (70-71)	36	665	18.5	3
Bob Niziolek (77-80)	49	664	13.6	5
Chuck Mosher (49-51)	36	663	18.4	5

ALL-TIME CAREER SCORING LEADERS

Player (Seasons)	TD	2Pt	EP-EPA	FG-FGA	Pts
Eric Bieniemy (87-89)	42	1-1	0-0	0-0	254
Bobby Anderson (67-69)	35	1-2	0-0	0-0	212
Rashaan Salaam (92-94)	33	0-0	0-0	0-0	198
Tom Field (79-83)	0	0-0	82-86	36-55	190
Byron White (35-37)	24	0-0	30-32	1-2	177
Merwin Hodel (49-51)	28	0-0	0-0	0-0	168
J.J. Flannigan (87-89)	27	0-0	0-0	0-0	162
Darian Hagan (88-91)	27	0-4	0-0	0-0	162
Charlie Davis (71-73)	26	1-1	0-0	0-0	158
Ken Culbertson (86-89)	0	0-0	85-87	23-41	154
Carroll Hardy (51-54)	23	0-0	14-19	0-0	152
James Mayberry (75-78)	25	0-0	0-0	0-0	150
Dave Haney (68-70)	0	0-0	86-92	21-34	149
John Bayuk (54-56)	24	0-0	0-0	0-0	144
Bob Stransky (55-57)	21	0-0	12-22	0-0	138
Lamont Warren (91-93)	23	0-0	0-0	0-0	138
Jim Harper (90-91)	0	0-0	71-74	22-35	137
Roger Williams (50-52)	12	0-0	61-81	1-1	136
Terry Kunz (72-75)	21	0-0	0-0	0-0	126
Fred Lima (72-73)	0	0-0	59-62	21-45	122

ALL-TIME TOTAL OFFENSE LEADERS

Player (Seasons)	Rush	Pass	Total	TDR
Kordell Stewart (91-94)	1289	6481	7770	48
Darian Hagan (88-91)	2007	3801	5808	54
Bobby Anderson (67-69)	2367	2198	4565	43
Eric Bieniemy (87-90)	3940	63	4003	42
Steve Vogel (81-84)	-411	3912	3501	27
David Williams (73-75)	959	2449	3408	25
Gale Weidner (59-61)	58	3033	3091	29
Bernie McCall (64-66)	725	2332	3057	10
Rashaan Salaam (92-94)	3057	0	3057	33
Zack Jordan (50-52)	748	2287	3025	21
Charlie Davis (71-73)	2958	0	2958	24
Ken Johnson (71-73)	727	2175	2902	21
Bill Solomon (77-79)	509	2115	2624	23
Mark Hatcher (84-87)	1470	1148	2618	25
James Mayberry (75-78)	2548	0	2548	25
Byron White (35-37)	1864	674	2538	25
Sal Aunese (87-88)	1009	1526	2535	19
Randy Essington (80-82)	-327	2773	2446	11
Jeff Knapple (76-77)	332	2107	2439	15
Lamont Warren (91-93)	2242	131	2373	25

ALL-TIME ALL-PURPOSE YARD LEADERS

Player (Seasons)	Rush	Rec.	KOR	PR	Total
Eric Bieniemy (87-90)	3,940	380	31	0	4,351
Byron White (35-37)	1864	234	506	973	3,577
Rashaan Salaam (92-94)	3 057	412	13	0	3,482
Charlie Davis (71-73)	2,958	131	75	0	3,164
Carroll Hardy (51-54)	1,999	38	853	225	3,115
Charles E. Johnson (90-93)	82	2,447	217	261	3,007
Lee Rouson (81-84)	2,296	699	0	0	2,995
James Mayberry (75-78)	2,548	171	265	0	2,984
Merwin Hodel (49-51)	2,102	540	255	13	2,910
Billy Waddy (73-76)	1,537	475	849	26	2,887
Michael Westbrook (91-94)	84	2,548	226	0	2,858
Kayo Lam (33-35)	2,140	111	331	236	2,818
Bob Stransky (55-57)	1,868	37	459	396	2,760
Bobby Anderson (67-69)	2,367	68	209	56	2,700
Lamont Warren (91-93)	2,242	432	0	0	2,674
Mike Pritchard (87-90)	585	1,241	693	-6	2,525
Cliff Branch (70-71)	354	665	755	733	2,507
Bill Symons (62-64)	734	537	1,051	153	2,475
Bill Harris (61-63)	1,486	235	556	134	2,411
Howard Cook (56-58)	1,463	99	373	459	2,394

ALL-TIME CAREER PUNTING (MINIMUM 50 PUNTS)

Player (Seasons)	No.	Yards	Avg.	Long
Barry Helton (84-87)	153	6,873	44.92	68
Keith English (85-88)	55	2,457	44.67	77
Zack Jordan (50-52)	139	6,013	43.26	72
Tom Rouen (89-90)	90	3,855	42.83	65
Mitch Berger (91-93)	168	7,177	42.72	74
Boyd Dowler (56-58)	106	4,441	41.90	63
ByronWhite (35-37)	124	5,104	41.16	84
Steve Doolittle (77-80)	57	2,343	41.11	69
Lance Olander (77-80)	107	4,370	40.84	62
Art Woods (79-82)	199	8,038	40.39	61
Homer Jenkins (53-55)	58	2,331	40.19	59
Bill Symons (62-64)	59	2,306	39.08	57
Stan Koleski (73-76)	195	7,614	39.05	62
Dick Anderson (65-67)	93	3,566	38.34	60
Don Evans (4648)	162	6,205	38.30	58
Allan Braun (83-84)	129	4,835	37.48	59
Dick Robert (68-70)	132	4,927	37.33	58
John Stearns (70-72)	114	4159	36.48	54
Chuck McBride (59-61)	145	5250	36.2	60

SINGLE-SEASON TACKLES (OVERALL)

Ray Cone (LB, 1982)	102	81 – 183
Bill Roe (LB, 1979)	73	89 – 162
Barry Remington (LB, 1985)	83	79 – 162
Greg Biekert (LB, 1990)	105	45 – 150
Eric McCarty (LB, 1987)	88	60 – 148
Ted Johnson (LB, 1994)	92	55 – 147
Jeff Geiser (LB, 1973)	46	100 – 146
Don DeLuzio (LB, 1986)	77	64 – 141
Greg Biekert (LB, 1991)	78	61 – 139
Greg Biekert (LB, 1992)	87	50 – 137
Laval Short (LM, 1979)	66	70 – 136

SINGLE-SEASON TACKLES FOR LOSS

24 (for 123 yards), Bill Brundige, 1969
23 (for 82 yards), Leonard Renfro, 1992
22 (for 81 yards), Garry Howe, 1990
21 (for 101 yards), Curt Koch, 1986
21 (for 104 yards), Alfred Williams, 1990
21 (for 122 yards), Ron Woolfork, 1992
18 (for 105 yards), Dan McMillen, 1985
18 (for 119 yards), Ron Woolfork, 1991
18 (for 84 yards), Sam Rogers, 1993
17 (for 74 yards), Randy Westendorf, 1977
17 (for 87 yards), Art Walker, 1989

SINGLE-SEASON QUARTERBACK SACKS

14 (for 86 yards), Dan McMillen, 1985
13 1/2 (for 99 yards), Ron Woolfork, 1992
13 (for 102 yards), Ron Woolfork, 1991
12 1/2 (for 76 yards), Alfred Williams, 1990
11 (for 82 yards), Bill Brundige, 1969
10 1/2 (for 92 yards), Alfred Williams, 1989
10 1/2 (for 61 yards), Leonard Renfro, 1992
10 (for 66 yards), Herb Orvis, 1971
10 (for 66 yards), Curt Koch, 1986
10 (for 60 yards), Garry Howe, 1990
9 1/2 (for 48 yards), Sam Rogers, 1993.
9 (for 70 yards), Laval Short, 1979
8 (for 51 yards), Laval Short, 1978
8 (for 61 yards), Dave Anderson, 1981
8 (for 39 yards), Chad Brown, 1991

SINGLE-SEASON PASS DEFLECTIONS

17, Eric Harris, 1969	8, Odis McKinney, 1976
13, Mickey Pruitt, 1986	8, Odis McKinney, 1977
12, Deon Fgures, 1991	8, Mike E. Davis, 1979
11, Michael Jones, 1987	8, Jeff Donaldson, 1981
11, Mickey Pruitt, 1987	8, Victor Scott, 1981
10, Lyle Pickens, 1985	8, Victor Scott, 1982
10, Alfred Williams, 1987	8, Barry Remington, 1985
9, Mike Spivey, 1976	8, Solomon Wilcots, 1986
9, Keith Pontiflet, 1988	8, Deon Figures, 1992
8, Jeff Raymond, 1968	

SINGLE-SEASON INTERCEPTIONS

7, Dick Anderson, 1967	6, Tim James, 1990
7, Cullen Bryant, 1972	6, Deon Figures, 1992
6, John Stearns, 1972	5, on 11 occasions

SINGLE-SEASON BLOCKED KICKS

4, Greg Thomas, 1991	2, Greg Thomas, 1990
2, Dick Anderson, 1967	

SINGLE-SEASON FORCED FUMBLES

6, Barry Remington, 1985	4, Kyle Rappold, 1987
5, Mickey Pruitt, 1986	4, Garry Howe, 1990
4, Dan McMillen, 1984	4, Eric Hamilton, 1991
4, Curt Koch, 1987	3, on several occasions

SINGLE-SEASON FUMBLE RECOVERIES

5, Stuart Walker, 1978	4, Mike Bynum, 1968
5, Mark Haynes, 1979	4, Lenny Ciufo, 1973
5, George Smith, 1983	4, Darrin Schubeck, 1984
4, Frank Bosch, 1967	3, on several occasions

ALL-TIME CAREER TACKLE LEADERS

Player (Position, Seasons)	UT	AT – TOT
Barry Remington (LB, 82-86)	245	248 – 493
Greg Biekert (LB, 89-92)	280	161 – 441
Ted Johnson (LB, 91-94)	253	156 – 409
Laval Short (DL, 76-79)	141	231 – 372
Chad Brown (LB, 89-92)	242	127 – 369
Michael Jones (LB, 86-89)	218	131 – 349
Mickey Pruitt (DB, 84-87)	207	133 – 340
Don DeLuzio (LB, 84-88)	175	129 – 304
Brian Cabral (LB, 74-77)	120	177 – 297
Kanavis McGhee (LB, 87-90)	179	118 – 297
Bill Roe (LB, 77-79)	116	156 – 272
Dick Anderson (DB, 65-67)	123	143 – 266
Alfred Williams (LB 87-90)	180	83 – 263
Jeff Geiser (LB, 72-i4)	102	159 – 261
Phil Irwin (LB, 68-70)	88	170 – 258
Mark Haynes (DB, 76-79)	142	114 – 256
Ruben Vaughan (DL, 75-78)	108	145 – 253
Billie Drake (LB, 70-72)	82	170 – 252
Alan Cmrite (LB, 80-84)	128	121 – 249
Don Fairbanks (LB/DL, 83-85)	120	128 – 248

ALL-TIME CAREER PASS DEFLECTION LEADERS

Player (Seasons)	No.	Player (Seasons)	No.
Mickey Pruitt (84-87)	32	Pat Murphy(68-70)	20
Deon Figures (8-92)	27	Michael Jones (86-89)	20
Alfred Williams (87-90)	25	Cmris Hudson (91-94)	20
Victor Scott (80-83)	24	Greg Biekert (89-92)	19

ALL-TIME CAREER QUARTERBACK SACK LEADERS

Player (Seasons)	No.	Player (Seasons)	No.
Alfred Williams (87-90)	35	Kanavis McGhee (87-90)	15
Ron Woolfork (90-93)	33	Chad Brown (89-92)	14
Dan McMillen (8285)	20	Garry Howe (89-90)	13.5
Laval Short (76-79)	19	Art Walker (86-89)	12.5
Curt Koch (84-87)	19	Joel Steed (88-91)	12.5
Leonard Renfro (89-92)	19	Steve Doolittle (78-80)	12
Bill Brundige (67-69)	18	Sam Rogers (92-93)	11.5
Herb Orvis (69-71)	15		

ALL-TIME CAREER INTERCEPTION LEADERS

Rk Player (Seasons)	No.	Yards	Avg.	TD
1 John Stearns (70-72)	16	339	21.2	0
2 Chris Hudson (91-94)	15	204	13.6	2
3 Dick Anderson (65-67)	14	151	10.8	0
4 Tim James (87-90)	13	120	9.2	0
5 Deon Figures (88-92)	12	96	8	0
6 Victor Scott (80-83)	10	203	20.3	3
6 Roy Shepherd (50-52)	10	157	15.7	2
6 Cullen Bryant (70-72)	10	139	13.9	1
6 Boyd Dowler (56-58)	10	75	7.5	0
10 Hale Irwin (64-66)	9	162	18	0
10 Jeff Donaldson (80-83)	9	120	13.3	1
10 Clyde Riggins (80-83)	9	76	8.5	0
13 Byron White (35-37)	8	153	19.1	2
13 Pat Murphy (68-70)	8	145	18.1	0
13 Jim Cooch (69-70)	8	92	11.5	0
13 Dave McCloughan (87-90)	8	91	11.4	0

AWARDS/HONORS

COLORADO'S ALL-BIG EIGHT HONORS

(First Team; AP; UPI; Coaches)

1948 Harry Narcisian, HB; Ed Pudlik, E
1950 Merwin Hodel, FB; Charles Mosher, E
1951 Tom Brookshier, HB; Don Branby, E; Merwin Hodel, FB; Jack Jorgenson, T; Charles Mosher, E
1952 Don Branby, E; Tom Brookshier, HB; Zack Jordan, HB
1953 Gary Knafelc, E
1954 Frank Bemardi, HB; Carroll Hardy, HB
1955 Lamar Meyer, E; Sam Salerno, T
1956 John Bayuk, FB; Jerry Leahy, E; Wally Merz, E; Dick Stapp, T
1957 Bob Stransky, HB; John Wooten, G
1958 Boyd Dowler, QB; Jack Himelwright, T
1959 Joe Romig, G; Gale Weidner, QB
1960 Jerry Hillebrand, E; Joe Romig, G
1961 Jerry Hillebrand, E; Walt Klinker, C; Joe Romig, G; Gale Weidner, QB
1962 Ken Blair, E
1965 Sam Harris, DE; Hale Irwin, DB; Steve Sidwell, LB
1966 John Beard, OG; Wilmer Cooks, FB; Bill Fairband, DE; Hale Irwin, DB
1967 Dick Anderson, DB; Frank Bosch, DT; Mike Montler, OT; Mike Schnitker, DE; Kirk Tracy, OG
1968 Bobby Anderson, QB; Rocky Martin, LB; Mike Montler, OT
1969 Bobby Anderson, TB; Bill Brundige, DE; Dick Melin, OG
1970 Dennis Havig, OG; Herb Orvis, DE; Don Popplewell, C
1971 Bud Magrum, MG; Herb Orvis, DT; Jake Zumbach, OT
1972 Cullen Bryant, DB; J.V. Cain, TE; Charlie Davis, TB; Bud Magrum, LB; John Stearns, DB; Jake Zumbach, OT
1973 J.V Cain, TE; Greg Horton, OT; Doug Payton, OG
1974 Rod Perry, DB
1975 Gary Campbell, LB; Don Hasselbeck, TE; Mark Koncar, OT; Terry Kunz, FB
1976 Don Hasselbeck, TE; Charlie Johnson, MG; Tony Reed, TB; Mike Spivey, DB
1977 Odis McKinney, DB; Randy Westendorf, DE; Leon White, C
1978 Mark Haynes, DB; Matt Miller, OT
1979 Mark Haynes, DB; Stan Brock, OT
1980 Steve Doolittle, LB
1981 Pete Perry, DE
1982 Victor Scott, DB
1983 Victor Scott, DB; Dave Hestera, TE
1984 Ron Brown, WR; Jon Embree, TE
1985 Barry Helton, P; Mickey Pruitt, SS
1986 Barry Helton, P; Mickey Pruitt, SS; Eric Coyle, C; Barry Remington, ILB; Curt Koch, DT
1987 Barry Helton, P; Mickey Pruitt, SS; Eric McCarty, ILB; Kyle Rappold, NT
1988 Eric Bieniemy, HB; Keith English, P; Kanavis McGhee, OLB; Erik Norgard, C
1989 Jeff Campbell, KR; J.J. Flannigan, TB; Joe Garten, OG; Darian Hagan, QB; Kanavis McGhee, OLB; Darrin Muilenburg, OG; Tom Rouen, P; Mark Vander Poel, OT; Arthur Walker, DT; Alfred Williams, OLB
1990 Eric Bieniemy, TB; Joe Garten, OG; Darian Hagan, QB; Garry Howe, DT; Tim James, FS; Jay Leeuwenburg, C; Dave McCloughan, CB/KR; Kanavis McGhee, OLB; Mike Pritchard, WR; Joel Steed, NT; Mark Vander Poel, OT; Alfred Williams, OLB
1991 Greg Biekert, ILB; Chad Brown, OLB; Eric Hamilton, SS; Jay Leeuwenburg, C; Leonard Renfro, DT; Joel Steed, NT
1992 Greg Biekert, ILB; Ronnie Bradford, CB; Chad Brown, OLB; Deon Figures, CB; Jim Hansen, OT; Chris Hudson, CB; Leonard Renfro, DT; Michael Westbrook, WR; Ron Woolfork, OLB
1993 Shannon Clavelle, DT; Kerry Hicks, NT; Chris Hudson, FS; Charles E. Johnson, WR; Rashaan Salaam, TB; Ron Woolfork, OLB
1994 Tony Berti, OT; Shannon Clavelle, DT; Christian Fauria, TE; Chris Hudson, CB; Ted Johnson, ILB; Rashaan Salaam, TB; Kordell Stewart, QB; Bryan Stoltenberg, C; Michael Westbrook, WR

OFFENSIVE PLAYER-OF-THE-YEAR

1989 Darian Hagan, QB
1990 Eric Bieniemy, TB
1993 Charles E. Johnson, WR
1994 Rashaan Salaam, TB

DEFENSIVE PLAYER-OF-THE-YEAR

1965 William Harris, DB
1969 Bill Brundige, DE
1989 Alfred Williams, OLB
1990 Alfred Williams, OLB
1992 Deon Figures, CB

NEWCOMER-OF-THE-YEAR

1969 Herb Orvis, DE
1976 Jeff Knapple, QB
1987 Sal Aunese, QB (Off.)
1990 Jim Harper, PK (Off.)

BIG EIGHT ALL-DECADE

1970-79 J.V. Cain, TE (1st-team); Herb Orvis, DE (1st-team); Tony Reed, RB (2nd-team); Cullen Bryant, DB (2nd-team)
1980-89 Barry Helton, P (1st-team); Mickey Pruitt, DB (1st-team); Jeff Campbell, KR (1st-team); Kanavis McGhee, LB (honorable mention); Victor Scott, DB (honorable mention)

BIG EIGHT COACH-OF-THE-YEAR

1956 Dal Ward
1965 Eddie Crowder
1985 Bill McCartney
1989 Bill McCartney
1990 Bill McCartney

BIG EIGHT HALL-OF-FAME (YEAR INDUCTED)

Byron White (1975)
Joe Romig (1976)
Dick Anderson (1978)
Mike Montler (1979)
Bobby Anderson (1980)
Herb Orvis (1982)

ALL-AMERICA FIRST TEAM

Year	Player, Position	Honored By
1937	*Byron White, HB	AP, UPI, INS, NEA, LIB, COL, Sporting News
1952	Don Branby, E	AP
1956	John Bayuk, FB	Sports Illustrated
1957	Bob Stransky, HB	NEA, INS, FWAA/Look
1958	John Wooten, OG	AFCA/General Mills
1960	*Joe Romig, OG	UPI, AFCA Kodak, FWM/Look, Football News
1961	Jerry Hillebrand, E	AP, FWAA Look
	*Joe Romig, OG	UPI, NEA FWAA/Look, AFCA Kodak, SportingNews
1967	*Dick Anderson, DB	AP, NEA
1968	*Mike Montler, OG	AP, AFCA Kodak
1969	*Bobby Anderson, TB	AP, UPI, NEA, Sporting News
	Bill Brundige, DE	FWAA Look
1970	*Don Popplewell, C	AP, UPI, NEA, CP, Walter Camp, FWAA/Look
	Pat Murphy, DB	Walter Camp
1971	Herb Orvis, DE	CP, AFCA Kodak, Walter Camp, Sporting News, Universal
	Cliff Branch, WR	Football News
1972	*Cullen Bryant, DB	UPI, NEA, AFCA/Kodak, Sporhng News
	Bud Magrum, LB	FWAA
1973	J. V Cain, TE	Sporting News
1975	Pete Brock, C	Sporting News
	Mark Koncar, OT	AP
	Dave Logan, SE	Sporting News
	Troy Archer, DT	Time Magazine
1976	Don Hasselbeck, TE	Sporting News
1977	Leon White, C	AFCA Kodak
1978	Matt Miller, OT	UPI
1979	Mark Haynes, DB	AP
	Stan Brock, OT	Sporting News
1985	*Barry Helton, P	AP, UPI, Walter Camp
1986	*Barry Helton, P	AP UPI, Sporting News
1988	*Keith English, P	AP UPI, Walter Camp, Sporting News, Football News
1989	*Joe Garten, OG	AP, UPI, AFCA/Kodak, FWAA
	*Tom Rouen, P	AP, UPI, Walter Camp, FWAA
	*Alfred Williams, OLB	UPI, AFCA/Kodak, FWAA, Football News
	Darian Hagan QB	Sporting News
	Kanavis McGhee, OLB	Walter Camp
1990	#Eric Bieniemy, TB	AP, UPI AFCA/Kodak, FWAA, Walter Camp, Football News, Sporting News
	#Joe Garten, OG	AP, UPI, AFCA/Kodak, FWAA, Walter Camp, Football News, Sporting News
	#Alfred Williams, OLB	AP, UPI, AFCA/Kodak, FWAA, Walter Camp, Football News, Sporting News
1991	#Jay Leeuwenburg, C	AP, UPI, AFCA/Kodak, FWAA, Walter Camp, Football News, Sporting News
1992	*Deon Figures, CB	AP, UPI, FWAA, Walter Camp, NEA, Football News, Sporting News
	Mitch Berger, P	UPI
	Michael Westbrook, WR	NEA
1994	#Rashaan Salaam, TB	AP, UPI, AFCA, FWAA, Walter Camp, Football News, Sporting News
	*Chris Hudson, CB	AP, UPI, FWAA
	Michael Westbrook, WR	AFCA, Walter Camp

* consensus   # unanimous

HEISMAN TROPHY

(Presented to the nation's top player)
1937 Byron White, HB (2nd, 264 points)
1961 Joe Romig, OG/LB (6th, 279 points)
1969 Bobby Anderson, TB (11th, 100 points)
1971 Charlie Davis, TB (16th, 28 points)
1989 Darian Hagan, QB (5th, 242 points)
1990 Eric Bieniemy, TB (3rd, 798 points)
    Darian Hagan, QB (17th, 17 points)
    Mike Pritchard, WR (5Oth, 2 points)
1991 Darian Hagan, QB (20th, 12 points)
1992 Deon Fgures, CB (30th, 4 points)
1993 Charles Johnson, WR (15th, 24 points)
    Michael Westbrook, WR (61st, 1 point)
1994 Rashaan Salaam, TB (lst, 1743 points)
    Kordell Stewart, QB (13th, 16 points)

BUTKUS AWARD

(Presented to the nation's top linebacker)
1990 Alfred Williams (winner)
1994 Ted Johnson (runner-up)

MAXWELL AWARD

(Presented to the nation's top player)

1994 Rashaan Salaam (runner-up)

OUTLAND TROPHY

(Presented to the nation's top interior lineman)
1990 Joe Garten (runner-up)

THORPE AWARD

(Presented to the nation's top defensive back)
1992 Deon Figures (winner)
1994 Chris Hudson (winner)

JOHNNY UNITAS AWARD

(Presented to the nation's top senior quarterback)
1994 Kordell Stewart (one of six finalists)

DOAK WALKER AWARD

(Presented to the nation's top running back)
1994 Rashaan Salaam (winner)

WALTER CAMP TROPHY

(Presented to the national player-of-the-year)
1994 Rashaan Salaam (winner)

NATIONAL FOOTBALL HALL-OF-FAME (YEAR INDUCTED)

Byron White (1952)   Dick Anderson (1993)
Joe Romig (1984)

NATIONAL COACH-OF-THE-YEAR

1989 Bill McCartney (unanimous: UPI, AFCA/Kodak, FWAA, Walter, Camp, Sporting News, Maxwell Football Club, CBS/Chevrolet)

FOLSOM FIELD – TOP 25 CROWDS

1. 53,553 vs. Oklahoma, Nov. 4, 1978 (L, 7-28)
2. 53,538 vs. Nebraska, Oct. 9, 1976 (L, 12-24)
3. 53,457 vs. Wisconsin, Sept. 17, 1994 (W, 55-17)
4. 53,380 vs. Oklahoma, Oct. 30, 1976 (W, 42-31)
5. 53,262 vs. Nebraska, Oct. 21, 1978 (L, 14-52)
6. 53,199 vs. Oklahoma, Oct. 15, 1994 (W, 45-7)
7. 53,022 vs. Nebraska, Oct. 9, 1982 (L,14-40)
8. 52,955 vs. Kansas State, Oct. 22, 1994 (W, 35-21)
9. 52,908 vs. Missouri, Oct. 29, 1977 (L, 14-24)
10. 52 904 vs. Okla. St., Oct. 8, 1977 (W, 29-13)
11. 52 877 vs. Nebraska, Nov. 4, 1989 (W, 27-21)
12. 52,868 vs. Washington, Sept. 29, 1990 (W, 20-14)
13. 52,707 vs. Oklahoma, Nov. 15,1986 (L, 0-28)
14. 52,692 vs. Notre Dame, Oct. 1, 1983 (L, 3-27)
15. 52,454 vs. Oklahoma, Oct. 17, 1992 (T, 24-24)
16. 52,440 vs. Nebraska, Oct. 25, 1986 (W, 20-10)
17. 52,391 vs. Miami, Fla., Sept. 25,1993 (L, 29-35)
18. 52,355 vs. Iowa, Sept. 26,1992 (W, 28-12)
19. 52,319 vs. Nebraska, Nov. 2, 1991 (T, 19-19)
20. 52,315 vs. Missouri, Oct. 12,1991 (W, 55-7)
21. 52,277 vs. Nebraska, Oct. 30,1993 (L, 17-21)
22. 52,235 vs. Kansas State, Oct. 24, 1992 (W, 54-7)
23. 52,164 vs. Colorado State, Sept. 5, 1992 (W, 37-17)
24. 52155 vs. Wyoming, Sept. 7, 1991 (W, 30-13)
25. 52147 vs. Minnesota, Sept. 21, 1991 (W, 58-0)
25. 52,147 vs. Missouri, Oct. 9, 1993 (W, 30-18)

LETTERMEN

A Abbett, Henry 1919; Abbott, Dudley 1902; Adams, George 1957-58-59; Adams, John 1925; Adams, John 1940-41-42; Adams, Victor 1915-16-17-19; Adams, Wilbur 1915-16-19; Adkins, Doug 1989; Affolter, John 1899-1900; Agnew, Derek 1992-93; Akerbrett, T. 1922; Albers, Bill 1945-46; Alderson, Dave 1981-82-83; Aldrich, Stuart 1970-71-72; Alexander, Charles 1920-21-22; Alexander, Loy 1983-84-85; Alison, Bruce 1981; Allen, Aubrey 1942-43-46-47; Allen, Bill 1950-51-52; Allen, Charles 1902-04; Allen, Carlin 1918; Allen, Frank 1913-14; Allen, Harry 1942; Allen, Larry 1972-74; Anderson, Blake 1994; Anderson, Bobby 1967-68-69; Anderson, Chris 1994; Anderson, Craig 1991-92-93; Anderson, Dave 1943; Anderson, Dick 1965-66-67; Anderson, Ken 1933-34-35; Anderson, Malcolm 1937; Andrew, John 1902; Andrus, Ralph 1910-12; Antonio, Joe 1936-37; Appleby, John 1936; Apuzzo, Gerald 1949; Archer, Troy 1974-75; Arendt, Paul 1969-70; Armstrong, Andy 1977-78; Armstrong, Sandy 1980-81-82-83; Armstrong, Tony 1983-84; Arnett, Bill 1892-93-94-95-98; Arnold, Rick 1984; Arriza, John 1962; Aunese, Sal 1987-88; Austin, Evan 1897; Austin, Jeff 1975-76

B Babcock, Colton 1927; Bagnall, Don 1927; Bailey, Boyd 1932-33-34; Bailey, Dewey 1902-03; Bailey, Dick 1933; Bailey, Glen 1968-70-71; Bain, Dale 1984; Baker, Ken 1957; Balich, Matt 1954-55; Ballage, Howard 1976-77-78; Banks, Estes 1964-65-66; Barbour, Bill 1892; Barnes, Bob 1940; Barnett, Norm 1992-94; Barr, Alvin 1905-06-07-08; Barris, Don 1939; Bartelt, Dave 1966-67-68; Bartlett, Chris 1926-27; Bartz, Dick 1962; Bayuk, John 1954-55-56; Beard, John 1965-66; Beard, Shaun 1983-84; Bearss, Bill 1962; Beaton, Dan 1930-31; Beaty, Calvin 1982-84; Beck, Steve 1985-36; Becker, Jack 1955-56; Becker, J.B. 1903; Beebe, Willie 1978-79-80-81; Beery, Arlie 1948-49-50; Belcher, L. 1918; Belders, George 1940; Bell, Bob 1961; Bell, Joe 1978-79-80; Bell, Matt 1989; Bellar, Steve 1969; Bennett, Byron 1955; Bennett, John 1984-85; Bennett, Mike 1970-72; Beresford, Stu 1928; Berg, John 1974; Berger, Homer 1922; Berger, Mitch 1991-92-93; Berk, Mike 1981; Bernardi, Frank 1952-53-54; Berti, Tony 1993-94; Beseman, Carr 1948; Bessee, C.W., 1914; Bevans, Tom 1971-72; Beveridge, George 1922; Beverly, Craig 1983; Biekert, Greg 1989-90-91-92; Bieniemy, Eric 1987-88-89-90; Bigelow, KK 1941; Birney, Fletcher 1930-31; Black, Ryan 1994; Blair, Ken 1960-61-62; Blair, Steve 1967; Blake,AB. 1915; Blanchard, Bill 1968-69; Bland, Rich 1971-72-73; Blasongame, David 1952; Bliss, John 1969; Blottiaux, Pat 1992; Blount, Blake 1968-69; Bluhm, Conrad 1890; Blunt, Brad 1968; Bohn, Bill 1923-24-25-26; Bolan, Mike 1960; Bolen, Ernest 1929-30-31; Boman, Jon 1989-90; Bortles, Bart 1966-67; Bosch, Frank 1965-66-67; Bowler, Sam 1908-09; Bowman, Kyle 1904; Boyd, Jim 1957; Boyd, John 1935-36; Brace, Doug 1974-76; Bradford, Byron 1927; Bradford, Ron 1989-90-91-92; Bradley, Larry 1977; Bradley, Paul 1930-31; Branby, Don 1950-51-52; Branby, Harlan 1954-55; Branch, Cliff 1970-71; Bratten, Jim 1968-69-70; Braun, Allen 1983-84; Braun, Cleon 1980-81-82; Breckenridge, Bob 1919; Breinig, Chuck 1948-49; Breitenstein, Bob 1925-26-27; Brenneman, Dick 1948; Briddle, Monte 1955-56; Bridenbaugh, Dick 1940; Briggs, Paul 1942-43-46-47; Brill, Marty 1937-38-40; Britton, Virgil 1932; Britzman, Homer 1920-21; Broady, Jack 1938; Brock, Pete 1973-74-75; Brock, Stan 1976-77-78-79; Brock, Willie 1975-76-77; Brookshier, Tom 1950-51-52; Brotzman, Don 1940-41-42; Browder, Stan 1978-79; Brown, Chad 1989-90-91-92; Brown, Charlie 1956-57; Brown, David 1987-88-89-90; Brown, Henry 1937; Brown, Jim 1918-19-20; Brown, John 1936-37; Brown, Ken 1970; Brown, Ron 1981-83-84-85; Brown, Sean 1990-91; Browne, Kenny 1994; Broyles, Tom 1944-45; Brundige, Bill 1967-68-69; Brunelli, Lee 1987; Brunner, Jeff 1990-91-93; Brunson, Larry 1970-71; Brusse, Joe 1904; Bryan, Rick 1976; Bryant, Cullen 1970-71-72; Brynestad, John 1950; Buirgy, Bob 1931; Buka, Sydney 1933; Burg, John 1931; Busick, Bob 1970; Bustler, Bernard 1928-29-30; Butero, Paul 1977-78-79; Butler, Rod 1979-80; Bynum, Mike 1966-67-68; Bynum, Rick 1979-80; Byrne, Steve 1974

C Cabral, Brian 1975-76-77; Cain, J.V 1971-72-73; Cain, Tom 1951; Caley, Bill 1893-95; Caley, Elwin 1901-04-05; Call, Larry 1956-57; Campbell, Bryan 1989-90; Campbell, Bruce 1979-80; Campbell, Gary 1972-74; Campbell, Jeff 1986-87-88-89; Campbell, Kirk 1957-58-59; Campbell, Nathan 1993; Canfield, Don 1944; Capra, Dave 1968-69-70; Caranci, Roland 194041-42; Card, Justin 1937-39-40; Carl, Lance 1986-87; Carlson, Bill 1900-01; Carlson, George 1928-29-30; Carlson, George 1898-99-1900-01; Carlson, John 1899-1900-01; Carmean, Lansin 1924; Carmichael, Bob 1967; Carmichael, Earl 1910; Carney, Pat 1890-01-02-03; Carroll, Fred 1892-93-95; Carroll, E.J. 1900; Carroll, Wayne 1982-83-84; Carruth, Rae 1992-94; Carver, Harold 1941; Case, Bill 1948-49-50; Castetter, Jim 1926; Catanzaro, Sam 1949; Catt, Tom 1978; Cesarek, Frank 1962-63; Chace, Brad 1978-79-80; Chamberlain, Max 1925-26-27; Chambers, Lloyd 1942; Chambers, Pat 1983; Chapman, Gerry 1915-16; Chase, Harry 1894-95-96-97-98; Cheney, Erv 1934-36-37; Chilson, Hatfield 1923-24-25; Chinatti, Howard 1977; Christensen, Dale 1961-62; Christensen, Mart 1902-04-05-06; Chrite, Alan 1980-81-82-84; Cilento, Mike 1975-76-77; Cimmino, Denis 1973; Ciufo, Lennie 1971-72-73; Clapper, Bob 1947-48; Clark, Ed 1957-58-59; Clark, Gary 1969-70; Clark, Jeff 1974; Clark, Leroy 1956-58; Clarke, Frank 1955-56; Classen, Ken 1944; Clavelle, Shannon 1992-93-94; Clay, Field 1895-96-97; Clay, Walt 1942; Clements, Bob 1932; Cleveland, Rick 1972-73; Click, Harvey 1939-40-41; Coffin, Claire 1904-05-06-07-08; Coffin, Claude 1902-03-04; Coleman, Bill 1986-87-88-89; Coleman, Ed 1960-61; Collier, Dennis 1992-93; Collier, Ozell 1972-73; Collins, Bill 1967-68-69; Collins, JoJo 1984-85-87-88; Colter, Spencer 1991; Colvin, Jeff 1983; Combs, Jay 1939; Cone, Martin 1981-82-83; Cone, Ray 1980-81-82; Confer, Pat 1976; Connell, Jim 1926-27; Connors, Joe 1955; Conrad, Frank 1967; Cooch, Jim 1968-69-70; Cook, Howard 1956-57-58; Cook, Pete 1947-48; Cooks, Wilmer 1965-6647; Cooney, Mark 1971-72-73; Cooper, Henry 1910-11; Cooper, Henry 1972; Cooper, W.H. 1914-15; Copeland, Morris 1984-85-86; Corson, Tom 1965-66-67; Cortese, Bob 1964; Costello, George 1916-17-19; Counter, Jim 1932-33-34; Counter, Nick 1959; Csikos, Bill 1965-66-67; Couzens, (?) 1902; Cox, Eddie 1969-70; Coyle, Eric 1982-84-85; Crabb, Claude 1960-61; Crandall, Merritt 1893-94-95-96; Creese, Don 1942-46-47; Creese, Loren 1938-39-41; Crompton, Bill 1926-27; Crosby, Willis 1930-31; Crotts, Frank, 1915; Crouter, Ed 1910-11-12; Crutchmer, Clyde 1973-74; Culbertson, Ken 1987-89; Cullins, Ron 1977-78; Cundall, Larry 1959-60; Cunningham, T.J. 1992-93-94; Curlee, Ken 1928-29; Curlee, Neil 1926; Curtis, Ralph 1950-51-52; Cush, Anthony 1920; Cyphers, Pete 1977-79

D Dadiotis, Pete 1976-77-78; Dages, Al 1974; Daiss, Bob 1945; Daigneault, Charles 1941; Dal Porto, Bob 1943; Dal Porto, Steve 1968-69-70; Dalthorp, Jim 1950-51-52; Darley, George 1890-02; Darovec, Dave 1971; Davenport,Neil 1910-11; Davidson, Hugh 1950-51; Davies, Joe 1936-37; Davis, Bud 1950; Davis, Charles 1978-79-80-81; Davis, Charlie 1971-72-73; Davis, Dave 1978; Davis, Dean 1985-86; Davis, Dwayne 1989-90-92-93; Davis, Elton 1994; Davis, Harmon 1931; Davis, Kent 1980-82-83-84; Davis, Kevin 1980; Davis, Mike E. 1976-78-79; Davis, Mike L. 1975-76; Davis, Todd 1935; Davidson, Morgan 1937-38-39; Dawson, H.M. 1895; Dawson, Eugene 1902-04; Dean, J.B. 1946; Dean, J.B. Jr. 1972-73; Decker, Aaron 1930; Deitrich, Dick 1951-52; DeGoler, Scott 1988-89-90; DeLine, Dave 1984-86-87; DeLuzio, Don 1985-86-88; Delmonico, Tony 1947-48-49; Demo, Bernelle 1952-53; Demos, Nick 1957; Dennis, Desmond 1994; Denvir, John 1959-60-61; DeRose, Mark 1980; Descenzo, Bob 1943; Desmarais, Gregg 1988; Detmer, Koy 1992-94; Dickey, (?) 1924; Dickey, Joe 1944-45; Dillon, Ed 1895-96-97; Dobler, Bill 1916; Donaldson, Dave 1943; Donaldson, Jeff 1980-81-82-83; Donnell, Larry 1965-66-67; Donnell, Bill 1972-73-74; Donnelly, Jim 1978; Donovan, John 1912-13-14; Doolittle, Steve 1988-89; Dorough, Joe 1945; Dove, Eddie 1956-57-58; Dow, Royal 1936; Dowler, Boyd 1956-57-58; Dowler, Joe 1959; Downing, Lyle 1912; Doush, O. 1918; Doyle, T.J. 1900-01; Dozier, John 1924; Drain, Vernon 1932-33-34; Drake, Billie 1970-71-72; Driskill, Walt 1933-34-35; Drummond, Dennis 1965-66; Duenas, Joe 1971-72-73; Duncan, Tom 1968-69; Dunham, Cliff 1970; Dunn, Pat 1978-79-80; Dunn, Tom 1986; Dunning, Hal 1950-52; Durward, Art 1890; Dwight, H.B. 1902; Dyet, Brian 1990-91-92-93; Dykstra, Lemar 1944; Dyson, Dion 1987

E Easley, Charlie 1890-91-92; Eastman, Harold 1916; Eastman, Leslie 1917; Easton, Evan 1917; Eaton, iohn 1940; Eckel, Clarence 1912-13; Eckel, Larry 1982-83-84-85; Ecklund, Bill 1944; Edmundson, C.L. 1890; Egging, Guy 1980-81-82-83; Elder, Marcellous 1989-90-91; Elizondo, Felipe 1981; Elkins, Bill 1958-59-60; Elliott, Choice 1928-29-30; Ellwood, Rick 1972-74; Embree, Jon 1983-84-85-86; Embree, Sean 1991-92-93; Embree, W.M. 1894; Emmerling, John 1969-70-71; Engel, Ray 1956-57-58; Engel, Steve 1968-69; English, Keith 1988; Eppick, Karl 1918; Eschenburg, Herman 1915-16; Esington, Randy 1980-81-82; Ethridge, Larry 1962; Eurich, Bill 1958-59-60; Evans, Don 1944-47-48; Evans, Ed 1915-16; Evans, Tom 1950-51-52

F Fabling, John 1943-46-47; Faciane, Dwayne 1984; Fairband, Bill 1964-65-66; Fairbanks, Don 1982-83-84-85; Faison, Derek 1968-69; Farler, John 1965-66-67; Farnworth, Nat 1905-06-07; Fauria, Christian 1991-92-93-94; Fawcett, Bill 1949; Ferguson, Larry 1973-74; Fernandez, Charlie 1974; Ferrando, Drew 1985-86-87; Ferraro, Larry 1963-64-65; Ferrier, John 1948; Field, Tom 1979-80-82-83; Figner, George 1951-52; Figures, Deon 1988-90-91-92; Finley, Lawrence 1945; Firm, John 1982-83; Fischer, Bill 1951-52-53; Fischer, Larry 1965; Fisher, Carl 1952-53; Fisher, Richard 1990-92; Flannigan, J.J. 1987-88-89; Flinn, Willard 1938-3940; Foote, Percy 1901-02-03-05; Forbes, Alvin 1902; Ford, Eddie 1978; Ford, Garrett 1993; Forney, Mike 1994; Foster, Brian 1969-70-71; Fowler, O.S. 1899-1900-01-02-03; Frank, Bill 1961; Franklin, Walt 1917-19-20-21; Frederic, Bob 1945; Freund, Dick 1954; Frezieres, Grant 1947; Fulghum, Carl 1917-19-20-21; Fullmer, Derek 1984-85-86; Fusiek, Ed 1968-69-70; Fry, (?) 1902

G Gamble, Harry 1891-92-93-94-95-96; Gammon, Harry 1914; Garcia, Jim 1902; Gardner, Brigham 1943; Garrett, Jim 1890-91-92; Garrison, E.F. 1890; Garten, Joe 1987-89-90; Gartland, Frank 1912; Garvin, Dave 1958-59; Garwood, Harold 1896-98-99-1900; Garwood, Omar 1898-99-1900; Gaunty, Steve 1975-76; Geiser, Jeff 1972-73-74; Geist, Randy 1971-72-73; Gelwick, Clyde 1932-34; Gentry, Letcher 1913; Gibbs, Darrell 1938; Gibbs, David 1987-88-89-90; Giek, Tom 1954-55-56; Gilbert, Bob 1936; Gilligan, Frank 1909-10; Givens, Howell 1890-92; Glass, Alabama 1952-53; Glaze, Ralph 1901; Glendenning, Ed 1912-14; Glenn, Jeff 1984; Gohde, Gary 1958; Golder, Dick 1954-55-56; Goodman, Harvey 1972-73-74; Gorman, Don 1950; Gorman, Russ 1949; Gould, Greg 1988-89; Graham, Nick 1961-62; Graham, Royal 1894; Graham, Vern 1939-40; Grant, Howard 1929; Graves, Dane 1948-49-50; Graves, Steve 1965-66; Gray, Lamarr 1988-89-90; Gray, Ron 1951-52; Green, Mike 1979-80; Greene,A.L. 1930; Greenwood, Don 1951-52; Greer, Charles 1965-66-67; Gregory, Roland 194647-48; Greig, Bill 1915; Gress, Jere 1927-28; Griffin, Dave 1976-77-78; Griffin, J.S. 1915; Griffin, Steve 1973-74; Griffith, Jack 1941; Grimm, Dan 1960-61-62; Grosvenor, George 1931-32-33; Grove, Gene 1937; Guest, Rodell 1991; Gulbrandson, Bob 1943; Gulley, William 1984-85; Gunter, Roger 1979-80-81; Guthrie, Paul 1914

H Hagan, Darian 1989-90-91; Hagan, Mike 1977-78; Haggerty, Steve 1972-73; Hagin, Don 1948-49-50; Haigh, Tom 1978; Hakes, Steve 1975-76; Halamandaris, Bo 1980; Haley, Jim 1930-31; Hall, Dave 1943; Hall, Wilbur 1962; Hallock, Bud 1938; Hamilton, Eric 1989-90-91; Hamilton, Jerry 1981; Hammett, Lee 1965; Hammond, Chad 1992-93; Hammond, Van 1979; Hancock, Tom 1948-49-50; Handy, Dick 1923; Haney, Charles 1940; Haney, Dave 1968-69-70; Hanna, Scott 1989; Hannah, Eric 1987; Hansen, Egon 1934; Hansen, Jim 1989-91-92; Harden, Reggie 1978-79-80; Hardison, Scott 1980; Hardy, Carroll 1951-52-53-54; Hardy, Dale 1944; Hardy, Lyman 1934-36; Harkins, Dick 1955; Harper, Dick 1961; Harper, Jim 1990-91; Harper, Tim 1984-85; Harris, Eric 1968-69; Harris, Bill 1961-62-63; Harris, John 1928; Harris, Sam 1964-65-66; Harris, William 1965-66-67; Harrison, Graham 1980; Harshbarger, Marty 1963; Hartling, Gary 1976-77-78; Hartman, Stanford 1932-33-34; Hartman,Warren 1910-11-12; Hartshorn, Fred 1923-24; Harvey, E.C. 1915; Harvey, William 1986-87; Hasart, Mart 1980-81-82; Hasselbeck, Don 1973-74-75-76; Hatch, Willard 1897-1900; Hatcher, Mark 1984-85-86-87; Hauptmann, Greg 1968; Havens, Chris 1969-70-71; Havig, Dennis 1968-69-70; Hawkins, Lyndell 1979-80; Hayes, Cole 1986-87-88; Haynes, Mark 1976-77-78-79; Hayward, Julian 1989-91; Heaghan, Gerald 1928; Healey, Roscoe 1913-14-15; Healey, Jach 1923-24-25; Heap, Bob 1951; Heasley, Russ 1989-90; Heath, Bruce 1965-66-67; Heaton, Arch 1909-10; Heck, Ralph 1960-61; Heckman, Scott 1913; Hedgecock, Glenn 1940-41-42; Heeb, Charles 1937-38-39; Helton, Barry 1985-86-87; Hemingway, George 1987-88-89-90; Henderson, DeOscia 1962-63; Hendrickson, Stan 1941-42-47; Henriques, Maurice 1993; Henry, Al 1943; Henry, Lendon 1994; Henry, Mark 1989-90-91; Henson, Gary 1959-60; Herbst, Ralph 1956-57-58; Heron, Steve 1982-83; Hestera, Dave 1981-82-83; Hickey, Jim 1937-39; Hicks, Kerry 1992-93-94; Hill, Bob 1937-38; Hill, Chuck 1983; Hill, Dave 1951-52-53; Hill, James 1990-91-92-93; Hill, Nate 1901; Hillebrand, Jerry 1959-60-61; Hilton, Tom 1974-76; Himelwright, Jack 1956-57-58; Hixon, Howard 1894; Hixon, T. 1896; Hodel, Merwin 1949-50-51; Hogan, Tom 1919; Hogarty, Barry 1895-97-98; Hogbin, Randy 1982-83; Hokanson, Vic 1965-66-67; Hold, Jim 1961; Holden, Delos 1890; Holland, Darius 1991-92-93-94; Hollingsworth, Al 1962-63; Holmes, Don 1979-82; Holmes, Elmer 1936; Holmes, Mike 1977; Hood, Kevin 1980-81-82; Hopper, Riley 1922; Horine, Larry 1950-51-52; Hornberger, Jeff 1977-78; Hornung, Stan 1980; Horton, Bill 1951-52-53; Horton, Greg 1971-72-73; Houck, Gerry 1970-71; Houk, Cliff 1961; Howard, Greg 1977-78; Howard, Isaac 1966-67-68; Howard, Tim 1982; Howard, Wellington 1898-1900; Howe, Ben 1962-63-64; Howe, Garry 1989-90; Howeil, Jim 1957-59; Huber, Kirk 1913-14; Huber, Monte 1967-68-69; Hubka, Arlin 1955; Hudson, Chris 1991-92-93-94; Huffer, Ken 1951-52-53; Humbie, Bob 1977-78-79; Humphry, Harry 1936; Hunt, Bobby 1972-73-74; Hunt, Roger 1951-52-53; Hunter, Derek 1980-81; Hutchins, Rob 1988-89-90; Hyson, Dick 1955-56

I Ili, Junior 1981-83-84-85; Indorf, Ellwyn 1956-57-58; Ingram, E.J. 1890; Irvin, Terry 1980-81-82-83; Irvine, Stan 1962-63-64; Irwin, Hale 1964-65-66; Irwin, Heath 1993-94; Irwin, Phil 1968-69-70; Ivers, Wayne 1912-13-14; Ivey, Roger 1991-92

J Jack, Del 1921-22; Jackson, James 1991; Jacobsen, Pete 1968-69; Jacobson, Oscar 1939-40; James, Homer 1890-91; James, Robbie 1991; James, Tim 1988-89-90; James, Vic 1980-81; Jameson, Meredith 1932; Javernick, Harry 1954-55; Jebb, A.B. 1900; Jenkins, Homer 1953-54-55; Jenkins, Ray 193940-41; Jindra, Bob 1945; Johnson, A.C. 1894; Johnson, Art, Dale 1979-80; Johnson, Beattie 1912; Johnson, Bert 1957-58-59; Johnson, Brian 1981; Johnson, Charles E. 1991-92-93; Johnson, Charles S. 1989-90; Johnson, Charlie 1975-76; Johnson, Darryl 1983; Johnson, Derek 1982; Johnson, Fred 1948-49-50; Johnson, Fritz 1923-24-25; Johnson, Gene 1967-68; Johnson, Hilary 1949-50; Johnson, Jesse 1977-78-79; Johnson, Ken 1971-72; Johnson, Melvin 1974-75-77; Johnson, Reed 1959-60-61; Johnson, Richard 1981-82; Johnson, Robert 1981-82; Johnson, Ron 1951-52-53; Johnson, Ted 1991-92-93-94; Johnson, Terry 1987-88-89-90; Johnston, Bill 1903-04; Johnston, Hal 1904; Jones, Cameron 1987; Jones, Dave 1954-55-56; Jones, Elton 1984-85; Jones, Greg 1992-94; Jones, Michael 1987-89; Jones, Steve 1979; Jones, Buck 1945-47-48-49; Jordan, Leonard 1904-05; Jordan, Zack 1950-51-52; Jorgenson, Jack 1949-50-51; Joseph, Vance 1991-93-94; Joslin, Chuck 1954-55-56; Jump, Lawrence 1937; Jump, Ray 1947-48-50

K Kafkaloff, Wade 1978; Kahl, Kent 1991; Kancilia, Willie 1979; Karnopp, Charles 1903; Karnoscak, Don 1953-54-55; Katovsich, John 1992; Kavanaugh, George 1904; Kay, Rick 1970-71-72; Kearns, Dick 1938; Keenan, Craig 1984-85; Keim, Don 1922; Keim, Thurman 1908-09; Kelley, Karry 1976-77-78-79; Kelleher, Jim 1973-75-76; Kelly, Dan 1966-67; Kelly, Paul 1967; Kelsey, Brian 1968; Kemp, Frank 1911-12; Kemp, Phil 1915-16; Kenlon, Mike 1978; Kennedy, Martin 1890-91; Kennelly, Dan 1977; Kensinger, Jeff 1973; Kerin, Mike 1974-75-76; Ketchem, T.H. 1898; Kettelson, Phil 1977-78-79; Keys, Jack 1992; Keyworth, Jon 1970-72-73; Kidd, James 1993-94; Kimmel, Joe 1907-08; Kingdom, Scott 1980; Kingsbury, Al 1903; Kirchner, Bruce 1977-78; Kissick, Erich 1986-87-88-89; Klamann, Bob 1951-52; Klein, Kelly 1974; Klinker, Walt 1959-60-61; Kmetovic, Tom 1967; Knafelc, Gary 1951-52-53; Knapple, Jeff 1976-77; Knieval, Ken 1943-4445; Knight, Greg 1986; Knowles, Bob 1941-42; Knowles, Carl 1911-12-13; Knowles, Ed, 1913-14; Knowles, RR. 1905-06-07-08; Knowlton, Dick 1951-52-53; Knutson, Jon 1991-92-93-94; Koch, Curt 1984-85-86-87; Koelbel, Walt 1944-45-46-47; Kohlman, Pat 1973-74; Koleski, Stan 1973-74-75-76; Koncar, Mark 1973-74-75; Kormylo, John 1974; Kozlowski, Mike 1977-78; Krahenbuhl, Doug 1979-80-81; Kralicek, Bili 1969-70-71; Krause, Paul 1975; Kresnak, Tom 1962-63-64; Krone, Frank 1948-49; Kubinski, Steve 1978; Kucera, Bill 1953-54-55; Kunz, Terry 1972-74-75; Kusayanagi, Miles 1984-85; Kuxhaus, Gary 1967-68-69

L LaGarde, Robert 1976-77; LaGuardia, Skip 1962; Lam, William 1933-34-35; Lamont, Bill 1953-54-55; Lancelot, Tim 1984-85; Lang, Bob 1928; Lavington, Leon 1935-36-37; Lawrence, Bob 1985-86; Lawrence, Ralph 1927; Layton, Harry 1890-91-92-93-94; Leahy, Gerry 1954-55-56; Leavitt, Avery 1904; Lee, Jeff 1976-77-78; Lee, Jerry 1969-70; Lee, Robert 1964-65; Leeuwenburg, Jay 1989-90-91; LeFevre, Harry 1921; Lefferdink, Merle 1932-33; LeMasters, Ray 1963-64-65; Lentz, John 1940; Leomiti, Donnell 1993-94; Lepsis, Matt 1993-94; Lesher, Don 1934-35; Levine, Abe 1936-37-38; Lewark, George 1964-65-66; Lewis, Brian 1984; Lewis, Clayton 1942; Lewis, McCreery 1897; Lightner, Ken 1984; Likovich, Tom 1974; Liley, Louis 1937-38; Lillie, Charles 1917-20; Lillo, Larry 1979-80; Lima, Fred 1972-73; Linder, Ray 1931-32; Lindsey, Greg 1990-91-92-93; Lindwall, Roger 1955; Lines, George 1908-12; Lisco, Dick 1944-45; Lockard, Vem 1939-40-41; Locke, Terry 1962; Logan, Dave 1972-73-74-75; Lolotai, Tiloi 1974-75-76; Loper, N.B. 1917; Lord, Bill 1918; Lotz, Les 1954-55-56; Loser, Earl 1921-22-23-24; Loucks, Alan 1927-29-30; Lowen, Charles 1927-29-30; Lowen, Charles 1937; Loyd, Mike 1969-70; Lund, Tom 1962-63-64; Lusk, Dick 1966

M Mackenzie, Tom 1974-75; Mackie, John 1899-1901; Maddalena, Bob 1943; Magrum, Bud 1971-72; Mahoney, Scott 1969-70-71; Mandril, Chuck 1971-72; Mangnall, Tim 1976; Manire, Bob 194849; Mankowski, Dick 1962-63-64; Maphis, Sam 1954-55; March, Ralph 1933-34; Marchiol, John 1964; Marquez, Mike 1985-86-87; Marshall, Derek 1983-84; Marshall, Lee 1952-53; Martin, Mike 1964-65-66; Martin, Rocky 1967-68; Martin, Scott 1983; Martinez, Jerry 1973-74-75; Masten, Bob 1969-70-71; Matthews, Bo 1971-72-73; Mattingly, Wayne 1973; Mauff, Bob 1904; Mauler, Larry 1973-74-75; Maumau, Viliami 1994; Maurer, Don 1958-59; Mavity, Leon 1961-62-63; Maxedon, Leon 1961-62-63; Maxedon, Dave 1978-80; Mayberry, James 1975-76-77-78; Mayer, Ron 1994; McBride, Chuck 1959-60-61; McBride, Ken 1962; McBride, Paul 1913-14; McCabe, Brian 1977-78-79; McCain, Addison 1900-02; McCall, Alvin 1938; McCall, Bemie 1964-65-66; McCandless, Bob 1951; McCandless, Byron 1899; McCarter, Chuck 1975-76-77; McCarty, Eric 1984-85-86-87; McCartney, Tennyson 1994; McCary, Phil 1912-13-14; McCloughan, Dave 1987-88-89-90; McClung, Paul 1939-40-41; McClure, George 1893; McClure, Greg 1993; McClurg, Jerry 1963-64; McConnell, Charles 1890; McConnell, Giley 1912-13; McCoy, C.E. 1895-96; McCoy, Mike 1974-75; McCreary, Joe 1984-85-86-87; McCullough, Bob 1959-60-61; McDonald, Bill 1971-72-73; McDonald, C.A. 1899; McEwen, Jack 1946-47; McFadden, John 1908-09-10-11; McGhee, Burt 1933-35; McGhee, Kanavis 1987-88-89-90; McGill, Earl 1894; McGlone, Bill 1923-24-25-26; McGlone, Frank 1931-32-33; McGuire, John 1962; Mclntosh, Bill 1891-92-93; Mclntosh, Bob 1943; McIntosh, Harry 1948; McKelvey, Warren 1928-29-30; McKenzie, Jack 1958; McKim, Jim 1957; McKinley, Bill 1943; McKinney, Odis 1976-77; McLean, Don 1921-22-23; McLean, Ken 1931-32-33; McLemore, Chris 1982-83; McMillen, Dan 1982-83-84-85; McMurray, Bill 1898-99; McNary, Bill 1923-24-25; McNutt, Maurice 1901-02; Mead, Ken 1923-24-25; Meadows, John 1961; Meckley, Dick 1942; Melin, Dick 1967-68-69; Mellet, John 1921; Melville, Dick 1962; Merkerson, Ron 1994; Merritt, Leon 1994; Merten, F.H. 1898-99; Merz, Wally 1954-55-56; Metoyer, Mike 1973; Meyer, Lamar 1950-54-55; Middlemist, Pete 1929-30-31; Middlemist, Pete Jr. 1954; Mikel, Chuck 1983; Miller, Jim 1895; Miller, J.O. 1898; Miller, Malcolm 1947-4849; Miller, Matt 1976-77-78; Miller, Vem 1939-40-41; Mills, Ed 1903; Mills, Wamer 1909-10-11; Milton, Noble 1961-63; Mitchell, Andy 1994; Mitchell, Bill 1952-53; Mitchell, Erik 1992-93-94; Modrich, Laurence 1934; Moles, Clint 1992; Moline, (?) 1924; Monczka, Tim 1962-63-64; Mondt, Bill 1956-57-58; Monson, Andrew 1902-03; Montera, Frank 1959-60-61; Montler, Mike 1966-67-68; Moore, Charles 1905-06; Moore, Clint 1991-92-94; Moore, Gene 1935-36-37; Moorhead, Emery 1974-75; Morgan, Kile 1967-68; Morgan, Mark 1981; Morley, Bud 1956; Morrill,

166 *Buffaloes Handbook*

Read 1907; Morris, Bobby 1975-76; Morris, Chuck 1962; Morris, Don 1945; Morris, Roger 1963; Morrison, Joe 1906-07-08; Morrow, Dick 1944; Morton, Bob 1951-52-53; Mosher, Chuck 1949-50-51; Motley, Mike 1989; Mottl, Kerry 1965-67; Muilenburg, Darrin 1986-87-88-89; Muir, Jim 1891; Muncie, Don 1981-82-83-84; Munson, Bob 1957; Murphy, Dave 1933-34-35; Murphy, Pat 1968-69-70; Musfeldt, Curtis 1994; Muth, Bob 1918-19-20-21; Muxlow, Bill 1975-76; Myers, Bill 1942; Myers, John 1943

N Nabholz, Jeff 1994; Nady, Gary 1956-57; Naeole, Chris 1993-94; Nagel, Bob 1958-59-60; Nairn, John 1984-85-86-87; Nall, Webb 1976; Narcisian, Harry 1947-4849; Nash, Shelby 1983; Neary, Don 1953-54; Neighbors, Doy 1932-33-34; Nelson, Chester 1928; Nelson, Doug 1946-4748-49; Nelson, Ed 1933-34; Nelson, M.J. 1986-87-88-89; Nelson, Ray 1911-13-14-15; Nelson, Robley 1931-33; Nelson, Tate 1990; Nery, Ron 1984; Nevarez, Hugo 1984; Newcomb, Ed 1890-91-92; Newton, Clem 1908-09; Newton, George 1930-31-32; Nigbur, Tom 1967-68; Newman, Bob 1915; Nichols, D. 1922; Nichols, Willie 1969-70-71; Nix, Joe 1948-49-50; Nixon, John 1890; Niziolek, Bob 1976-77-79-80; Nobble,Alva 1917-19-20-21; Norgard, Erik 1987-88; Nuttall, O.T. 1936-37-40

O O'Brien, George 1893; O'Brien, Joe 1982-83; O'Brien, John 1907-08-09-10; O'Conner, Harry 1899-1900-01; O'Dell, Dick 1965-66; O'Donnell, Chris 1988-89-90-91; Ogle, Rick 1968-69-70; Olander, Lance 1977-78-79-80; Oliver, Jim 1944; Oliver, Lloyd 1939-40-41; Oliver, Marvin 1958; Oliver, O.C. 1986-87-90; Olson, Ryan 1994; Ortner, Roy 1907; Orvis, Dave 1971-72; Orvis, Herb 1969-70-71; Orvis, J.C. 1990; Osbom, Kirk 1962-63-64; Osbom, Steve 1962-63; Osbom, George 1975-76-77; Oviatt, Al 1932-33-34-35; Owens, Everett 1902-03-04

P Pace, Charles 1943-45; Paddock, A.A. 1908; Painter, H.T. 1908; Parker, Brad 1980-81-82; Parlapiano, Dave 1949; Parmater, Jack 1962-63-64; Parr, Greg 1970-71-72; Pate, Emest 1901-02; Patrick, Frank 1975-76; Patrick, Neal 1981; Patterson, Dan 1968-69; Patterson, J.S. 1899-1900-01; Paul, Whitney 1973-74-75; Pauline, Kevin 1985; Payton, Doug 1972-73-74; Pearson, Chuck 1959-60; Peate, Ed 1931-32; Peercy, Dave 1964-65; Penney, Bazil 1927; Pennock, UR. 1891; Peoples, Bruce 1971-72; Peper, John 1944; Perak, John 1987-88; Perini, Dave 1968-69; Perkins, Horace 1974-75-76; Perkins, Jason 1991; Perkins, Jim 1959-60-61; Perry, Clarence 1891; Perry, Pete 1980-81; Perry, Rod 1973-74; Perry, Tom 1975-76-77; Peters, Joe 1939; Pexton, Frank 1925; Philleo, Rialto 1924-25; Phillips, Alvin 1976; Phillips, Jim 1968-69-70; Phillips, Mike 1994; Phillips, Scott 1991-92; Phillipson, Bob 1944-45-46; Pickens, Lyle 1984-85; Pigg, Frank 1911; Pike, Bob 1950; Piper, Don 1953; Pisani, Dean 1988; Pitman, Don 1962; Pixler, Jack 1947; Plantz, Larry 1965-66-67; Pleasant, Sid 1929-30-31; Plested, Bill 1923; Pletcher, Gary 1963; Polk, William 1993; Polumbus, Tad 1965-66; Pontiflet, Keith 1986-87-88; Popplewell, Don 1968-69-70; Portis, Larry 1963; Pottier, Chuck 1968; Powars, Frank 1913-14; Prator, Ralph 1926-27-28; Pratt, Eric 1986; Price, Daryl 1993; Price, Jack 1962-63; Price, Jim 1943-46; Prince, Ernest 1908; Pritchard, Mike 1988-89-90; Pruett, Mike 1967-68-69; Pruit, Sherman 1956-57-58; Pruitt, Mickey 1984-85-86-87; Pudlik, Ed 1946-47-48-49; Pudlik, John 1938-3940; Pugh, Kazell 1977-78-79; Pughe, Frank 1901; Punches, Dick 1949-50; Punches, Harold 1938-39-40; Punches, Max 1938-39-40; Putnam, Wesley 1890-91-92

Q Quackenbush, Jim 1985-86-87; Quarnberg, Lex 1937-38-39; Quinlan, Art 1921-22-23; Quinlan, Clarence 1928-29-30

R Rader, Paul 1899; Rafferty, Vince 1981-82-83; Rafferty, Wayne 1986-87; Railey, Bill 1929-30-31; Raisis, Jim 1960; Ralph, Dan 1979-80; Ramsey, Bill 1926; Randall, John 1915-16; Randolph, Ward 1907-09; Rappold, Kyle 1985-86-87; Raso, Soilie 1942; Rasmussen, Scott 1986-87-88; Rautenstraus, Roland 1943-44; Raveling, Jerry 1952-53; Ray, Wayne 1930; Raymond, Jeff 1967-68; Reagan, Francis 1927-29; Reece, John 1948-49; Reed, J.H. 1916; Reed, Tony 1975-76; Reeves, Paul 1939; Reid, Murray 1906-07-08; Reilly, Maurice 1941-42-46-47; Reinhardt, Ed 1983-84; Reinhardt, Tom 1985-86-87-88; Reliford, Marcus 1988; Remington, Barry 1982-84-85-86; Remington, Mark 1980-81; Renfro, Leonard 1990-91-92; Rettig, Tony 1982-83; Reuter, Ray 1968; Rice, Dave 1975; Rich, John 1909-10-11; Richardson, Lorne 1970-71-72; Rickels, Laverne 1950-51; Rieger, Ron 1969-70; Rife, Dave 1959-60; Riggins, Clyde 1981-82-83; Ritchhart, Del 1933-34-35; Robert, Dick 1968-69-70; Roberts, Ray 1903-04-05; Roberts, Roy 1906-07-08; Roberts, Tim 1977-78-79; Robertson, F.W. 1915; Robertson, Harry 194748; Robinson, Brad 1988; Robinson, Carl 1917; Robinson, E.C. 1896-99; Robinson, John 1928-30; Roe, Bill 1977-78-79; Rogel, Frank 1934-35-36; Rogers, Allan 1941; Rogers, Frank 1963-64-65; Rogers, John 1896-97-99; Rogers, Joe 1898; Rogers, Milt 1959; Rogers, Rodney 1985-86-87; Rogers, Sam 1992-93; Roller, Douglas 1904-05-06; Romans, A.B. 1900; Romig, Joe 1959-60-61; Rooney, Bill 1893; Rooney, Jack 1937-38-39; Rooney, Tom 1943; Rose, Paul 1988-89-90; Rosenthal, Jerry 1953; Rosga, Steve 1992-94; Ross, Tim 1992; Rossi, Tom 1978; Roth, Bart 1974-75-76; Rothwell, Matt 1895-989; Rouen, Tom 1989-90; Rouson, Lee 1981-82-83-84; Rubalcaba, Alvin 1982-83-84; Rubidge, Harold 1900-01-02; Rubright, Earl 1930; Russell, Matt 1993-94; Rust, Melvin 1890; Ryan, Pat 1984-85-86-87; Ryder, Bill 1952

S Sabatino, Bill 1964-65-66; Salaam, Rashaan 1993-94; Salavea, Okland 1988-89; Salberg, John 1904-05-06; Salerno, Bob 1956-58-59; Salerno, Sam 1953-54-55; Salvatore, Steve 1980-81-82; Samuelson, Carl 1917; Sanders, Dave 1985; Sandhouse, Ray 1916; Saunders, Harold 1937-38-39; Savage, Ray 1918-19; Savoy, Phil 1994; Sawyer, Ken 1923; Sawyer, Paul 1929-30-31; Sazama, Kevin 1979; Schaefer, Bob 1892-93-94-96-97; Schlagel, Ken 1954-55-56; Schlesener, Neil 1989; Schneiter, Walt 1954; Schnitker, Mike 1966-67-68; Schnorr, Dennis 1968-69-70; Schrepferman, Chet 1918-19-20; Schrepferman, Dick 1946-47; Schroeter, Rob 1972; Schubeck, Darin 1984-85-86; Schwayder, Irving 1941; Schweninger, Loren 1959-60-61; Scott, Charlie 1979; Scott, Homer 1954; Scott, Leonard 1940; Scott, Ralph 1945-46; Scott, Ron 1965-66-67; Scott, Victor 1980-81-82-83; Scoville, Dave 1924-25-26; Scribner, Bill 1958-59-60; Sears, Harold 1917; Sebro, Bob 1979-80-81; Sells, Virgil 1914; Semenko, Mel 1958-59-60; Senna, Tony 1991; Sens, Mark 1971-72-73; Shannon, Gus 1941-42-46; Shapiro, Charles 1917-18; Sheldon, Harold 1926; Shelley, Don 1952-53; Shelton, Woody 1950-51-52; Shepherd, Roy 1950-51-52; Shilling, Walter 1897-98; Shinnick, Pete 1985-86; Shoen, Ed 1972-73-74; Shoop, Mark 1980-81-82; Short, Laval 1976-77-78-79; Shoulin, Hubert 1942; Shugren, Maurice 1916; Sidwell, Dave 1967-68; Sidwell, Steve 1963-64-65; Siegmund, Fred 1905; Sievers, George 1927; Simmons, Dalton 1992-93-94; Simmons, Michael 1987-89-90; Simons, Bill 1946-4748-49; Simons, Henry 1934-35; Simpson, Bob 1973-74-75; Singleton, Derek 1980-81; Sisson, Joe 1924; Slattery, Frank 1912; Slevin, Mike 1994; Sloan, Bill 1912-13-14; Slovek, John 1936; Slusher, Jim 1909; Smart, Don 1937-38-39; Smith, Charles 1927-28; Smith, Conley 1984-85-86; Smith, Don 1937-38; Smith, George 1982-83-84; Smith, Howard 1904; Smith, Howard 1921-22; Smith, Irish 1979; Smith, Jim 1941-42-46; Smith, Jim 1985-86-87; Smith, Kyle 1994; Smith, Lou 1935-36-37; Smith, Mark 1993; Smith, R. Bruce 1968-69-70; Smith, Rico 1990-91; Smith, Sam 1984-85-86-87; Smith, William 1927-28-29; Smotherman, Terry 1958; Smotherman, Trevor 1988; Somerville, Ted 1961-63-64; Solomon, Ariel 1989-90; Solomon, Bill 1978-79; Spangler, G. 1897; Spencer, Bob 1927-28-29; Spicer, Bob 1942-46-47-48; Spivey, Mike 1974-75-76; Spring, Walter 1913-15; Springston, Greg 1966-67; Staab, Otto 1932-34-35; Stampley, Tim 1979-80; Stander, Jim 1951-52-53; Stanley, Walter 1980-81; Stapp, Bob 1957; Stapp, Dick 1954-55-56; Stapp, Dean 1926; Starks, Bob 1919-20; Starks, Wayne 1957; Starr, Scott 1992; Stasica, Leo 1939-40; Stavely, John 1970-71-73; Stearns, Carl 1942; Stearns, John 1970-71-72; Stearns, Rick 1972-73-74; Steed, Joel 1988-89-90-91; Stefan, Tim 1984-85; Steffen, Jerry 1958-59-60; Steffenhagen, L. 1936; Stemmons, John 1963; Stenzel, Ray 1931-32-33; Stephenson, John 1967; Stevens, Dick 1948-50; Stevens, Fran 1935-36-37; Stewart, Bob 1950; Stewart, Kordell 1991-92-93-94; Stewart, Paul 1923-24; Stillwell, Mort 1922; Stipanovich, Ted 1978; Stirrett, Elmer 1907-08-09; Stocker, Harry 1907-08-09; Stoltenberg, Bryan 1992-93-94; Stone, Tom 1986-87-88; Strain, Bob 1918; Strait, Alan 1987; Stransky, Bob 1955-56-57; Streeter, Tommy 1984-85; Stripling, Steve 1974-75; Strobel, John 1946-47-48-49; Stroup, HA 1895; Sturm, Herman 1903; Suess, Willard 1920; Sutherland, Sam 1987; Sutrina, John 1976-77-78; Swigert, Jack 1950-51-52; Sylvester, Alfred 1916; Sylvester, Mike 1980-81-82-83; Symington, Chris 1985-87; Symons, Bill 1962-63-64

T Taibi, Carl 1969-70-71; Talbot, R.A. 1915; Taney, John 1935; Tanner, Art 1945-46-47; Tarver, John 1970-71; Tate, David 1985-86-87; Taylor, Dick 1963-64-65; Taylor, F.W. 1943; Taylor, Wallace 1932; Teets, Bernard 1929-30-31; Tesone, Tom 1973-74-75-77; Teter, Roy 1912; Thayre, Harry 1898-99-1900-01; Theiler, Roland 1945; Thistle, Dave 1983-84; Thomas, Dave 1905-06-07; Thomas, Greg 1989-90-91; Thomas, L.M. 1943; Thomas, Ryan 1991; Thomas, Vic 1948-49-50; Thompson, Bob 1954; Thompson, Pete 1948-49-50; Thompson, Ray 1937-38-39; Thompson, Rick 1976; Thompson, Warren 1919-20; Thornton, Jackie 1975; Thurston, Brant 1978-79-80; Thurston, Guy 1979-80; Tobin, Duke 1992-93; Tomlinson, Rex 1937-38; Tonkin, A.B. 1900-01-02-03; Tope, Mike 1975-76-77-78; Torri, Jeff 1982; Touhy, George 1921; Trachsel, Floyd 1936-37-38; Tracy, Kirk 1965-66-67; Tracy, Steve 1966-67-68; Troudt, Darrell 1977; Troutman, Herchell 1994; Trowbridge, Roland 1917; Trudigan, Bill 1903-04-05-06; Turcotte, Jeff 1972-73-74; Turman, Wilson 1896-99-1900-01; Turrell, H.C. 1899

U Uhlir, Jim 1954-55-56; Umphrey, Rich 1979-80-81; Unger, Art 1935-36-38; Usher, Jack 1945; Uteck, Larry 1972

V Vance, (?) 1901-02; Vander, Poel, Mark 1988-89-90; Vandeventer, Cliff 1950-51; Van Gundy, Cecil 1911; Van Meter, Harold 1907; Van Valkenburg, Frank 1963-64-65; Vardell, Ken 1959-60-61; Varriano, Rich 1968-69-70; Vaughn, Ruben 1975-76-77-78; Veeder, Mike 1966-67; Venzke, Lee 1950-51-52; Vest, Howard 1956; Vidal, Lou 1920; Visger, George 1977-78-79; Vivian, Dave 1960; Vogel, Steve 1981-82-83-84; Volkmann, Chester 1928; Voskeritchian, Neil 1994

W Waddy, Billy 1973-74-75-76; Wadlow, Rich 1969-70; Wagner, Eddie 1933-34-35; Wagner, Rex 1946; Waite, George 1925-26; Wales, George 1893-94; Walker, Arthur 1986-87; Walker, Eddie 1979; Walker, Russ 1979; Walker, Stuart 1976-77-78; Walsh, Ward 1968-69-70; Walter, Fred 1913-14-15; Walters, Marc 1986; Waltfer, Karl 1922; Wanless, F.R. 1894-95; Ward, Ricky 1980-81; Warkley, John 1909-11-13; Warner, Mel 1955-56-57; Warren, Lamont 1991-92-93; Warshauer, Ted 1944; Washington, Mark 1980; Waters, George 1942; Watkins, Jerry 1962; Watkins, John 1959; Watson, Greg 1977-78; Weatherspoon, Anthony 1984-85-86; Webb, James 1984-85; Webster, B.M. 1892; Weidner, Gale 1959-60-61; Weiner, Rudolph 1906-07; Weiss, A 1918; Weiss, Chuck 1958-59-60; West, Bob 1944-45; West, Derek 1991-92-93-94; Westbrook, Michael 1991-92-93-94; Westbrooks, Greg 1973-74; Westendorf, Randy 1974-75-76-77; Wheeler, Rick 1985-87; Whitaker, Marv 1969-70; Whitaker, Milton 1894-95; White, Byron 1935-36-37; White, Clayton 1931-32-33; White, Leon 1973-74-75-77; Whitehead, Harry 1899-1900-01-02; Whitmore, AC. 1898; Wiesner, Derek 1982-83; Wightman, (?) 1911; Wilbon, Alien 1993-94; Wilcots, Solomon 1983-84-85-86; Wilkins, Kenny 1993-94; Willard, Lee 1918-19-20-21; Willett, Greg 1979-80-81; Williams, Alfred 1987-88-89-90; Williams, David 1973-74-75; Williams, Larry 1974-76; Williams, Mike 1981; Williams, Roger 1950-51-52; Williams, Ted 1918; Wilscam, Tom 1959-60; Wilson, Art 1905; Wilson, Bob 1950; Wilson, Emerson 1953-54-55; Wilson, Fritz 1890; Wilson, J.J. 1902; Wilson, Rollin 1944-45; Wiley, O.K 1902; Winningham, Sam 1948-49; Wise, Bob 1945-46-47; Wissmiller, Roger 1962-63; Witcher, Maury 1926-28-29; Withrow, W.E. 1899; Witte, Jerry 1966-67-68; Wittemeyer, George 1926-27; Wolcott, F.H. 1898-99-1900; Woll, Troy 1984-85-86-87; Woulfe, Mike 1960; Wolff, John 1925-26-27; Wood, Ellis 1979-80-81-82; Woods, Art 1980-81-82; Woods, Ted 1960-61; Woodward, Dick 1940-41-42-46; Woolfork, Ron

1991-92-93; Wooten, John 1956-57-58; Worden, Gene 1955-56-57; Worden, Stewart 1944; Wuellner, Bob 1944; Wurst, Mike 1960
Y Yago, Roger 1990; Yates, Scott 1979; Yegge, Bernard 1917; Young, Brad 1978-79; Young, Bruce 1988-89; Young, Darrin 1987; Young, Dave 1960-61; Young, Pat 1960-61; Young, Steve 1974-75
Z Zaharias, Dave 1966; Zanoni, August 1930; Zeigler, Bob 1926; Zeigler, John 1942; Zetterberg, Mark 1976; Ziegler, Walter 1914; Zimmers, Ray 1907; Zisch, John 1946-47-48; Zordani, Jim 1984; Zuckerman, Sam 1920; Zumbach, Jake 1971-72.

TRIVIA ANSWERS

1. New York City (guard Harry Layton) and Bisbee, Ariz., (quarterback Tom Edmundson).
2. 1894, in the second game of CU's fifth season. The Buffs went to Denver and beat the DAC, 12-4.
3. Nebraska. CU lost, 23-10, in Boulder. Nebraska also was the opponent in CU's first road game outside the state. In a 1903 game at Lincoln, the Buffs lost, 31-0.
4. Each stadium opened in 1924. The oldest Big Eight venue, Oklahoma State's Lewis Field, opened in 1920. Kansas' Memorial Stadium opened in 1921.
5. He was killed in France, fighting in World War I.
6. 26,740.
7. 71-17-3. Wyoming is 2-22-1 against the Buffs, and Colorado State is 15-49-2.
8. 1970. AstroTurf was installed for the 1971 season, and CU's first game on its Boulder carpet was a 56-13 romp past Wyoming on Sept. 18. CU's last home game on real grass was a 45-29 mowing of Kansas in November, 1970.
9. Oklahoma State's Barry Sanders, the 1988 Heisman Trophy winner. Sanders averaged 295.5 all-purpose yards per game.
10. 1937. That year, led by the great Whizzer White, the 8-1 Buffs averaged 374.4 total yards per game, 310 rushing yards per game and 31 points per game. Their only loss came in the Cotton Bowl, a 28-14 setback to Rice. In its eight victories that year, CU outscored opponents 248-26. The Buffs were ranked 17th in the final Associated Press poll, announced before the bowl game was played. Rice was 18th.
11. George Carlson (1931), Clayton White (1933), Whizzer White (1938), Joe Romig (1962), Jim Hansen (1992).
12. Scoring, with 122 points.
13. 1952, when CU's average home attendance was 24,188, a record at the time. Two of the five home games that year were sellouts.
14. Jack Swigert.
15. The Buffs of 1956, who were ranked 20th. They beat Nebraska (16-0) in Boulder, Clemson (27-21) in the Orange Bowl and finished 8-2-1. Oklahoma was the 1956 national champion.
16. CU's sports information director. Casotti graduated from CU in 1949 and became the athletic department's historian after retiring as the longtime SID of the Bills.
17. 1966, during an Oct. 1 game against Kansas State. The Buffs won, 10-0, one week after upsetting 10th-ranked Baylor on the road, 13-7.
18. Whizzer White wore 24, Joe Romig wore 67 and Bobby Anderson wore 11.
19. Romig, who logged straight A's his last six semesters at CU, is a physicist in Boulder. He was a two-time all-America lineman and has been inducted into the Big Eight's Hall of Fame and National Football Foundation's College Hall of Fame.
20. CU's Bobby Anderson, the 11th pick of the 1970 draft. The Broncos merged into the NFL in 1970.
21. Lima wore No. 3.
22. Mike Montler, an all-Big Eight selection in 1967 and '68.
23. Jon Keyworth, who carried five times for 9 yards in Super Bowl XII, which Denver lost to the Cowboys, 27-10.
24. 5-16 (.238). The Buffs haven't had a losing season in Big Eight games in any season since 1984.
25. In 1971, the Buffs were 10-2 and finished No. 3 in the polls. Ahead of them were No. 1 Nebraska and No. 2 Oklahoma.
26. Charlie Davis, 342, in a November 1971 game against Oklahoma State. Davis, from Houston, averaged 10.1 yards per carry and scored one touchdown. CU won, 40-6, at Folsom Field.
27. True. The Buffs are 0-9 in games against No. 1 teams. They are 0-3 against Nebraska, 0-5 against Oklahoma and 0-1 against Southern California. Twice the Buffs have lost 1-point games to No. 1 teams. And each time it was to OU, 14-13 in 1957 at Norman and 21-20 in 1975 at Norman.
28. CU is 568-349-36 (.615). Inside the Big Eight, the Buffs are 168-137-10 (.549) in 47 seasons.
29. Five. They came in 1961, 1976, 1989, 1990, 1991.
30. Jon Embree. Then an all-Big Eight tight end, Embree caught 51 passes (worth 680 yards) in 1984.

31. 1-10 in 1984 and 7-5 in '85.
32. The 1975 Bluebonnet Bowl. Played at Houston's Astrodome, CU lost to Texas, 38-21, in the now-defunct game. Logan caught three passes for 20 yards and a touchdown. At halftime, CU had a 21-7 lead. Logan, an all-America (Sporting News) wide receiver who chose CU over Nebraska, played nine years in the NFL.
33. Drake. The Bulldogs won 13-9 and 41-22 games against CU teams that were a combined 4-18. Drake recently reinstated football – at the I-AA level.
34. Iowa State was the only team CU beat each year. The Cyclones fell, 17-9, at Boulder in 1980 and they lost, 23-21, at Boulder in 1984.
35. 1978. That year, CU opened 5-0 but finished 6-5. In that 5-0 start, CU allowed 7 points in each game.
36. Les Steckel of the Minnesota Vikings and Jim Mora of the New Orleans Saints. Steckel was on the CU staff from 1973-76 and from 1991-92. Mora coached with the Buffs from 1968-73.
37. Don James, at Washington.
38. Miami (Ohio), Northern Illinois, Indiana. Mallory is one of only three coaches in NCAA history to take four schools to bowl games. The others are Earle Bruce (Tampa, Iowa State, Ohio State, Colorado State) and Lou Holtz (William & Mary, North Carolina State, Arkansas, Notre Dame).
39. 129-1. Oklahoma dealt the Buffs an 82-42 loss in 1980 at Folsom Field.
40. Missouri.
41. Doc Kreis, who coaches speed, strength and conditioning for the Buffs. He came to Boulder in January, 1993.
42. 20-0-1. The only blemish was a 19-19 tie with Nebraska at Boulder in November, 1991.
43. 51,478. Boulder's population is 89,025.
44. Offensive guard Joe Garten, running back Eric Bieniemy and outside linebacker Alfred Williams, all seniors.
45. He was 7-25-1 (.227) from 1982-84. After an 0-4 start in 1986, he was 79-21-5 (.776) over his last 105 games.
46. Washington State. CU went on the road to beat the Cougars, 12-0, before 30,923. It took McCartney seven home games to finally taste victory in Boulder, a 28-3 whipping of Kansas late in the 1982 season.
47. Keith English (1988) and Tom Rouen ('89). Rouen transferred to CU from Colorado State.
48. It's the most points allowed by the Fighting Irish in their 20-game bowl history. Notre Dame is 13-7 in bowl games, 1-2 against CU.
49. The player must graduate. The rule applies to athletes in all CU sports.
50. Miami (Fla.). The Hurricanes were coming off a national title in 1989.
51. Brian Cabral, a standout CU linebacker from 1975-77. Now the CU linebackers coach, Cabral earned a Super Bowl ring when the Bears beat the New England Patriots, 46-10, at the Louisiana Superdome. Cabral played six years with the Bears, two years with the Atlanta Falcons and one year with the Green Bay Packers.
52. Gregory, the CU running backs coach since 1991, played for Nebraska. McBride, the Huskers' longtime defensive coordinator, played for CU.
53. Wisconsin. CU blistered the Badgers, 55-17, in a September, 1994, night game that ESPN televised.
54. CU's Rashaan Salaam (1994), Miami's Vinny Testaverde (1986), Southern California's Marcus Allen (1981).
55. Fifth. Winner of seven bowl games, CU trails Oklahoma (20), Nebraska (15), Oklahoma State (nine) and Missouri (eight). Iowa State (0-4) is the only Big Eight school that's never won a bowl game.
56. He was 0-4 until winning the Orange Bowl, a 10-9 squeeze past Notre Dame, that produced CU's only national title in 1990.
57. Clemson, Miami (Fla.), Alabama, Houston, Notre Dame (twice) and Fresno State.
58. 1976. That year, CU produced 11 draft picks. All in the first 10 rounds.
59. Cornerback Mark Haynes went eighth to the New York Giants and offensive tackle Stan Brock, Pete's younger brother, went 12th to the New Orleans Saints.
60. Most completions (33), passing yards (418) and interceptions (five). The game, played at night in Boulder, ended in a 24-24 tie. Detmer was 33 for 50, including two touchdown passes.
61. Wisconsin. Salaam carried 26 times for a season-low 85 yards against the Badgers, but he scored four touchdowns to fuel the Buffs' 55-17 stampede. Salaam finished the 1994 season with 2,055 yards. He averaged 6.9 yards per carry and scored 24 touchdowns.
62. Madison, Wis. Neuheisel was born there Feb. 7, 1961.
63. Southern California, UCLA's hated crosstown rival.